FEMINIST RECONSTRUCTIONS IN PSYCHOLOGY

To, for, and with Ken,
as always

FEMINIST RECONSTRUCTIONS IN PSYCHOLOGY

Narrative, Gender, and Performance

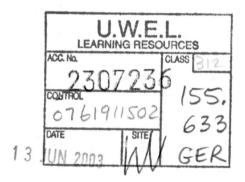
MARY GERGEN

Sage Publications, Inc.
International Educational and Professional Publisher
Thousand Oaks ▪ London ▪ New Delhi

For information:

Sage Publications, Inc.
2455 Teller Road
Thousand Oaks, California 91320
E-mail: order@sagepub.com

Sage Publications Ltd.
6 Bonhill Street
London EC2A 4PU
United Kingdom

Sage Publications India Pvt. Ltd.
M-32 Market
Greater Kailash I
New Delhi 110 048 India

Printed in the United States of America

Library of Congress Cataloging-in-Publication Data

Gergen, Mary M.
    Feminist reconstructions in psychology: Narrative, gender, and performance / by Mary Gergen.
        p.   cm.
    Includes bibliographical references and index.
        ISBN 0-7619-1150-2 (cloth: alk. paper)
        ISBN 0-7619-1151-0 (pbk.: alk. paper)
        1. Feminist psychology.   I. Title.
    BF201.4 .G47   2000
    150'.82—dc21   00-010058

This book is printed on acid-free paper.

01   02   03   04   05   06   07   7   6   5   4   3   2   1

Acquiring Editors:	Jim Nageotte and Rolf Janke
Editorial Assistant:	Heidi Van Middlesworth
Production Editor:	Sanford Robinson
Editorial Assistant:	Victoria Cheng
Typesetter:	Lynn Miyata
Indexer:	Molly Hall
Cover Designer:	Michelle Lee

Contents

Acknowledgments

Each of the chapters in this book has been written specifically for it. However, I wish to acknowledge the following sources, in which various chapters were originally published in different forms.

Chapter 2: Revised version of "Life Stories: Pieces of a Dream." In G. Rosenwald & R. Ochberg (Eds.), *Storied Lives* (pp. 127-144). New Haven, CT: Yale University Press. Copyright 1992 by Yale University Press. Adapted with permission.

Chapter 3: Revised version of "Narratives of the Gendered Body in the Popular Autobiography" (with K. J. Gergen). In R. Josselson & A. Lieblich (Eds.), *The Narrative Study of Lives* (pp. 191-218). Newbury Park, CA: Sage. Copyright 1993 by Sage Publications. Adapted with permission.

Chapter 4: Revised version of "Talking About Menopause: A Dialogic Analysis." In L. E. Thomas (Ed.), *Research on Adulthood and Aging,* by permission of the State University New York Press. Copyright 1989 by the State University of New York. All Rights Reserved.

Chapter 8: Revised version of "From Mod Masculinity to Post-Mod Macho: A Feminist Re-Play." *The Humanistic Psychologist,* 1990, *18,* 95-104.

PART I

Straight Talk

An Introduction

I am tempted to call this brief introduction the seduction. Despite the title, this straight talk is not about sex, lies, or even videotape. This siren call is placed here to offer an enticement into a particular orientation that has kept this book in my dreams, fantasies, and thoughts for a long time. As I endeavor to create an origin myth for the beginnings of this book, I look back to a moment of epiphany in which I said to myself, "What if?" What if one took seriously the critiques of science that had been converging on psychology since the revival of Kuhn's *The Structure of Scientific Revolutions* in 1970? What if one tried to reconfigure psychology so that the arguments that created the "crisis" conversations in diverse arenas in the social sciences could be addressed in a fruitful manner?[1] What if one did psychology in that empty space of possibility beyond the domain of the everyday and the taken for granted? What if one could do it differently? How would it look? Did I dare to try?

These provocative questions came upon me suddenly, but with excellent preparation, as I now see it in the wonderful afterglow of events past. It is difficult to separate the various strands of influence that are woven together in the creation of such a moment. One cannot determine which events produced the woof and which the warp in the making of a vision. How important were all the conversations beginning in the mid-1970s with Kenneth Gergen and other close friends and colleagues, many of whom had visited our home, to discuss the latest events in the developing schism in social psychology? What influence did the encounters with Erving Goffman have, in which he outrageously called into question all that was taken as doctrine in the empirical social sciences? How central was the graduate course in the philosophy of the behavioral sciences with Professor Joseph Margolis at Temple University, which I greedily dissected later with my fellow graduate student Walter Paynter? Or our seminar with Willis Overton, who presented contrasting models of development, a first step in constructionism? What was the influence of the introduction of "postmodern" ideas, first concentrated in the work of French intellectuals, especially feminists, and then spreading across the Atlantic and into every crevice of American cultural life? Surely the word *postmodern* has become an echo through all of my work. Although I have grown to understand myself as a social constructionist, it is also clear that social constructionism is a page from the postmodern text. From another angle, it is important to recognize that my biography as a feminist, which began in the "second wave of feminism" and its powerful demands for equality, was tempted by the rites of those who held that women are a special breed of superior creatures apart from the social order, and then later became challenged by the potentials of a new feminism that could be integrated with postmodern perchances.

I know that these influential strands, as well as many others, led me to write a paper in which I brought together the lessons of critique and the politics of feminism—a way that took seriously the exhortations both to leave certain practices behind and to enhance the agendas of feminism. For the feminist critiques, I was indebted to many feminist scholars who had preceded me in the production of arguments against the scientific practices in these traditional, male-dominated fields.[2] My hope was that out of this tumult, new paths for doing psychology could be blazed (M. M. Gergen, 1988b). This paper, written over a decade ago, concerned the ways in which a feminist perspective, informed by these philosophical critiques, would challenge the dominant paradigm of psychology, bringing to it a fresh assembly of possibilities.

Five facets of doing psychology seemed especially in need of reform. The first challenge involved the traditional view of the scientist as noninterventionist. This tenet suggested that *the scientist is or should be an uninvolved and unbiased spectator who simply collects the data from subjects* once the research study is underway. The supposed advantage of this perspective was that the neutrality and distance from subjects imposed upon the scientist would result in no relationship bias to influence the independence of subjects' responses. Subjects would not act in order to please or to displease the scientist. Yet as feminists, including myself, argued, any form of interaction between scientist and subject constitutes relatedness. To have "no relationship" is a social/physical impossibility. An alternative compatible with this critique would be to incorporate into the scientific endeavor the view that the investigator and the other are interdependent: that is, involved in a partnership of some sort. The necessity and nature of this relationship became the first premise in the effort to create new methodologies.

A second source of difficulty within the traditional scientific metatheory was the proposition that *general laws of human behavior can be established through experimental methods.* In general, psychologists work under the assumption that by testing the responses of a selected sample of subjects in a controlled experimental setting, basic laws of human behavior can be obtained. But several aspects of this enterprise are problematic. The most basic difficulty has to do with the practical value of creating these so-called "general laws." What good is it to note how people behave under controlled laboratory conditions if these conditions bear no resemblance to ordinary life? I also noted the problems with interpreting results when people are stripped of their relational connections and placed in a quasi-featureless environment, seemingly out of time and place. Would the same subjects act similarly in any other venue? Also of concern was the nature of the subject pools on which these general laws were based, which, very often, were American college sophomores taking introductory psychology. Not even the most ardent experimentalist would hold that this sample was an adequate representation of humankind, except under the rarest of circumstances. In a feminist alternative, researchers would be humble about the generalization of their findings from unrepresentative samples. They would recognize the limitations of gathering information from people who are acting in a condition of disconnection from their normal social groups in strange settings. Rather than working in this manner, researchers would incorporate into their studies a recognition of the social embeddedness of the research participants. This approach would expand on the relevance of their findings to ordinary life events.

The temporal specificity of the research enterprise was also noted. Everything occurs within specific time-space coordinates. Thus, psychology, as a culturally sensitive science, can be seen as the historical contingency study of similar events (K. J. Gergen, 1973). Universality of results, exact replicability, or transhistorical lawfulness would be renounced as scientific goals. Researchers would be aware of not only the socially constructed nature of the phenomenon under study but also of their own historically embedded conditions. Researchers are people as well as scientists and are bound by temporal effects. This form of reflexivity is essential to a view that eschews foundational truths and accepts the historically situated nature of all activity.

The third point of my critique and reassessment was focused on the issue of values. *Traditional science had made claims to a stance of value neutrality.* Somehow, during the conduct of science, personal values were to be left aside to keep the enterprise free of selfish considerations. This seemed to me an impossible state of affairs to achieve. Rather, as many feminists had already noted, value implications are embedded in every choice of words, in every theoretical framework, and even in the manner in which statistical findings are described. Thus, value neutrality had lost a great deal of credibility as a way of framing scientific work. Instead, to quote feminist sociologist Shulamit Reinharz (1985),

> The feminist critique of social science supports the view that since interest-free knowledge is logically impossible, we should feel free to substitute explicit interests for implicit ones. Feminism challenges us to articulate our values and, on the basis of these, to develop new theories and formulate new research practices. (p. 163)

How liberating these words feel, and how dangerous. New forms of psychology would stake out value-based claims for all the world to see. (At least, that is the principle at stake.) The obvious advantage to this approach is that the effort to disguise or suppress value-laden terms or perspectives would be reduced; the obvious disadvantage is that those who are skeptical of the value orientation are forewarned of the position of the psychologist. Thus, a greater skepticism about research itself is called forth. But is that outcome necessarily a negative one?

The fourth assumption challenged the notion that *facts are independent of the scientist who establishes them.* This is still a standard notion within most of psychology, as well as in other sciences. Many critics have disagreed with this view of objectivity. The feminist perspective suggests instead that all aspects of scientific work require acts of choice and interpretation. Whatever is, in terms of the invisible hand of nature, is unknowable until it is created in systems of symbolic significance. Scientists in an important sense are required to select the relevant vocabulary in which to couch their research; they choose the theoretical framework and explanatory systems in which to place their procedures; they run statistical tests that meet the demands of their research communities; and they produce forms of data display—graphs, figures, tables, and/or sentences—in which to present their findings. As a result, most critics, including feminists, argue that findings are not simply found; they only seem to be.[3] To integrate this orientation into the new way of doing science, it is important that all researchers, including feminists, be willing to acknowledge that research results depend upon their own interpretive skills and the regulatory forms that membership in a community of scholars requires. The preferences of those who support one's work have a powerful impact on how research is reviewed, published, and received. In this sense, the regulation and control of the work of scientists is based not on logical considerations but on the necessity of conforming to one's scientific peers. Once these issues are clarified, it is possible for psychologists to be sensitive to the choices they make in naming things and measuring things and to avoid the pitfalls of a seemingly objective approach to science.

Another critical concern involved an assumption I believe is generally prevalent in the culture: that *scientific methods are superior to other forms of knowledge acquisition.* The scientific community has somehow managed to wrestle the mantle of truth from the shoulders of theologians, philosophers, judges, and historians to place it upon its own. Because of the assumed superiority of scientific truths over others, scientists have often become uninterested in the insights that others have to offer in terms of "reality" claims. In the social sciences, research participants' opinions about the experiences they undergo in a psychology study, for example, are usually disregarded unless they have been elicited by standardized measurements. The strict design control over how experiments, surveys, interviews, and even case studies are produced is indicative of the authority vested in the scientist. Following the design of the study precisely is expected; any deviant activity on the part of the participants or researchers is undesired. If psychologists look beyond their own domains for theoretical insights, it is most often to the "harder" sciences of neurobiology, computer science, or evolutionary biology. A feminist alternative would allow for a collaborative approach to research, in which an openness to the potentials of participants to offer ideas and to give reactions and evaluations to the researcher would be solicited and appreciated. Psychologists would also be encouraged to investigate and appreciate the insights of those in other fields, especially the "unscientific" ones. This mode could lead to a reflexive position regarding one's research. When one realizes that what has been done could have been done otherwise, then one can reflect upon one's actions and ask whether this mode of study is the best or the only mode that one could have chosen. Although there is no end to this questioning and no final answer, the asking itself is of benefit in breaking the mask of authority that represents the personification of the scientist. Of course, it also opens the door to questions about what criteria should be considered as leading to the "good."

Having considered all of these alternative options together, I began to dream of how to create a multifaced psychology that would in some fashion instantiate these new possibilities. Ultimately, the chapters of this book are the result of this quest—to experiment with alternatives to the dominant traditions in psychology. The title of the book, *Feminist Reconstructions in Psychology,* signals that each way of doing things could have, and perhaps should have, been otherwise. There is a partiality, sometimes a tentativeness, and an optional quality to what I have said I have done. In this important sense, the postmodern admonition to avoid closure is honored. The projects I describe are presented not as prototypes but rather as intimations of future possibilities. Nothing is meant to serve as "the last word." One of the advantages of this approach is that it invites others to develop similar ideas in an entirely different manner. Another advantage is to blunt the criticisms of those who see the limits to any or all of what I have done.

I discovered along the way to practicing a new psychology that it is very difficult and not altogether wise to bypass traditional solutions to research problems at all times. Overall, in these chapters, some more than others, there is a melding of more traditional approaches with more unconventional ones. When I found myself not at the margins of the discipline but directly in the middle, I became rather disconcerted. I could not imagine any alternatives to traditional practices, or I was not unaware that I had replicated them. Eventually I concluded that the notion of margin versus middle is an overworked polarity in itself. The borders between insider and outsider are not so clear and clean as one might wish or pretend. The suspicions that I have developed concerning binary oppositions have also been a postmodern gift. At the same time, the changing nature of the field, which has grown and developed in many fascinating ways since its inception, has created a situation in which provocative interventions from 10 years ago have become part of the conventions today. In particular, the notion of gender as socially constructed is so accepted now as to seem mundane. What was conceived of as a disruptive jolt calling for revolution has become in some circles merely a gentle rocking of revision. As I read and reread what I have written, there are times when I wish I could go back to do some things differently. Yet perhaps there is also inspiration in the "failures."

Because of my involvement in surveying innovative methods I am aware of the strong desire among scholars in communications, cultural studies, and women's studies, among others, to find new ways of investigation within their subject areas. In the concluding chapter of the *Handbook of Qualitative Research* (M. M. Gergen & K. J. Gergen, 2000), qualitative researchers in the social sciences and humanities reported on how they are working with others on approaches developed in their own fields of origin, which are similar to those advocated and adopted in this book.[4] With all of these cross-currents converging at this methodological meeting point, there are illustrative projects that give psychologists an opportunity to expand their repertoires in every topical area.

Although this book is intended to offer liberatory avenues for all psychologists, it is addressed to feminist scholars especially. The topics, the aims, and the primary participants in my research and my imagined audience are women, as well as all who call themselves feminists or friendly bystanders. I'd be happy if the leaders of the political parties in the government wanted to read it as well, but this is far beyond my expectations. However, because the critiques of the field and the search for alternatives have been taken up by a diversity of writers, there may be some question as to why I describe these alternative figurations of doing psychology as feminist. Could they as well be called by some other name? In many cases, I think the answer is yes. Critical theorists, sociologists, socialist liberals, queer theorists, men's studies specialists, socialists, Marxists, Maoists, libertarians, independents, radical lesbians, Paglians, and many others may note great overlaps between the alternatives proposed within this book and what they might claim as their own. I have called these alternatives feminist because they all can be coordinated within a perspective on psychology that defines the position of a social constructionist feminist. Others might prefer other names in keeping with their strongly held positions. As one must always remind oneself, naming is a political act. In Chapter 1, I discuss in great detail the ways in which feminism and social constructionism, the postmodern epistemology that has recently evolved to counter the hegemonic presence of logical empiricism, create a strong, flexible intellectual position that is well suited to the study of gender and women's issues. Much more is said about the union of these two strands of thought as the book progresses.

The chapters explore the ways in which I have been experimenting as a feminist social constructionist psychologist in the past 10 years. Each of the chapters is designed to highlight different aspects of or approaches to doing psychology. In some chapters, the importance of narrative methods is highlighted; in others, literary or historical references are influential; in many, a reflexivity about the nature of the work and my place in it is foregrounded; in one, a focus group application is found; and at the conclusion of the volume, two exemplars of performative psychology, a relatively new way of working with audience responses, are placed. The finale is a not-quite-closed summary, designed to express both a feeling of completion, even if partial and temporary, and an invitation to reflection on the potential of a relational form of psychology on the horizon. There are times for openings, and also for closings, or we could not continue to act into living.

Each chapter also focuses on a particular topical issue related to gender. Regardless of the topic or the method, the general framework is designed within a social constructionist metatheory. Every project is the outcome of involvements of diverse parties, situated within a variety of social settings. One might say I have participated in a variety of "language games" with others and that from them I draw out a story that I relate on these pages. Because of these multiple coconstructions, of which I was only a part, what I am writing is not the truth about what happened; at the same time, it is not a pack of lies. From a constructionist perspective, truth and falsehoods exist only within traditions of talk. A fact or a lie depends upon the linguistic conventions of those speaking to make it so. A convincing example of this to me is the question of whether or not the sun rises or sets. It depends on who is asking and why. Additionally, as a reader you enter into my renditions with your own resources, and from that vantage point, whatever it is, you make sense of them. I see my work as an offering to begin a conversation or to extend or expand an existing one with the reader. I deeply hope that you will experience a sense of intrigue, pleasure, and refreshment in this work, as well as creative/critical bursts that will lead you in directions from which I in turn will someday profit. I anticipate not only that my practices will be helpful to some of you and your future students in their work but that the work of others to which I refer within these pages will lead you into unexplored niches where rich treasures will be revealed.

I also hope that this book will facilitate an expansion of the boundaries of psychology and through this effort create new means of going on together. Although there is a critical edge to some of my comments, especially concerning the nature of psychological research, my purpose is not to alienate those who have been vital contributors to the field. I hope that my views are perceived more as an embrace that welcomes a diversity of practices, than as a stranglehold that prescribes new orthodoxies and suffocates the old. In my enthusiasm to suggest a narrative of change, I do not wish to be disrespectful of the achievements of the past. This doubleness of stance cannot always be sustained, and if I lose my balance from time to time, I hope your tolerance will be forthcoming.

And this is enough straight talk. Straight has its place, but it cannot be taken too seriously. Nothing arouses skepticism about my own talk and others' more than an all-too-constant refrain, without a reflexive verse. One needs a hint of irony, a joke, or even a patch of silence as an escape from sober proclamations. Straight talk requires some bending; the curves come next.

NOTES

1. The so-called "crisis" literature, especially as it was developed in Europe, included such volumes as Buss (1979), K. J. Gergen (1973, 1978, 1985), Harré and Secord (1972), Henriques, Hollway, Urwin, Venn, and Walkerdine (1984), Israel and Tajfel (1972), Rappoport (1984), Rommetveit (1980), and Strickland, Aboud, and Gergen (1976).

2. Among the many works that influenced my ideas were those of Bart (1971), Bernard (1973), Bleier (1984), Deaux (1985), Eagly and Carli (1981), Fausto-Sterling (1981), Fine (1980), Griscom (1992), Haraway (1988), Harding and Hintikka (1983), Henriques et al. (1984), Irigaray (1985a, 1985b), Jaggar (1983), Keller (1985, 1992), Longino (1981), Mednick and Tangri (1972), O'Leary, Unger, and Wallston (1985), Reinharz (1985), Roberts (1981), Rosaldo and Lamphere (1974), Sherif (1979), Shields (1975), Smith (1991), Spender (1980), Stanley and Wise (1983), Unger (1983), Vaughter (1976), Weisstein (1971), and Wilkinson (1986).

3. Sociologists of science had made strong arguments to this effect at this time. Among the most influential were Latour and Woolgar (1979) and Mitroff (1974).

4. These approaches have also had a strong resonance with other work documented in a bibliographic article (M. M. Gergen, Chrisler, & LoCicero, 1999) written for a special issue on innovative methods for *Psychology of Women Quarterly* (Crawford & Kimmel, 1999), as well as featured in *Toward a New Psychology of Gender* (M. M. Gergen & Davis, 1997).

1

The Emergence of Feminist Postmodern Psychology

If you come to a crossroads, take them!

—Rachel Hare-Mustin (1991)

Inviting readers into an appreciation of feminist postmodern psychology in just one chapter is a formidable challenge. (As I revise it for the hundredth time, I realize it could have been a book in itself.) My aim is to tell the story of feminist psychology from the traditional empiricist approach of the 1970s, through the introduction of the feminist standpoint position in the 1980s, and finally to the radical disjuncture of the postmodern turn in the 1990s. Many versions of this history can be and have been told[1]; this is one that serves to emphasize the evolving nature of feminist psychology in terms of its underlying assumptions about what it is to be a feminist science. As such, it provides a background for the chapters that follow.

Over the past three decades, feminist psychology[2] has grown enormously in countries characterized as "Western" in culture, and it is emerging in others as well. With this energetic expansion has come a weakening of the dominant scientific movement that gave it birth and, in its place, an ever-increasing willingness to challenge its ancestry. Celia Kitzinger (1991b), a prominent British psychologist, has described this tension in the following manner: "Feminist psychology is fundamentally a contest over meanings . . . what questions can be asked, and what constitute legitimate answers" (p. 49). The increasing fragmentation of perspectives, values, and intellectual commitments among psychologists has stimulated exciting and sometimes contentious dialogues about what constitutes proper questions and legitimate answers, even within feminist psychology itself.

A decade ago, I believed that the unification of feminist voices both within psychology and across all disciplines was an important political and intellectual goal, and I wrote of "the power for transformation that one clear song of feminism might some day hold" (M. M. Gergen, 1988a, p. x). Today I believe that this vision is no longer dreamable or even desirable, even in one discipline. What is possible for feminist psychologists does not depend upon unity. The range of pursuits within feminist psychology is not a discouraging formation,[3] nor is the rising chorus of different voices to be regarded as problematic. Rather, from a postmodern position, a new appreciation of this diversity becomes possible. Although this tolerant viewpoint may seem to beg the crucial question of defining how scientific endeavors are to be conducted, it does offer a valuable alternative toward scientific as well as toward other cultural practices—that is, the view that no one set of standards is or should be hegemonic. For some, this alternative may pose unacceptable challenges to previous understandings of science. Yet the current beliefs about what constitutes "good" science have also constrained many feminist psychologists. More will be said later in this chapter about the value of diversity in the production of psychologies of gender. For now, I would venture that the freedom to explore more broadly is a growing desire among many feminist psychologists (see the two-part special issue on innovative methods in *Psychology of Women Quarterly* edited by Crawford & Kimmel, 1999). My argument, in brief, is that the emergence of a feminist postmodern position may afford opportunities for new conversations, new resources for reaching politically valued ends, and innovative methods of research in the psychology of gender.

In what follows, three distinct forms of study in feminist psychology are reviewed. To give life to these differences within the chapter, particular attention is paid to the question of how *gender identity* is defined in these various approaches. I have chosen this topic because it is basic to all forms of feminist psychology. In clarifying the term *gender identity,* the question of what constitutes "difference" also becomes relevant. That is, within each perspective, assumptions are made as to whether women and men are essentially the same or opposite to one another, or whether they are neither the same nor opposite until someone says they are.[4] The tension over the notion of difference is significant in feminist psychology because it is related to the question of what the major purpose of feminism is. For some feminists, the goal of the movement is the resolution of gender differences. Thus, if women and men are truly equal, and if fairness prevails in all things, then differences become unimportant. For other feminists, the goal of the movement is to focus on the special qualities of women and to promote a culture in which feminist values prevail. For them, a focus on difference is inherent to the celebration of women's identity and feminism. The postmodern approach is to question—but not to deny—all linguistic categories, and especially to resist the reification of universal, atemporal ones, including gender.

THE FEMINIST-EMPIRICIST POSITION:
THE (FAIRLY) COMFORTABLE MAJORITY

In 1986, the feminist philosopher Sandra Harding published *The Science Question in Feminism,* in which she distinguished three feminist epistemologies: feminist empiricist, feminist standpoint, and feminist postmodern. These three positions are widely recognized within the humanities and to some extent within the social sciences as well. Though Harding's tripartite distinction was not specifically intended to apply to psychology, I believe it can be useful in clarifying similarities and differences among feminist psychologists. Looking more closely at the ways each can be applied to psychological practices, we may be inspired to create hybrids and new forms altogether.

The World of the Modernist: Enlightenment's Creation

The Scientific Enterprise

Harding's description of feminist empiricism corresponds to dominant traditions within academic psychology today. The source of this psychology is found in the methodology of the natural sciences, which itself springs from the philosophical heritage of the Enlightenment. Although the vast array of meanings attached to the notion of the Enlightenment cannot be discussed in detail here, we may briefly pay tribute to the impact of this once revolutionary movement on contemporary life, including the creating of scientific activity. The intellectual world as we know it would not exist without the services of those within the modernist movement who freed us from the constraints of earlier ways of thinking that confined inquiry solely to the search for God's truth as revealed in creation (Nicholson, 1990; Nicholson & Seidman, 1995). The political struggle born of the modernist imagination—from Galileo's early trials with the medieval church to the defense of evolutionary theory in the 20th century—led to the development of empirical forms of discovering knowledge, which became the foundation for contemporary scientific research. Modernists believed in a truth that, rather than being defined as what God's ordained theologians had to say, was available to all those who freely and carefully made inquiries based upon observations of the natural world. Progress was built on the accumulations of scientific studies, and truth was the end result.

Science in an important way was conceived as a sensual activity. The means for discovering truth were grounded in the senses. What investigators saw, heard, touched, or otherwise perceived provided the basis for proving something true or false. Thus, evidence was public. This was indeed a powerful departure from reliance on disciples, priests, or philosophers, who could deduct the principles of the universe from unquestioned a priori assumptions. In this move to empirical science, a democratic spirit of inquiry challenged all that had stood before it. It was no wonder that this new approach to acquiring knowledge created such a powerful stir. The question of how to communicate the findings—the sensory experiences derived from observations—was dealt with by assuming that certain prescribed ways of describing phenomena would produce adequate reflections of the events themselves. Particularly with the use of mathematics, seemingly the purest form of knowledge, the transmission of knowledge from the physical to the symbolic could be achieved without undue distortions. Other rules of conduct to ensure accuracy included operationalizing terms, so that their definitions were clearly tied to the objects observable in the world; using common measurements that could be easily recognized, replicated, and reported among scientists; avoiding poetic language, such as metaphors and other figures of speech, which relied upon imaginary instead of factual realms; depending upon logical reasoning to accurately draw conclusions from sense data; avoiding emotional involvement with one's findings; and developing rigorous reporting forms that organized research into preestablished formats. In sum, scientists held that with proper procedures, the language of science could effectively "mirror" the empirically derived facts of nature, create an "objective" field of inquiry, and culminate in general laws of nature, which could be universally applied (K. J. Gergen, 1994; Higgins & Kruglanski, 1996). This reasoning, which should sound very familiar to all of us, has been the justification of the majority of natural and social science practices until today.[5]

Modernist Culture and the Place of Psychology

Just as the scientific world has been shaped by Enlightenment ideas, so has the culture more generally. From or with these ideas has sprung the modern world we inhabit, including its liberal humanist political philosophy, which serves as the basis of democracy. One aspect of this heritage has been to foreground the single individual as the source of thought, volition, and action (Sampson, 1981, 1991). It is this person who perceives via the senses and who can incorporate this information into various forms of knowledge and behavior. The focus on the individual as the organizer of knowledge has paved the way to a science of the individual—that is, psychology.[6] This interest has stimulated curiosity concerning differences among people's subjective states and whether they can be clarified and contained in general scientific laws about human minds and behaviors. The challenge of psychology has been to do just that.

In many other ways, the modernist world was also congenial to the production of psychology. As incorporated into General Electric's motto, "Progress is our most important product," the notions that we can accumulate knowledge, that science can lead us to a better world, and that the values of scientific method are generalizable to all other facets of social life are significant principles. Most institutions and individuals in Western culture value progress, orderliness, rationality, efficiency, and objectivity in their interactions with people and things. In fields as different as Bible translation, management theory, and engineering, modernism altered the ways in which work was done. The modern translations of the Bible, for example, simplified the language by altering or erasing poetic verses that were considered too obscure in their meaning. Early 20th-century management theorists advocated metaphors of machine functioning to prescribe more efficient human productivity on factory lines. In the fields of architecture and engineering, modernism stressed functionality over decoration and the straightforward over the fanciful. The skylines of American's major cities, pierced by soaring skyscrapers devoid of any decorative flourishes, illustrate the application of the modernist motto "Form follows function" to urban design. The predominance of scientific methods that led to enormous cultural innovations in the 1960s, including landing a man on the moon, producing a polio vaccine, inventing birth control pills, improving weather prediction, and creating "just-in-time" inventory control of production via computers, greatly reinforced those who employed and were affected by such modern techniques.

Psychology as a Modernist Science

The optimism created by the belief that science could eventually solve all significant social problems played into the development of psychology and helped to create its powerful position in the social sciences. The promise of a truly modernist psychology was to create forms of understanding that could encompass human behavior and eliminate previously intractable social ills such as crime, poverty, prejudice, mental illness—and the list goes on. Psychology's prominent place at the table where scientific research funds are doled out reminds us of the modernist expectation that psychology will solve significant social problems scientifically.

Over the last century, mainstream psychological research has responded to this challenge by evolving standards of practice in emulation of the natural science models. This research is characterized by a search for general laws on the basis of a highly evolved methodology, replete with sophisticated statistical methods. One of the most important rules of the game, as mentioned in the introduction to this book, is that research be produced from an unbiased or value-neutral position, or one as close to that standard as is humanly possible (Tetlock, 1994). The eventual goal of psychology is the prediction and control of human activity. Although some aspects of this formulation have mellowed with time, the guardians of the tradition keep a fierce eye on those who do not honor this perspective (e.g., Kimble, 1984, 1995).

We speak of hard data as being better than soft data, hard science better than soft science, hard money better than soft money. . . . This is of course a male metaphor, so since discovering this, I have substituted a metaphor based on female sexual experience and refer to wet and dry data.

—Pauline Bart (1971, p. 1)

The Feminist-Empirical Turn

Supporting the Modernist Science Methodology

Feminist empiricists in psychology are modernists in that they generally agree with their peers as to what constitutes "good" scientific practices within the field. All prominent textbooks in the psychology of women are based upon this scientific legacy (Kahn & Yoder, 1989). Two of the leading journals in the field, *Psychology of Women Quarterly,* sponsored by the American Psychological Association, and *Sex Roles,* reflect this commitment to empirical research methods in their editorial policies and in their publishing practices. Upon becoming editor of *Psychology of Women Quarterly* in 1995, Nancy Felipe Russo (1995) described *Sex Roles* as comparable in its emphasis on traditional empirical methods of study with *Psychology of Women Quarterly* and described *Feminism and Psychology,*[7] a British journal that regularly publishes research based on qualitative methods, as "exciting and innovative and . . . a wonderful foil for the scientifically-oriented perspective of *PWQ*" (p. 2). From this perspective, *scientific* is aligned with certain methods and forms and not others. As is the case with other psychologists, feminist empiricists, especially those using statistical measures and experimental methods, have tended to value quantitative research over qualitative work. Reasons for this preference are many, including clarity of research design, ability to control the variables, the possibility of making causal statements, and, perhaps most important, attaining social influence within the field. Noted feminist researcher and author Rhoda Unger (1988) has bluntly summarized this view: "If such tools may not be used by feminist psychologists there is little likelihood that their insights will be taken seriously by the rest of the discipline" (p. 137). The tension between being a feminist and being a respectable scientist is foreshadowed in this statement.

Feminist psychologists are by definition committed to a political stance that is not value neutral, and this creates a barrier to being wholly accepted by the mainstream community, which supports objectivity in all matters. If the true scientist is one who takes a value-neutral stand, then the feminist psychologist, with a public value commitment, is in danger of being discredited as biased and unscientific. The conflict is historically rooted, as Letitia Anne Peplau and Eva Conrad noted in 1989: "The fundamental issue for feminist psychology is the dilemma of combining feminism—a value orientation with action implications—and the tradition of psychology as an empirical science striving for objectivity and value-neutrality" (p. 381). To counter this threat, many feminist empiricists hold that their political values are influential in the way they approach psychological research—for example, in selecting what areas they research and in avoiding sexist practices of all kinds—but most insist that their feminist values in no way corrupt the integrity of their scientific activities.

Feminist-Empiricist Critiques of Mainstream Psychology

Though identifying with mainstream standards of scientific excellence, feminist empiricists have distinguished themselves from their nonfeminist peers in their fight against sexist practices within the field (Lott, 1985; McHugh, Koeske, & Frieze, 1986).[8] Their chief criticism has been that standards of scientific integrity and objectivity have been violated to the disadvantage of women. To prevent these abuses, empiricists generally turn to the scientific method itself. This view is expressed in Harding's (1987a) review of the empiricist position: "Androcentric biases are eliminable by stricter adherence to the existing methodological norms of scientific inquiry. It is 'bad science' . . . which is responsible for . . . biases [against women] in the results of research" (p. 182), not the innate form of science itself. Feminist empiricists have argued strongly for internal reforms in research practices in order to produce a more gender-equitable psychology.

These feminists have decried sexism in many ways—for example, in pointing out how women's issues have been avoided in more prestigious journals, how gender as a variable has been ignored, and how research results have been interpreted to the advantage of men.[9] Over the last 20 years, feminist empiricists have greatly affected the ways in which psychological research is conducted. No longer is it possible for researchers to do studies on men and then claim that the findings apply to both sexes. Far fewer studies are done using men only. Certain topics that once were discouraged from mainstream journals have made some headway—for example, articles are published on gender differences in physiological states, sexual harassment, health issues, and parenting.

Other examples of reforming psychology are also evident. One clear-cut success for feminists is the inclusion of explicit guidelines against sexist language in manuscripts submitted for publication to professional journals published by the American Psychological Association. This guideline is now widespread in all forms of publications in the field and in other professions influenced by psychology. Feminist empiricists have also been involved in the professional development of women in psychology, and the combination of mentoring and political activism has made a difference in the governance structures of the professional organizations, among others. Great strides have been made in areas of professional inclusion—fairness in graduate school selection, hiring for entry-level jobs, gains in numbers in terms of promotion and tenure decisions, and access to leadership positions across many areas of the field. Though women in academic life are still predominantly in lower-ranking positions and the social inequality of women beyond the ivory tower still leaves much to be accomplished, feminist-empiricist psychologists continue to wage campaigns to empower women in all areas of life. The capacity of empiricist feminists to advance feminist causes remains significant. They hold the majority of positions of influence within the field and elsewhere where feminist psychologists are invited. In joining with the majority of research psychologists, as empirical scientists, they gain a measure of respectability that offsets their commitment to gender issues (Eagly, 1995; Unger, 1988).

Feminist Empiricists and Gender Identity

Feminist empiricists seldom ask the question: Who is the subject of our research? Contemporary psychological studies, except for the postmodernist, are grounded in three basic assumptions about this subject: (a) The unit of psychological investigation is the single individual; (b) each individual is normally equipped with a biological sex, which is designated female or male; and (c) each of these sexed individuals is socialized into a gender role during the course of development. Feminist empiricists, along with others, uphold a distinction between *sex,* which is pure biology, and *gender,* which is our socialized femininity and masculinity (Unger, 1989). Psychologists of women generally study gender-related topics within these definitional constraints.

"If you're married and want to stay that way, you learn to keep your mouth shut." With relatively few exceptions, feminists have learned this lesson in their marriage with the discipline of psychology. . . . Feminist psychology itself tends problematically to reproduce the individualism and conservatism of the larger discipline.

—Michelle Fine and Susan Gordon (1991, p. 20)

The single, independent, individual as the unit of analysis is supported, in part, because the responses of the individual form a necessary preamble to the production of data designed for statistical analysis. One of the results of the focus on the individual is that social conditions become translated into trait or state terms describing the interior of the individual. For example, the effects of living in an impoverished neighborhood in which there is a lack of resources are translated into individual personality traits, such as having a high score on an "external control" variable, a learned-helplessness scale, or a test for clinical depression. Feminist empiricists generally do not question how the practice of exploring the psyche of the individual might itself contribute to the oppression of women as a social group (Parlee, 1991). Yet there are arguments that suggest that it does. As Mary Brown Parlee (1991) has described it, "At the conceptual level, theoretical frameworks and interpretations have in general continued . . . to reframe structural forces as individual attributes or internal psychological 'variables' . . . while neglecting other social and political analyses" (pp. 40-41). For Parlee, as well as for other feminists, socialist or Marxist in particular, this tendency to turn away from societal critique and to focus on individuals, who are the "carriers" of social ills, suppresses the possibility of including social structure within explanatory frameworks. Large-scale social changes cannot emerge from an analysis that is limited to variables related to the interior of the individual.

This tendency to individualize all conditions and problems also occurs within empirical descriptions of therapy and remediation. In the therapeutic setting, the therapist tries to assist in the reformation of the individual patient, who is defined as the locus of distress and disability (M. M. Gergen, 1994; Hare-Mustin, 1994). Evidence that women have been disproportionally diagnosed as "depressed," "anxious," or "hypochondriacal" supports the view that women have certain weaknesses that men do not have and that individuals are the source of their problematic state (Marecek, 1993). The same can be said of the diagnoses prevalent among men, such as alcoholism and violent outbursts. The focus on individuals as the loci of pathology forces oppressive social and political systems into theoretical invisibility and can result in blame being placed on individuals for their failures to adjust or be emotionally stable in what might be viewed, via other analyses, as pathological surroundings (see Hare-Mustin & Marecek, 1986, for a detailed analysis of this outcome).

Because most psychologists swim like fish in the waters of individualism, it can be difficult to grasp what is controversial about psychologists studying the individual psyche (Sampson, 1993). Later in the chapter, when postmodern selves are considered, questions are raised about the notion that what we study in gender psychology are biologically determined females and males who are socialized as autonomous selves into gendered beings.

Feminist Empiricists and the
Question of Sex Differences

In terms of contributing to the substantive body of literature in psychology, empirical researchers have investigated many gender-related topics. Yet perhaps the primary concentration of inquiry has been on so-called sex differences, how significant they are, and how they relate to gender stereotypes. The classic volume edited by Eleanor Maccoby and Carol Jacklin (1974), which summarized vast stores of sex difference research, helped to undermine certain assumptions about the "opposite" sexes by noting the lack of differences between them. More recently, meta-analysis, a major statistical innovation, has been helpful in examining sex difference research.[10] Meta-analysis is often able to discover contextual influences that place limitations on any sweeping generalizations about sex differences. This approach has been used to great advantage by feminist empiricists to investigate important issues such as the direction and power of sex differences in mathematical achievements (Hyde & Linn, 1986), leadership (Eagly & Johnson, 1990), helping behavior (Eagly & Crowley, 1986), group performance (Wood, 1987), conformity (Cooper, 1979), aggression (Eagly & Steffen, 1984), and influenceability (Eagly & Carli, 1981; Lockheed, 1985). According to Janet Hyde and Marcia Linn (1986), active researchers in this area, meta-analysis is capable of providing "powerful quantitative answers to questions, thereby smashing many myths about gender differences" (p. 73). In the main, these studies have supported the view that gender differences are rarely as great as common stereotypes of female-male differences suggest. Women are not necessarily poorer at mathematics or leadership abilities, nor are they more persuasible or helpful. How aggressive women and men are depends greatly upon how the variable is measured, as is true of most of the traits under study. In reaching these conclusions, feminist empiricists rely heavily on the validity of the studies under review, which is itself a sign of their complicity with the dominant paradigm. In terms of outcomes, their research tends to support liberal humanist values, which emphasize the worth of the individual and equality between the sexes, and which do little to support notions of either female superiority or female inferiority. In general, for feminist empiricists, the notion of "opposite" sexes in terms of psychological qualities is almost always wrong. Further, feminist empiricists tend to believe that women fare best in society if they are granted equal status with men and that attempts to segregate women by disposition, ability, or skill inadvertently foster subordination in important areas of life. The strong controversy over whether a "Mommy track" for working mothers was a positive or negative option for women in business outlines this difference of opinion among feminists, with empiricists being more inclined to be opposed to such arrangements because of the various dangers of unequal status definitions.

Feminist Empiricism and Reflexivity

Perhaps as a result of this solid history of research success, feminist empiricists have not developed a tradition of skepticism regarding the paradigm in which they work. A strong belief in the adequacy of the scientific enterprise also suppresses attention to the tensions, conflicts, and criticisms of scientific practices that have arisen in psychology and in neighboring disciplines. Allied with powerful groups in the profession, many feminists ignore these challenges and support existing paradigmatic practices (Smith, 1991).[11] Though protecting the profession in the short term, this lack of critical reflexivity threatens to create an isolation from changing intellectual climates in the rest of the culture and, I believe, will eventually endanger its very existence as a relevant social discourse.[12] Within feminist psychology, however, currents of curiosity and resistance born of earlier rebellions are likely to keep this isolationist tendency at bay. In addition, the willingness to tolerate alternative practices created by marginalized contributors may provide feminist psychology with a flexibility unavailable within mainstream psychology.[13]

THE TRANSITION FROM EMPIRICISM TO
THE FEMINIST STANDPOINT POSITION

Certain limitations of traditional psychology, noted by feminist empiricists and nonempiricists alike, helped to create the grounds for an alternative perspective, one that moved away from a gender-neutral, equality-based psychology, in which masculine traits and traditions are often unwittingly supported and enhanced, to a more woman-centered one (Morawski, 1987). Resistance to the dominance of experimental research over other methods also led feminist psychologists to seek new directions. Many critiques viewed experiments as fulfilling certain scientific goals but as failing to satisfy others. One objection was that experiments, in their function as proving grounds for hypotheses, had no "ecological validity."[14] That is, findings created in the laboratory, even though brilliantly designed to test theory, might be incapable of producing knowledge of the social world external to controlled settings. Though I believe most feminist empiricists hope that their research on gender differences has relevance to the so-called "real world," when findings from empirical studies are applied to areas outside the laboratory, problems of applicability arise. For example, such difficulties can be inferred from a careful study on leadership by Alice Eagly and Blair Johnson (1990). In a discussion of their meta-analysis of gender and leadership, the authors noted that the laboratory studies of differences between men and women as leaders contained findings that were contradictory to studies done in the applied settings. That is, in studies of people in leadership positions in the "real world," women and men were judged as more similar in styles of leadership than in laboratory settings. Given this lack of generalizability from the laboratory to the field, the utility of the laboratory studies might well be questioned, for leadership positions do not exist in the laboratory, except in artificially contrived ways. Of course, a proponent of meta-analysis might note that the discrepancies in results were located by virtue of the analysis. Thus, ironically, a meta-analysis served the purpose of questioning the utility of laboratory studies for applications to the world outside.

Another practice within mainstream psychology of special concern to feminists of all theoretical persuasions is the use of manipulations and deceptions of subjects in research settings. For many decades, feminist empiricists, along with other psychologists, engaged in projects that from today's standpoint are open to question from an ethical standpoint. Examples come easily to mind. In a research project on romantic relations, women were deceived into thinking they had been asked out on a date in order to evaluate their response to the attractive male confederate (Walster, 1965); in another study, a woman confederate, dressed to look either attractive or ugly, was used to lure men into various romantic activities (Kiesler & Baral; 1970); and in a well-known experiment on the effects of physical attractiveness on dating behavior, psychologists secretly rated undergraduates on their physical appearance as they interacted with them and then lied to them to make them think their blind date for a dance had been arranged by a computer on the basis of compatibility, not by physical appearance, as it actually was (Walster, Aronson, Abrahams, & Rottman, 1966). As various critiques mounted over the years against this type of research, as research interests shifted toward "cognitive" issues, and for many other reasons as well, deception in research projects has lessened. However, in principle, the total control over subjects and manipulation as needed within the experimental setting has never been rejected by many feminist empiricists.[15]

The feminist critique of the control/manipulate school of psychology has most often stemmed from a value position that is critical of the power dynamics of the research endeavor in which the researcher is master and the subjects are servants within the research design. In such arrangements, it is claimed that the patriarchal nature of the society becomes replicated and justified in the name of science (Lykes, 1989). Feminist psychologists began to modify their roles in research in order to create more parity between the subject and the researcher. In this move, the unviolated voice of the subject became more respected as the source of scientific knowledge (M. M. Gergen, 1988b). The heartland of scientific activity became that of discovering women's stories of their everyday lives. For some feminist psychologists, especially those involved in therapy and education, this move toward a nonmanipulative, observational research format created a promising new mode for engaging with gender issues.

THE FEMINIST STANDPOINT POSITION: WOMEN'S TRUTH(S)

By listening to the stories women tell about their lives . . . we have found that . . . women's sense of self and of worth is most often grounded in the ability to make and maintain relationships.

—Jean Baker Miller and Irene Pierce Stiver (1997, p. 16)

Trading the God's-Eye View for the Goddess's Hearth

Harding (1986b) referred to the second epistemological position as the feminist standpoint position.[16] In agreement with the empiricist claims, feminist standpoint philosophy supports the view that knowledge is derived from experience. These feminists argue that traditional science has been developed by men, whose life experiences have been historically very different from women's. Thus, the claims of universality made by scientists should be modified to be called "Men's Science." Those who first took up the feminist standpoint position also argued that it was time to build another science, not one that appeared to be universal, as in the famed "God's-eye view" position claimed by traditional scientists, but one that represented women's knowledge (Haraway, 1988). For many feminist standpoint theorists, this new position not only would be distinct from the men's standpoint but also would provide a superior type of knowledge. It would be better because the work and life experiences of women are closer to the realities of life than those of men, who live in artificial work settings, removed from the nitty-gritty concrete detail of the real world (Hartsock, 1983). This argument was both pleasing to many feminists, who had long tried to wrestle against the pervasive notions of their inferiority expressed by male scientists and philosophers, and problematic to defend. How could one standpoint be inherently better than another? As Harding (1987a) described it,

> Knowledge is supposed to be based on experience, and the reason the feminist claims can turn out to be scientifically preferable is that they originate in, and are tested against, a more complete and less distorting kind of social experience. (p. 184)

In her view, the feminist standpoint position is reached through the process of intellectual and political struggle against male oppression. "Thus the standpoint theorists offer a different explanation than do feminist empiricists of how research that is directed by social values and political agendas can nevertheless produce empirically preferable results of research" (Harding, 1987a, p. 185).

From within the standpoint position, knowledge is again vested in individuals, and it can be gathered from their self-disclosures. The research methods used to obtain these insights are usually qualitative (Gavey, 1989; M. M. Gergen et al., 1999). Such methods are preferred because they avoid the pitfalls of traditional standardized measures that squelch or deform the localized and personal knowledge of research participants and support the hierarchy of researcher over researched. The standpoint position holds that participants in research should be allowed to tell their own stories in their own ways. As a "gynocentric feminism," the standpoint position takes a preferential and sometimes compensatory stance toward women (Belenky, Clinchy, Goldberger, & Tarule, 1986; Black, 1989; Young, 1990).

Socialist/Marxist Influences and the Standpoint Position

There have been diverse forms of standpoint alternatives over the last two decades, including important contributions from Marxist and other socialist sources.[17] These theories involve a social critique dependent upon a materialist base[18] (Hartsock, 1983; Miller, 1976). That is, special attention has been paid by these theorists to the impact of economic conditions on the lives of women. Foundational to these theories is the Marxist claim that issues of production, ownership, and exploitation in the capitalist marketplace are central to the shaping of the individual psyches of women. Exclusion from participation in certain areas of labor; confinement in low-paying, dead-end jobs; lack of opportunities related to unfair employment practices; and exclusion from ownership and wealth by discriminatory property and inheritanĉe laws, among other factors, have all influenced women's experiences of reality and their ways of knowing (Black, 1989; Farganis, 1994; Mies, 1987). These feminists are highly critical of theories that neglect economic factors while stressing psychological ones (Fraser, 1989; Griscom, 1992; Kitzinger, 1987; Mies, 1987; Smith, 1991). Socialist feminists most often assume that much that is particular about women's oppression, and the resultant personality structures that appear, would be changed with an economic and social system that did not privilege certain men over others.

Though many standpoint feminists have been trained in socialist/Marxist orthodoxy, over time most have distanced themselves from positions that do not specify women's concerns (Nicholson & Seidman, 1995). For example, the notion that *means of production* refers only to paid labor outside the home has been challenged or cast aside. As Nancy Fraser (1989) has argued,

> [The] classification of childbearing as symbolic reproduction and of other work as material reproduction is potentially ideological. It could be used, for example, to legitimize the institutional separation of childbearing from paid work, a separation that many feminists, myself included, consider a linchpin of modern forms of women's subordination. (p. 116)

In the last decade, with the worldwide disruptions of communist governments, the popularity of socialist/Marxist theories—feminist and otherwise—has suffered a steep decline. Though once a thriving root of feminist theory, especially in Europe, other versions of social theory and feminism are now gaining momentum. In these versions, materialist concerns are still evident, but the Marxist-style definitions and solutions that overlooked women's lives are missing (Burman et al., 1996; Fraser, 1989; Jaggar, 1983).

Emphasis on Embodiment

Feminist standpoint theorists also tend to emphasize the importance of embodiment in the production of knowledge. Where one stands, both metaphorically and physically, is an essential component of knowledge acquisition for the standpoint theorist, as the name suggests (Griffin, 1993; Grosz, 1994). As has been formulated by the social psychologist Dorothy Smith (1991), the essential biological characteristics of women give rise to relations with the world that are different from men's, and thus to different experiences and perceptions. According to Smith:

> The woman knower for whom we will write the systematic feminist consciousness of psyche and social relations stands outside textually mediated discourse, in the actualities of her local and particular world. She exists in and as body that is the

body of a woman, and is active and experiencing in the modes in which her body relates, anchors, organizes her being as a woman, at all times breasts, vagina, clitoris, and sometimes menstruation, childbirth, suckling and the shape her body takes toward the child. She is always where her body is. (pp. 158-159)

Smith has urged a method of study that progresses by accumulating the phenomenological reports of each person, so that by adding layer upon layer of different tellings, truth will emerge. Her approach

insists on beginning where people are, learning the society from multiple sites, exploring it together and . . . piecing together an account of our discoveries that expands our grasp of how our experience and activity are anchored in, shaped by and part of the extended social relations that are powered by and overpower our lives. (p. 167)

As an alternative to empirical psychology, feminist standpoint researchers have struggled against their notion of the invisible or value-neutral author and the palpability of an objective material world. Rather than accept the transparently knowable nature of the physical world, most standpoint theorists insist on the centrality of the authorial presence in determining the nature of "reality." Contained within the notion of the author's presence is that of the viewer's evaluation and intention in perceiving. There is no value-free or unbiased manner in which to report on the nature of the world. What is important is to acknowledge one's standpoint, to declare it, and to respect its centrality in the formation of one's views.

Listening to girls at the edge of adolescence . . . cracks the cosmic egg of patriarchy and, in so doing, provides an opening through which we can see more clearly the price all children—boys as well as girls—pay for living in a patriarchal culture.

—Lyn Brown (1994, p. 384)

Reclaiming the Lost Voices

One metaphor in particular that is strongly identified with the feminist standpoint perspective is that of discovering, uncovering, and proclaiming the lost voices of women. In her well-known book *In a Different Voice* (1982), based on interviews with women considering abortions, Carol Gilligan gave a new vocabulary to thousands of readers with her claim that moral choices might be based on caring about the relationships of those involved in a dilemma rather than on universal principles of justice. With her students and colleagues, in numerous other books and articles on such topics as learning, life span development, and mental illness and therapy, a new authority for women's views was developed (Belenky et al., 1986; Brown & Gilligan, 1992; Brown et al., 1988; Gilligan, 1982; Gilligan, Lyons, & Hanmer, 1990; Gilligan, Rogers, & Tolman, 1991; Tappan, 1991).

The valuing of marginalized voices has also been championed by others, including psychologists from various minority groups and those involved in cross-cultural work.[19] M. Brinton Lykes (1989, 1996), for example, has worked with women in Guatemala for many years. In bringing together women who have been preyed upon by hostile military forces, who have witnessed the destruction of their villages and the "disappearances" of families, Lykes has helped to give them the courage to tell the stories of their lives and rebuild their sense of hope and potential within a human community. One particular theme within this arena is that of "desilencing" women, of aiding them to reveal their hidden selves and their knowledge of the world, of giving them space to reveal secrets about themselves and about their husbands, bosses, and leaders that, if told, could challenge the political and personal power of men (Miller, 1976).

Desilencing women's secrets of sexuality, danger, passions, violence, oppression, dependence and fears could lead to the creation of political consciousness that might overcome man's power. This political scholarship might enable women to reconceptualize the structural features of their "personal problems" and could clearly create the space for powerful, social research designed to provoke activism.

—Michelle Fine and Susan Gordon (1991, p. 23)

Politics and the Feminist Standpoint Position

The political ramifications of the feminist standpoint position are central to its appeal for many psychologists. With its openly prowoman stance, it has stood as a compelling alternative to empiricist positions for many feminist scholars (Harding, 1991). The standpoint position has encouraged doubts about the standard scientific practices of empirical psychology. For these reasons, it is a highly controversial position but one of great value to many whose dedication to women's rights is not closeted at the laboratory door. It has also encouraged options for collecting data that have been considered inferior by traditional canons of methodological rigor. To collect the stories of people with as little interference as possible moderates the need for laboratory-derived research methods and supports those who are drawn to qualitative methods. In opposition to empiricism, the feminist standpoint position honors a close collaborative relationship between researcher and researched. This approach has had a strong impact on developmental, clinical, and educational psychology, as well as sociology, men's studies, and anthropology. Its influence has also been powerful among educators, therapists, women's studies scholars, and diverse types of support groups (Belenky et al., 1986; Brown, 1994; Jack & Dill, 1992; Miller, 1976; Miller & Stiver, 1997; Tappan, 1991).

The Feminist Standpoint Position
and the Question of Gender Identity

For the feminist standpoint psychologists, as for empirical psychologists, the object of study generally remains the single individual, often framed, however, as the oppressed subject. Standpoint researchers tend to worry that despite their sensitive methods of probing for individual narratives, the danger remains that individuals' truths cannot be told. Pressures to adhere to regulations within the public domain—to be nice girls—remains a central problem (Poland & Pederson, 1998). Thus, gathering data still presents a challenge to standpoint psychologists. In addition, the subject may not be able to "find" the proper words to describe her world. Dana Crowley Jack (1991), writing about depression, detailed the difficulties for women who want to express a subjective reality but have no language readily available. Jack hinted at the possibility that the agentic "I"—central to one's ability to function fully in the cultural realm—is lacking for women. She suggested: "One would expect women to invent phrases . . . to express a subjective reality different from the autonomous, individualistic "I," the self of Western psychology" (p. 30). Yet for Jack and other researchers, women may be silenced, their authentic selves buried by their oppressive conditions that forbid them "true" expression of their needs and wants (Belenky et al., 1986).

Studies of girls becoming adolescents have also focused on the loss of voice, the loss of expression, that accompanies entry into the adult world. Girls who spoke out about their views and feelings as 8-year-olds become bland, opinionless, and self-effacing at 12 (Brown & Gilligan, 1992). This developmental perspective posits a shift in the identity of girls as they become self-conscious about their entry into adolescence. As children, without a strong gender identity, they are bold and precocious, but as budding women, their identity shifts to a much more insecure and silent womanhood. From this viewpoint, girls become deformed by the pressures of the patriarchy, especially when they become valued commodities as fertile women. This distortion continues throughout life unless relieved by education, therapy, or eventually, in some cases, by menopause.

The Feminist Standpoint Position and
the Question of Difference

Differences—both psychological and biological—between men and women serve as a critical organizing principle for feminists taking the standpoint position. A radical interpreter of this standpoint is feminist theologian Mary Daly

(1978), who advocated a separatist position as the only refuge for women in a male-dominated world.[20] To renovate existing cultural forms at the deepest levels of organization, she invented a new feminist language to replace androcentric versions, and more. In her book *Gyn/Ecology* (1978), she wrote that the book "is a declaration/manifesto that in our chronology (Crone-ology) it is time to get moving again. It is a call of the wild to the wild, calling Hags/Spinsters to spin/be beyond the parochial bondings/bindings of any comfortable 'community'" (p. xv).

Spinsters smash our way out of the mirror coffins by our courageous/ contagious Revolting Risking. Our reckless Risking is unlike the ruthless "bravery" of necrophiliac bomb-makers, planet-polluters, who try to turn the earth into their Poisoned Apple.

—Mary Daly (1978, pp. 352-353)

Within this position, the notion of woman as a separate and essentially different gender has led to a reversal of stereotypic categorizing. Thus, suggestions are made that the supposed weaker or inferior sex is in fact superior to men in important ways. Rather than trying to be equal to or like men, which is more characteristic of the empiricist position, standpoint feminists advocate creating different forms of life—modifying or ignoring male forms, as well as their scientific methods and intellectual styles, in order to advance a more truly feminine way.

The central question for standpoint theorists is how to emphasize the female side of the sexual dichotomy and the potential that this unexpressed side has for changing conceptions of psychology, individual lives, and the social world. Whereas empiricist feminists have criticized other psychologists for doing research on men only or for segregating research topics by gender, feminist standpoint researchers have generally argued for women-first and women-only research. As a response to the notion made famous by Simone de Beauvoir (1953) that women have always been positioned as the "Other" in male-dominated systems, women become the "One" in this analysis. Jean Baker Miller's endeavors (Miller, 1976; Miller & Stiver, 1997), and those of the Wellesley Centers for Women with which she is associated, are attempts to "understand the forces acting on and in women, qua women—life as it has been and still is for most of us" (Miller, 1976, p. ix). Feminist standpoint psychologists tend to disregard the argument that without explicit distinctions being made between the sexes, no knowledge of either one can be obtained. Rather, they argue that attention can be given to women without creating the backdrop of the "Other," in this case, of men. They are willing to abandon binary categorizing of the sexes. Their quarrel with empiricists is that these feminists do not take seriously the extent to which they have been coopted by the male-dominated discourse in psychology and have given insufficient expression to alternative, female versions of reality (Gilligan, 1979).

The theoretical base for many feminist standpoint psychologists is adopted from object relations theory, especially as encountered in Nancy Chodorow's influential book *The Reproduction of Mothering and the Sociology of Gender* (1978). In this view, two very different trains of development are instituted by mothers in the care of their babies and by fathers, who are very removed from the childhood caretaker role. In this scenario, mothers treat their daughters as extensions of themselves, and thus of their own gender identities; they treat their sons as "other," as not-female. As young children, boys are required to become physically and psychologically distanced from their mothers. As they find their way, they take on a gender identity created from the more emotionally and physically distant male models available to them. This theoretical base serves as the scaffolding upon which countless feminist standpoint theorists have built their highly popular models of gender identity and difference.

Critiques of the Feminist Standpoint Position

Minority Voices and Silence

Despite its great appeal to many, the feminist standpoint position in psychology has many detractors as well. Various racial and ethnic minority groups have expressed serious reservations about existing points of view (Collins, 1986; Landrine, 1995; Lorde, 1984b; Moraga & Anzaldua, 1981; Sampson, 1993; Spelman, 1988; Yoder & Kahn, 1993). The African American scholar Barbara Christian (1989) has wondered how it is that one particular voice has become *the* voice of women in every social and historical context. She and others have pointed out that the standpoint from which women's truths have been told can in itself be regarded as the basis of oppression. The critical view suggests that this woman-story has most often been told by certain kinds of feminists—white, heterosexual, healthy, middle-aged, middle-class academic women. It is not the single story for all women—those who differ in color, class, age, physical ability, sexual orientation, or ethnicity claims. They have been shut out of the telling by certain advantaged feminists in the same fashion as they claim to have been excluded by men. Though many of these spokespersons have chastised the feminist academy for controlling the standpoint position, it is not clear from the standpoint position what to do about this dilemma. How does one "relativize" one's own story? I believe that the conceptual difficulties of what it means to tell one's own truth have remained unaddressed by both standpoint supporters and critics.

Yet if, as Sandra Harding (1987b) has alleged, the feminist standpoint position is one that is achieved through a sensitive focus on particular women's experiences, then there is the possibility of building a unified truth together by shaping the varieties of "told experiences" into a unity. This position has fallen by the wayside in recent years, in recognition that social, racial, ethnic, physical ability, educational, and other contextual differences make very complex the meaning of what a standpoint is. Often the solution to this dilemma of the single story among those within the standpoint position is to encourage a proliferation of voices, all of whom presumably can speak their own truths. With this strategy, the problem of whose "truth" is canceling out who else's "truths" can be avoided. Of course, other problems surface, such as where to draw the boundaries for storytelling rights, whether anyone can speak for anyone else at all, or whether a proliferation of stories serves a woman-centered cause (Alcoff, 1994; Macmillan, 1990). Harding, who has become a strong advocate of the feminist standpoint position, avoids the tactic of relativizating and historicizing truth, which would be the logical outcome of accepting that every woman's story is a transcendental Truth. Despite some intellectual incoherencies, supporters of the feminist standpoint position resist abandoning it as a viable scientific model, and some have intensified the search for a connection between the postmodern or constructionist position and this one. As Caroline New (1998) put it, "The feminist standpoint . . . as the imagined upshot of an investigative political programme . . . [involves] the *construction* of unity, yet it is also the *discovery* of real bases for that unity" (p. 370). As Harding (1986b) has argued, "Should feminists be willing to give up the political benefits which can accrue from believing that we are producing a new, less biased, more accurate, social science?" (p. 87). Her question appears to be rhetorical, as the answer is an obvious "no." Despite this powerful answer to this difficult conundrum, the intellectual scaffolding of such arguments appears to be weak.

Feminist-Empiricist Resistances

Although both feminist-empiricist and feminist standpoint psychologists have generally subscribed to the central Enlightenment tenets of individualism and scientific thinking, there are tensions between them. For me, the most crucial one involves the nature of language—in particular, the relationship between words and their referents. For the feminist empiricist, the world is available for naming, and there are rational choices to be made about which words are most appropriate given the nature of the phenomena; for the standpoint theorist, naming is a reflection of one's gendered experiences in the world. For the standpoint theorist, the choice of words may differ from the scientist's, but this difference is about the perspective from which the object is perceived. In neither position, however, is there any question about the link between world and word, an issue that will reappear when the postmodernist position is described.

A second tension between the two groups stems from their methodological differences. As has been discussed, empirical psychologists are more likely to prefer quantitative methods, although this tendency has weakened in recent years. Feminist standpoint psychologists are much more favorably inclined toward qualitative work, which is better designed to respect the integrity of personal narratives than analytical investigations.

FEMINIST POSTMODERNISM/POSTMODERN
FEMINISM: JOCKEYING FOR POSITIONS

Postmodernism invites us to engage in continual disillusionment of the grandiose fantasies that have brought us to the brink of annihilation.

—Jane Flax (1993a, p. 147)

Two Postmodern Moves:
Deconstructive and Reconstructive

Postmodernism as an intellectual and cultural movement is entangled in a very profound way with the modern period from which it is emerging (K. J. Gergen, 1991). Many scholars agree that postmodernism, as the name suggests, is the period that comes after modernism and stands in opposition to it. Others have suggested that postmodernism is an heir to or a continuing facet of modernism, not its repudiation. Some have even argued that it was a necessary precursor to modernism, or else modernism could not have been born (Foster, 1983; Jameson, 1984; Kvale, 1992). Whatever the viewpoint, the scholarly terrain encompassed by postmodern themes is immense; I shall not attempt to describe the complexities of this exciting transformative movement in intellectual and social history within this chapter, but I shall refer to some aspects of these discussions in order to arrive at a description of a feminist postmodern psychology.

Deconstruction

Postmodernism might be characterized by two positions—deconstruction and reconstruction. Each takes a skeptical stance on modernist views about the nature of *truth, knowledge,* and *language,* concepts that have been cornerstones of contemporary Western culture since the Enlightenment (Flax, 1990). The deconstructionist movement,[21] originating primarily within French intellectual circles, centers on the nature of language, especially by casting doubt on the ability of language to reference what there is in the world. One form for challenging the presumed function of language to "mirror" the world within deconstructionist circles is reminiscent of the 2-year-old's endless question: "Why?" The game can go on as long as the "becauses," and the answerer, do not wear out. Deconstructionists have demonstrated the possibilities of questioning all conventional meanings and word uses and of showing the ways in which seemingly firm facts about the world are unreliably in flux. This instability is what invalidates the notion of a foundational or absolute truth or field of knowledge, exempt from the vagaries of language. The deconstructionists point out that the closer one examines a word, the less clear one is about its meaning. Words are very flexible, and they have multiple potentialities for use. We cannot know what a word means unless we know what other words have surrounded it (Derrida, 1981). "The Big Apple" becomes New York City in one context, a large fruit in another, a huge painting by artist Karl Appel in another, and, finally, a computer. Though it would appear that such limitations resulting from the capacity to deconstruct every word we speak would mean that we could not communicate with one another, somehow we do manage to get on. But it must be by some means other than by being able to clearly and permanently define what we "mean" when we speak or write. The second position, one that rescues the problem of meaning from this conundrum, is the reconstructive one, which, I suggest, is what social constructionism has to offer us.

Social Construction

The social constructionist position, in its connection to the deconstructionist movement, might be regarded as its Janus-like Other. This metaphor of the two-faced Greek god guarding doorways allows us to grasp the simultaneously opposing aspects of these processes. One process involves deconstructing or dissolving meanings, and the other involves creating and supporting it. The creation of new discourse forms as "reality making" focuses attention on the communities of users instantiating social reality through language practices. As we talk and coordinate movements with each other, we construct the world. Through a continual process of supplementation in which we acknowledge each other's utterances, we cocreate reality. People nod, smile, say "Good morning," "Pass the butter," or "Let us pray," and others respond by nodding back, saying hello, passing the butter, and bowing their heads in prayer. Together, in diverse forms of habitual practices, we perform the world, whatever world there is, each and every moment.

Though social constructionism as a reconstructive practice shares an affinity with deconstructionist practices, the origins of social constructionist ideas are different and diverse. Contributors to the origins of the contemporary social constructionist scene are well known in many of the social sciences, particularly in sociology. Among the most familiar are the symbolic interactionists, as well as those who have called themselves social constructivists (especially Berger & Luckmann, 1966; Cicourel, 1968; Cooley, 1902; Garfinkel, 1967; Goffman, 1959; Kelly, 1955; Mead, 1934).

Primarily cognitive in their orientation, symbolic interactionists and social constructivists have created theories about meaning making that emphasize the integration of social influences within a single individual's mind. Through the formation of internal schemas, the world is shaped within each person. Instead of referring to the physical world, these writers emphasize mental perceptions or constructs created through interactions between the two. Two well-known exemplars of these approaches are George Herbert Mead and George Kelly. Mead's (1934) notion of the "Generalized Other," for example, defined as a summation of how people in the world perceive us, was a concept that each person developed through exposures to others. As a social constructivist, Kelly's personal construct theory (1955) defined how individuals structured their experiences in unique and private ways through mental schemas.

For the social constructionist, attention is riveted on the ways in which people coordinate their actions in the social realm (K. J. Gergen, 1994, 1999). Whatever physiological activity goes on to sustain an individual's ability to coordinate—whether in the brain, blood, or bile—is regarded as another field of study. Thus, the social constructionist tends not to be interested in exploring such topics. At the same time, social constructionists recognize that discourses of mental and physical life—including psychodynamic theory, sociobiology, genetics, and cognitive psychology—are powerful discourse forms among many people today. From a constructionist perspective, one can examine how various discourses influence people's ways of creating social life together. This is a general orientation of social constructionism, to be applied to all forms of "talk," including its own.

Multiple Communities of Meaning Making

Every community supports certain forms of discourse and resists others. For example, adolescents in peer groups develop certain vocabularies that sustain their relationships and their forms of what is real and good. Semiprivate languages serve to solidify the social connections among them. If certain ways of "wording" do not gain credibility, that reality does not come to exist for those within a particular group. For example, some of you may use words related to astrological predictions, channeling, UFO abductions, hypnotic trances, weather reports, MUDs, Tarot card readings, and chaos theory. Others of you may resist or be ignorant of these linguistic forms. For you, the worlds "made" by these communities barely exist. (They exist to the extent that you are aware of the social actions that produce them.) Though each community may have a circumscribed range of linguistic practices, people belong to many different linguistic communities, such as families, neighborhoods, schools, interest groups, political parties, and religious sects, which provide them with many resources in the meaning-making process. Each of these groups has its sphere of linguistic tools. If there are rival communities, meanings will be contested, so the reality created by their words will also be contested. Any reality is vulnerable to alternative constructions, with many overlapping, partial, and noncommensurable formulations coexisting in the same temporal and spatial arenas; one group's reality may be another's fantasy.

For social constructionists, the recognition of the socially dependent role of reality construction is necessary for the appreciation of the political nature of language. So, for example, if new forms of resistance to discriminatory practices are created through language, as "Black is beautiful" was in the 1970s, new options for political action are opened. Of special concern to feminists, until the discourse of sexual harassment was formulated, certain charges of sexual misconduct in the workplace could not be brought. Marital rape was a contradiction in terms in the United States before the 1980s, and it is still a nonevent in many parts of the world. Its introduction has had an impact on the rights of wives, which can affect their willingness to be sexually submissive to their husbands. For social constructionists, the ways in which people coconstruct their worlds in all walks of life in diverse contexts and times are a fascinating form of study. The question of how new forms of life may be developing through linguistic means is also vital. Exploration of how languages alter social life has become an increasingly lively research activity in the past decade (see K. J. Gergen, 1985, 1991, 1996; Harré, 1986; Hekman, 1990; Nicholson, 1990; Scott, 1988; Shotter, 1984, 1993; Weedon, 1987).

Doing Psychology Within a Postmodern Framework

To understand what it means to do psychology within this social constructionist frame, Thomas Kuhn's (1970) views on paradigms and paradigm shifts can usefully be recalled. Kuhn described groups of scientists interested in the same problems as developing certain definitional terms, quantitative analyses, research methods, experimental procedures, instrumentation, educational and apprenticeship processes, historical records, prestigious journals, authority figures, methods for adjudicating disputes, and forms of rejecting rival alternative approaches and findings. "Normal science," in Kuhn's terms, occurs when there is a solidarity among the circle of scientists who engage in the approved practices for problem solving—a paradigm as Kuhn defined it. When this state of concurrence is not found, the field is a pre-science, a pseudoscience, or a nonscience. Take your pick! Kuhn's work served to create skepticism about the Enlightenment quest for universal or general laws, theories, or principles—those pieces of knowledge that exist beyond the control, influence, or desire of any given individual or group.[22] Social constructionists agree with Kuhn that knowledge is situated, local, contingent, temporary, and inextricably intertwined with the situated nature of the community of knowledge makers (Haraway, 1988; Hekman, 1990; Lyotard, 1984). Absolute progress, approximating Truth more closely, accumulating knowledge, and conquering ignorance, though they may be heroic visions of how the future might be shaped for the conventional scientist, become chimerical goals. Thus, modernist scientists may believe they are faithful to the quest of discovering truth, but their "truths" are subject to the conditions of their discourse community and are not universal, noncontingent discoveries (K. J. Gergen, 1994; Gilbert & Mulkay, 1984; Knorr-Cetina, 1981; Latour & Woolgar, 1979).

Despite these social constructionist claims that truth is foundationless, all is not in flux. Neither chaos nor order has the final say. Strong social barriers, as well as highly approved forms of scientific conduct, created through customs, laws, and group practices, contribute to the maintenance of order within scientific discourse spheres. As long as hierarchical arrangements, local agreements, and social stability are the norms, meaning-making processes seem orderly. Change occurs as what is taken to be the nature of the Real oscillates between the coreproduction of prior practices and the coproduction of the new. This emancipatory pulsation within the postmodern frame creates the sense of progress within the field. With the constant shuffling and restacking of the decks of the Real, options for synthesis and change, for new configurations of power, and for new potentials are created.

The major difference between a socially constructed psychology and the mainstream is in the stance one takes as a scholar, researcher, or therapist to one's practices, not in any given practice in itself. Aware of the socially constructed nature of all "language games," the social constructionist psychologist is willing to acknowledge that all descriptions and explanations of the world could be otherwise if adequate social permission were granted. Whether one is naming variables, declaring levels of statistical significance, stating hypotheses, collecting stories of participants, doing emancipatory research interventions in the field, or creating summaries of qualitative measures, all claims are construed as forms of discourse, as approaches to truths within social conventions. Yet at the same time the social constructionist stance feels liberating. Forms of psychology are being produced that are beyond the wilder imaginations of the traditions. I will summarize a few of these projects in the following discussion of feminist postmodern psychology.

Feminist Appropriations of Postmodern Psychology

The French Connection: Helene Cixous, Luce Irigaray, and Julia Kristeva

To reiterate, the third feminist epistemological position defined by Sandra Harding (1986b) was the postmodern. In the 1980s, feminist postmodernism was most strongly associated with a small group of French intellectuals, among whom the most widely recognized in the United States were Helene Cixous, Luce Irigaray, and Julia Kristeva.[23] It was primarily to these writers that Harding turned to describe the postmodern position in feminism. It is ironic that although these women have been widely celebrated in the United States as postmodern feminists, they have not regarded themselves as such but rather have stressed their strong individual differences and their occasional unwillingness to be labeled as feminists, as well as their resistance to the label *postmodern* (Moi, 1985, 1987; Suleiman, 1990).

The focus of their work was in confronting and acceding to the rich array of intellectual forces operating within the burgeoning postmodern culture of France. Among the poststructuralist influences with which they grappled were Lacanian psychoanalysis and semiotic theory, including the work of Jacques Derrida (1978).

These French writers brought to the attention of feminists worldwide the significance of language as a creator of sexual boundaries between women and men. As feminist postmodern psychologist Chris Weedon (1987) described it, "Their work aligns rationality with the masculine and sees the feminine in forms and aspects of language marginalized or suppressed by rationalism: poetic language and the languages of mysticism, madness, and magic" (p. 9). In their celebration of "the feminine" over the masculine, they blurred the boundary between a gynocentric feminism of the standpoint position and the postmodern position. Within their own groups of followers, however, competition led to aggression. The turmoil—eventually taking the form of criminal violence—became overwhelming. Today, the nucleus of intellectual force they created has dissolved. However, their brave insurgent philosophical and poetic sweep continues to capture international attention (Moi, 1985).

> Listen to their voices (in translation) one moment. They speak of thresholds, of crossing over, of breaking and blurring the binary of one versus one.

Every time I read a text by a woman, I am left with the impression that the notion of the signifier as a network of distinctive marks is insufficient. . . . It is as if this emotional charge so overwhelmed the signifier as to impregnate it with emotion and so abolish its neutral status, but, being unaware of its own existence, it did not cross the threshold of signification or find a sign with which to designate itself.

—Julia Kristeva, quoted in Moi (1987, pp. 112-113)

Immanence and transcendence are being recast, notably by that threshold which has never been examined in itself: the female sex. It is a threshold unto mucosity. Beyond the classic opposites of love and hate, liquid and ice lies this perpetually half-open threshold, consisting of lips that are strangers to dichotomy.

—Luce Irigaray, quoted in Moi (1987, p. 120)

To admit that writing is precisely working (in) the in between, inspecting the process of the same and of the other without which nothing can live, undoing the work of death—to admit this is first to want the two . . . the ensemble of one and the other, not fixed in sequence of struggle and expulsion or some other form of death but infinitely dynamized by an incessant process of exchange from one subject to another.

—Helene Cixous, quoted in Moi (1985, p. 109)

Basted in the conversational jouissance of the French academy, turned on the spits of Lacanian psychoanalytic discourses, em-broiled in the turbulence of Feminist firewars, each—twisting and twirling the mustaches of her father-figures—forges ahead, passing through the envelopes, making marks, entering into our history, leaving the trails of angels' wings beating.

In 1986, when Harding was developing her typology, she was unable to find prominent North American or British Commonwealth feminists to represent the postmodern epistemological position. She did recognize, however, that something unique was emerging in intellectual circles. Since then, a multitude of activities have been forthcoming within postmodern feminism. However, in the transition from the Gallic to the Anglo worlds, postmodernism has changed, and the academic relationship between the two linguistic communities has remained distant. Yet some common themes prevail—issues of embodiment, identity, emancipation, patriarchal authority, language, and logical forms are mutually explored, although with different, and often incommensurable, modes of inquiry.

Feminist Psychology as a Social Constructionist Science
in North America and the British Commonwealth

In the past several years, North American and British Commonwealth country feminists in diverse specialities of psychology have increasingly appropriated various postmodern positions, especially social constructionism (Nicholson, 1995). The core notion of *gender,* for example, is defined as a socially constructed notion of identity, as are many others, such as sexual orientation, social class, and ethnicity. At present, these feminist psychologists might be generally grouped into two clusters of postmodern/social constructionists. The larger group includes those who are grounded in some form of theoretical foundation, such as materialism, realism, phenomenology, or psychoanalysis, or who are ambivalent about social construction and thus wavering between a realist and a constructionist position. The second group, which is in the minority, is composed of those who take a more radical position, which eschews any claims to founda-tional underpinnings.[24] These feminist psychologists, attempting to integrate social constructionist ideas with a politics of emancipation, struggle both within and beyond their traditions. They work at the integration of these two divergent discourses, postmodern and modernist (Farganis, 1994). At the same time, they are troubled by accusations from other feminists that they have "sold out" to the male leaders of postmodernity who deny the possibility of Truth or its discovery and who are skeptical, as well, of progressive movements, such as feminism (Benhabib & Cornell, 1987; Braidotti, 1991, 1994; Brodribb, 1992; Diamond & Quinby, 1988; Scott, 1988). Despite these critical conundrums and controversies, these feminists have begun taking social constructionist positions in their research and writings (see Bohan, 1993; Crawford, Kippax, Onyx, Gault, & Benton, 1992; Flax, 1990; M. M. Gergen, 1992a, 1992b; M. M. Gergen & Davis, 1997; Hare-Mustin & Marecek, 1990; Hekman, 1990; Kessler & McKenna, 1978; Kitzinger, 1987, 1991a, 1991b; Lather, 1991; Morawski, 1988a, 1994; Potter & Wetherell, 1987; Squire, 1989; Tiefer, 1988, 1995; Unger, 1988, 1989; Walkerdine, 1986; Wetherell, 1996; Wilkinson, 1986). For them, exciting options have been open-ing up.

Social Constructionist/Feminist
Psychology and Gender Identity

The category of *gender identity* has become vital to many social discourses, including psychology, law, fashion, biology, sociology, theology, and informal everyday talk. For social constructionists, verbal designations are also open to becoming contested categories—that is, categories that can be investigated as to what their social value is, how they function within society, and whether they are liberating for people—questions that center on the politics of the category (Butler, 1990, 1993; Hekman, 1990; Kroker & Kroker, 1993; Tiefer, 1995; Trebilcot, 1994).

By contesting categories of identity, which can be seen as a radical, even inflammatory, activity, social constructionists emphasize the differences be-tween themselves and other feminist psychologists. For many feminists, without the notion of gender identity there could be no feminism. For others, such as Chantal Mouffe (1995), "The deconstruction of essential identities should be seen as the necessary condition for theorizing the multiplicity of relations of subordination" (pp. 317-318). In her provocative text *Gender Trouble* (1990), philosopher Judith Butler provided many arguments for the importance of ques-tioning gender identity. She argued that instead of thinking of individual identi-ties—a teenage girl, for example—as preceding conversation and other social activity, one can view identities as existing only *within* certain temporally fixed social occasions and as a consequence of certain linguistic conventions. Whether one is a "teenage girl" or some other designation—for example, a "voter"—depends upon the context of interaction. Thus, identities are produced within social interactions, not prior to them, and, once accepted, they influence the man-ner in which one conducts oneself. In *Bodies That Matter* (1993), Butler continued her arguments against the commonsense assumptions of unconstructed realities, such as the existence of biologically sexed bodies. The outcome of her work is to place a question mark around all categories of identity. The point is not to prohibit any designated identity but to focus on the constructed, situated character of any naming.

Does being female constitute a "natural fact" or a cultural performance, or is "naturalness" constituted through discursively constrained performative acts that produce the body through and within the categories of sex?

—Butler (1990, p. x)

A postmodern position on identity suggests a critical analysis of the tendency to assume that the body is essentially sexed, "as mute, prior to culture, awaiting signification" (Butler, 1990, p. 148). Reconstituting the body as socially constructed does not, however, deconstruct the possibility of its sexed or gendered nature. One does not give up one's notions and practices of gender entirely. Rather, one recognizes oneself as "put" into a position within a culturally contrived frame.

Social Construction and the Question of Difference

This attack on the essentializing of identity unsettles as well the notion of sex differences (Bohan, 1996; Hekman, 1990). A critique of difference takes the form of questioning the traditional logical form of binary oppositions, in particular that of male versus female. The possibility of questioning the binary of man/woman, of doing away with two sexes, allows for the possibility of new distinctions to be made (Kroker & Kroker, 1993; Poovey, 1988). A social constructionist feminist might argue that the problems suffered by women in being contained within the male/female binary provide a basis for disenchantment with the entire notion of opposites. Among them, a major concern is that women are perceived as carrying qualities that are the polar opposite of dominant male characteristics, such as rational, cultured, and strong, and thus are seen as irrational, animalistic, and weak. The feminist postmodern position is that once this stranglehold of "logic" is broken, the entire edifice of Western, male-dominated world making, along with its seemingly value-neutral approach to problem solving, is also in jeopardy. Within this frame, the opportunity exists for feminists to defy all conventions. Every social form that has been created to control, classify, bound, edge, and formulate becomes subject to skepticism and to disrespect. Every grand narrative about how women and men should live together is cracked. Here, the notion of blurred boundaries becomes prominent and political.

Theorist Rosi Braidotti (1994) invokes the metaphor of the nomad to describe the self in the world: "The nomadic subject is a myth, that is

> to say a political fiction, that allows me to think through and move
> across established categories and levels of experience: blurring
> boundaries without burning bridges" (p. 4).

This daring maneuver—to undo the binary— leaves many feminists feeling stranded despite its advantages. Some lament, along with Harding (1986a), that just as women gain voice in the political arena, the oppressor as well as the oppressed becomes deconstructed. That is, if the category of gender is erased, challenges to male domination cannot be made. If there are no men, there cannot be a patriarchy. Others write to maintain some connection to the female body and to avoid what seems to be an overly abstract, noncorporeal theoretical stance. A significant challenge to a full-blown constructionism came from Elizabeth Grosz's book *Volatile Bodies* (1994), in which she introduced the metaphor of the Mobius strip to create a sense of connection between embodied selves within a socially constructed framework. Interestingly, some Anglo-American post-modernists who have been trained within psychoanalytic communities are also inclined to back away from the final deconstruction of terms such as *woman, gender,* and *sex* (Flax, 1983, 1987, 1990, 1993b; Hollway, 1989).[25] For some, the validity of gender differences is sustained through a reliance on object relations theories within psychoanalysis (Chodorow, 1978, 1989; Keller, 1985). The Unconscious seems to be a refuge for vestiges of "realism" among feminist postmodernists, who normally eschew such foundational ideas. It is important, I believe, for the postmodern feminist to challenge any form of foundationalism, psychoanalytic or materialist. As Butler (1990), too, has queried, "Is psycho-analysis an antifoundationalist inquiry that affirms the kind of sexual complexity that effectively deregulates rigid and hierarchical sexual codes, or does it main-tain an unacknowledged set of assumptions about the foundations of identity that work in favor of those very hierarchies?" (p. xii). Her analysis suggests the latter.

From a social constructionist position, a Freudian discourse of gender rela-tions is not excluded as one possible way to regulate a complex and disordered rhetorical space. Feminists might argue in favor of a discussion of "unconscious processes" not because it is True that unconscious processes exist or because they are necessary to grasp otherwise unfathomable phenomena, but because making them "real" allows for different theoretical or practical interchanges to occur. Yet it must be periodically reinstantiated that the notion of "unconscious processes" is a temporary, fictive, and partial construction of reality, not the Truth. For many radical constructionists, such as myself, psychoanalytic dis-courses interfere with the development of theories that are relational rather than intrapsychic.[26] The psychoanalytic discourse diverts attention from the notion that it is the social network of people that is significant in constructing identities to that of the deep interior of the single isolated individual (K. J. Gergen, 1994). Social constructionists argue that if the origins of social process are construed as vested in the unconscious recesses of the single psyche, there is no theoretical space left for positing relational theories of social interaction. Other theoretical positions that might be taken are those that consider sex/gender distinctions as open to question and that regard the notion of "natural" itself as a constructed category (Martin, 1987; Tiefer, 1995; White, Bondurant, & Travis, 2000). The task, according to Butler (1990), is "to expose the foundational categories of sex, gender, and desire [and thus difference] as effects of a specific formation of power" (p. x). What political possibilities are the consequence of the refusal to allow categories of identity? What can we become when we are not bound by these prior categories? Is this a question that is answerable? What are the consequences of any answer that might be given?

Postmodernity, as a set of precepts, would alter both feminist theory and practice, for it disallows a variety of positions on which activists wish to group a movement. Ultimately, it is a position that could ruffle hard feminist feathers.

—Sandra Farganis (1994, p. 44)

Challenges to the Postmodern: Empiricist and Feminist Standpoint Critiques

Empiricists and feminist standpoint theorists often resist either directly or indirectly social constructionist claims. Empiricists often ignore the philosophical and linguistic issues raised about their own practices, thereby avoiding doubts about continuing to support the status quo. Feminist standpoint theorists in general staunchly defend the significance of women's experiences and value orientations, despite the postmodern argument that "experience must be historically interpreted and theorized if it is to become the basis of feminist solidarity and struggle" (Mohanty, 1995, p. 82). They resist the notion that the stories women tell of their lives are ventriloquated through the narratives that the culture has made available to them. Even feminists who are critical of aspects of both empiricism and standpoint positions resist jumping on the postmodernist bandwagon. Sandra Harding (1986b), for example, has formulated the major criticisms of empiricist and feminist standpoint positions and yet is unwilling to support a postmodern one. She has written, "Both of the feminist epistemological strategies we examined are legitimate targets of . . . skepticism, since they assume that through reason, observation, and progressive politics, the more authentic 'self' produced by feminist struggles can tell 'one true story' about 'the world'" (pp. 188-189). At the same time, she prefers her standpoint position over postmodernism and has defended it vigorously, in large measure because it seems to be more compatible with her feminist agenda (Harding, 1991). Other scholars also draw back from the abyss of postmodernism. As Margo Culley (1991) suggested,

> Most feminists and Black Studies scholars are cautious about the extreme skepticism of post-modernist thought. For it is more than ironic that just as the female and/or ethnic subject has emerged as a strong voice in the academy and on the streets that the concepts of subject and agency themselves have come under attack. (p. 7)

Voices are not in unison in this unsettling time. Some Black Studies scholars do speak from a postmodern position. The prominent author bell hooks (1990) has said:

> We have too long had imposed on us from both the outside and the inside a narrow, constricting notion of blackness. Postmodern critiques of essentialism . . . can open up new possibilities for the construction of self and the notion of agency. (p. 28)

For hooks, the potentials of a social constructionist approach for creating new images far outweigh the disadvantages of a lack of foundations that other static positions attribute to it.

The crux of the matter for some feminists is to remain respectable scientific citizens. They resist the powerful critiques of postmodernists in order to maintain the possibility of a scientific triumph within the existing system. In this vision, feminist psychologists will somehow be recognized by the established order for finally getting it right about issues of gender differences and identity. From a postmodern feminist position, this orientation seems defeatist in that it suggests that the only route to an adequate feminist psychology is via the well-traveled paths of masculinized scientific inquiry.

> Do I exaggerate? Do I invent enemies of postmodern feminism to spice up the story? Consider: "Poststructuralist [postmodernist] feminism is a high cult of retreat. Sometimes I think that, when the fashion passes, we will find many bodies, drowned in their own wordy words, like the Druids in the bogs" (Weisstein, 1993, p. 244).

Postmodern Backtalk: Responsive Relations and Risky Enterprises

Although the postmodern perspective attracts criticism from various feminist quarters, it has many laudable aspects that are frequently overlooked by the critics. For example, the view that all linguistic categories are both socially constructed and potentially deconstructable can be productive, as well as frustrating, for every variety of feminism. This notion allows for a skeptical stance toward all antifeminist rhetoric. Categories that are harmful to women, such as certain diagnostic categories of mental illness, can be closely scrutinized and, if need be, rejected (Hare-Mustin, 1994). New categories can be invented and sustained, in part, as they are seen to function satisfactorily within a feminist framework. The persistent attacks against postmodernism for its "relativism" are more a polemic than a productive intervention. It is necessarily the case that if one does not claim any form of foundational or universal originating statements, then one is left without any absolutes. This line of critique is a positivist position in science that refuses to recognize that value positions are integrated into every scientific endeavor, whether one is aware of it or not. Rather than disdaining or resisting ethical considerations, a postmodern position allows for the integration of boldly stated value positions within forms of analysis. As a social constructionist, one may be scientifically oriented and yet claim a feminist value investment as long as one does not regard any aspects of one's grounding as foundational or true. In this respect, the feminist standpoint position and the postmodern one need not be at odds. The question of difference between them concerns certainty, not value orientation. That is, both social constructionist and standpoint feminists can declare their views concerning feminist values. The distinction made here is that the social constructionist will not claim that her views are universal, essential, or transhistorical.

A social constructionist psychology also allows scholars to entertain and invent new forms of action related to both practical and theoretical endeavors. Opportunities arise for constructing generative as well as investigative research (K. J. Gergen, 1978). A form of generative activity can be examined in the applied area of organizational consulting. Most traditional organizational consultants practice a problem-solving strategy when they encounter dilemmas in institutional settings. Recently, a new approach called appreciative inquiry has been developed in which consultants engage a large network of involved participants in a process designed to be appreciative of the aspects of the organization that are working well and with which they are personally engaged (Cooperrider & Dutton, 1998; Cooperrider & Srivastva, 1998; Hammond, 1996; Hammond & Royal, 1998). In one case, in which women and men were not getting along well and a sexual harassment suit was about to be filed, the researchers engaged the company in an exercise in which they described times when women and men got along extremely well with one another (Cooperrider, 1998). Through reconstructing the nature of "reality" within the company, generative outcomes were produced, which had positive consequences for the organization.

More generally, within social constructionist work, innovative methods are encouraged as the interpretation of what constitutes scientific work is enlarged to include diverse endeavors. With this new freedom come opportunities to act reflexively, to engage in open dialogues with others who do not share one's particular views, to respect the differences that are inevitable across the discipline and beyond it, to experiment with new modes of communicating, to share one's work with others, both collegially and with those one hopes to help through cooperative ventures, to continually recognize that all that one has done is open to deconstruction, with one's own and with other voices, and to accept that no grand truth will be found, but that all one stands for is partial, mutable, and historical.

Powerful/Playful Feminist Practices

What aspects unite diverse research projects into the general framework of feminist social constructionism? What makes a text belong under the loosely flung tent of constructionism? First, nothing is by definition excluded. With a constructionist vision of potentials, all activities and all methods are permitted. Acceptability is determined more by a researcher's stance toward a project than by the nature of the work itself. Yet although it is important to stress the potential inclusiveness of social constructionism, some general themes are especially recognized as linking diverse practices with one another. Let me mention five of the themes I consider typical of social constructionist work, along with a small sample of projects that I would suggest are prototypical of these themes in social constructionist/feminist psychology.

Theme 1: Critique as Scientific Activity

Social constructionists openly express their metatheoretical positions within their work. Among the results are forms of critique. Frequently they examine the ways that the taken-for-granted "realities" of our cultures limit us in our ways of knowing the world and the modes by which we build up and change our notions of the real. Often these projects are critical of existing scientific practices. For example, Richard Walsh-Bowers (1999) challenged the ways in which the *Publication Manual of the American Psychological Association* has forced thousands of scholars into one narrowly defined form for writing psychology.[27] By combining his inspection of the manual with his interpretations of how psychology is shaped as a discipline by seemingly objective and proper methods, he illustrated his point of view, which at heart is highly critical of this seemingly positive societal artifact.

Theme 2: Value Statements Are Integrated
Into Scientific Work—The Personal Is Political

As previously mentioned, social constructionist work allows one to integrate one's value orientation and political philosophy into various forms of action. The lines demarcating scientific investigation, social activism, participatory research, and persuasion are blurred in the process. Michelle Fine's work, as both a theorist and an educator, is developing a legacy of critical social constructionist work. Her feminist values have been foremost in all of her texts as she has experimented with new writing forms, research modalities, and educational methods. Fine and her colleagues and students often create unusual venues for research, including projects that involve a high degree of contact between researcher and participants in settings where casual interactions are likely. They frequently insert dialogues into their texts to give a greater sense of immediacy, particularity, and flavor to their generalities. For example, in one project, Fine (1997) spent 1 year listening to students and teachers in a New York school discuss topics related to sex education. She discovered many ways in which the curriculum sustained the ideas that girls should not be sexually desirous, that sex is dangerous, and that evil befalls those who engage in sexual activities. Fine described this approach to sex education as enhancing the woman-as-victim stance, which she opposed. To give substance to her claims, she included a sample of dialogue taken from one of her observations.

Teacher:	What topics should we talk about in sex education?
Portia:	Organs, how they work.
Opal:	What's an orgasm?
	[*Laughter*]
Teacher:	Sexual response, sensation all over the body. What's analogous to the male penis on the female?
Theo:	Clitoris.
Teacher:	Right, go home and look in the mirror.
Portia:	She is too much!
Teacher:	Why look in the mirror?
Elaine:	It's yours.
Teacher:	Why is it important to know what your body looks like?
Opal:	You should like your body.
Teacher:	You should know what it looks like when it's healthy, so you can recognize problems like vaginal warts. (pp. 384-385)

Theme 3: The Limits of Language
Are the Limits of Our Worlds

Central to social constructionism is the notion that there is no one best way to relate language forms to whatever there is. Language, in this sense, creates the world and frames the truths that can be told. Feminist constructionists have been particularly interested in experimenting with linguistic forms, including writing with multiple voices, exploring various narrative forms, and creating new writing styles for presenting research practices.

Writing Multiple Voices. The ethnographic approach yields many innovative possibilities for feminists within a constructionist framework, including ways of integrating multiple voices into research endeavors. In their edited volume *Composing Ethnography: Alternative Forms of Qualitative Writing,* Carolyn Ellis and Arthur Bochner (1996) presented several chapters composed of multiple voicings. In the introduction, they shared their views about ethnography through a conversational device. In one chapter, "Silent Voices: A Subversive Reading of Child Sexual Abuse," author Karen V. Fox (1996) provided a three-part scenario based on her own interviews, participant observation, and telephone conversations with a convicted sex offender and with a stepdaughter who was abused many years ago as a child; Fox described herself as a survivor and researcher of child sexual abuse. As the fictional conversation spread across the pages of the chapter in patches of dialogue, the geographic sense of diverse positions was made visual. The process allowed for many perspectives to emerge that would normally be suppressed by a more singular authorial voice.

Searching for Narrative Forms. Narrative psychology is perhaps the most developed social constructionist form. The next two chapters of this volume, for example, are devoted to this endeavor. Among the many narrative publications, the series called *A Narrative Study of Lives,* edited by Ruthellen Josselson and Amia Lieblich (Josselson & Lieblich, 1993, 1995; Lieblich & Josselson, 1994), is an especially active outlet for this work in psychology. Chapter 3, which was originally published in one of these volumes, illustrates how narrative forms can be explored. These volumes, which highlight themes such as identity, ethics, experience, and aging, provide a showcase for a diverse collection of narrative work. The emphasis is on how the culture's narrative forms provide the boundaries by which we know ourselves and what we have accomplished. As the author Jill F. Kealey McRae (1994) concluded, "Telling one's story is a means of becoming" (p. 215).

Creating Novel Forms of Representation and Writing. The work of Patti Lather, along with Chris Smithies, with a support group of women who were HIV positive or who had AIDS, broke with traditional forms of research endeavors and writing styles. In *Troubling With Angels: Women Living With HIV/AIDS* (1997), Lather and Smithies joined these women to help them write about their lives and at the same time to integrate the reactions of the researchers and other informational sources into one text. With an eye to a general audience as well as the social science community, the compiling authors were encouraged to invent a new form. The book itself was first published as a desktop endeavor in order to rush it into print so that some participants could see their words published before they died. Later, the book was professionally published and distributed. The book is composed of variegated-sized ribbons and blocks of text, with the women's accounts in the support group taking the major portion of the text. Lather and Smithies also gave their individual accounts in various segments of the book. In addition, in blocks of text throughout the book, resource materials related to women and HIV were placed. The book experimented with auto-biographical entries, conversations, press releases, commentary, figures, and illustrations. Such an endeavor created the effect of a more entangled and supportive set of relationships between researchers and participants than is presented in more traditional forms of writing.

Theme 4: Reflexivity

The voice of the researcher/writer is never absent in a social constructionist project. One of the functions of this practice is to create some form of commentary on the ongoing representations of the work. In a sense, one presents the positioning of the project and then lays it open to question. Rather than sealing the structure of the form so that it becomes as strongly resistant to examination and critique as possible, a frequent practice in scientific writing, the reflexive moment allows for drawing attention to the choices made, the limits inherent in the formulation of the project, and what might have been otherwise. Reflexivity is a looking backwards, but always from another vested position. It is not a panacea that eliminates bias or preferential tellings. Yet it is a helpful move in opening the work to alternative interpretations.

Jill Morawski's book *Practicing Feminism, Reconstructing Psychology, Notes on a Liminal Science* (1994) expressed liminality in a way that disturbs the ordinary conventions of books in which chapters have distinct breaks. The chapters are separated by interchapters to encompass the notion of liminality—that is, the state of being neither one nor another—a notion that is also central to Morawski's description of feminist psychology. The notion of constantly being reflexive about her presentations is stressed through this form. In her concluding commentary, she becomes reflexive about her choices as author, what she has included and omitted, and reasons for her approach. The creativity and reflexive moments of this book give it a voice that would be unimagined in more orthodox book forms.

Theme 5: Going Beyond Text Into the Performative

The blurring of the boundaries between various forms of discourse—scientific, social, aesthetic, and pragmatic—allows for experimentation at these fading intersections. Performative psychology—that is, psychology that uses modes of expression from the dramatic arts, visual arts, music, and other media—promotes the mingling of the scientific with the secular and the spiritual. This tendency to merge discourses runs counter to a century of effort within psychology to eliminate nonscientific terms from the field and to segregate the impact of the nonscientific world on itself. Various forms of experimentation in this domain are increasingly gaining attention within feminist postmodern psychology. Sexologist/psychologist feminist Leonore Tiefer's "Sexual Biology and the Symbolism of the Natural" (1997) calls into question the ways in which the word *natural* creates political and moral distinctions between the good and the bad, the well and the sick. Working in a urology department where men come to complain about erection functions, Tiefer pondered questions such as what an erection is, what its purpose is, and how "natural" it is to have one. To quote Tiefer (1997),

> The men don't want to have an erection to dry their socks on, they want it because they have learned that the *natural* expression of masculinity is to have one frequently and easily for the practice or capability of heterosexual intercourse. . . . The growing domain of impotence research and treatment is part of the contemporary construction of masculinity. (p. 372)

The irreverent and humorous image Tiefer has provided of an erection as not a clothesline serves a tongue-in-cheek didactic function that we will all probably remember for some time. By integrating diverse performative elements such as cartoons, jokes, and humorous anecdotes into her work, she exerts far more influence than a scholar who adheres to the traditional textual boundaries.

Psychologist Tracey Hurd (1998) has developed performative psychology in her adaptation of interview materials with mothers into poetic verse, following James Gee's (1991) formulations. The re-presentation of the interviewee's words as poetry allows for significant thematic aspects to be highlighted through emphasis on certain phrases, ordering of words (which are all taken from the transcript), and repetition.

A third domain of influence can be found among ethnographers who take as their founding disciplines such areas as anthropology and communication but who are doing performative psychology in terms of their topics of interest, research modalities, and forms of display. For example, in his efforts to combine research and performativity, Jim Scheurich of the University of Texas is exploring various means of moving beyond "writing for an audience" to create what he calls "intersections" or "engagements" with others. In one project, he worked together with two Latino students to produce activities and textual/visual images designed to present the migrant experience of Mexican Americans. Together they created a "manuscript" that is basically a collage of excerpts from government reports, newspapers, children's poems, novels, interviews, ethnographies, drawings, and other visual materials. The manuscript has a conventional introduction and conclusion but the rest is all collage (J. Scheurich, personal communication, April 1998).

On the basis of this manuscript, the research group created a multimedia performance piece. This production included music, a video, and a carousel of slides of migrants—all presented at the same time. Also, a script accompanied the presentation. Members of the audience read parts, and some parts were read in unison. The idea was to give the audience an experience—with no assumption that it was an accurate experience or the only possible experience —of Mexican American migrant life (J. Scheurich, personal communication, April 1998).[28] A fuller description of performative psychology and references to this work are found in the prelude to Chapters 7 and 8.

THE HEREAFTER

The remaining chapters of this book demonstrate various social constructionist/ feminist practices in psychology. The flow of the book is from this general overview downstream (or up, as I sometimes see it) to specific projects created out of this framework. The prose forms of the chapters are adapted to the mission of the moment, often experimental, and frequently functioning to disrupt traditional narrative lines. Although there is a profusion of topics and styles, they bear a family resemblance, and at the center of each is a feminist issue. The interpretive potential is open, but truth claims are nowhere to be found. What primarily sets these projects off from traditional empirical or experiential forms is a respect for the fragile, unstable, and temporary nature of the forms that shape our lives, our scientific enterprises, and these words. Though each project is grounded in a particular set of practices, constructions of reality, and conclusive commentary, nothing is assumed to be based on a firm foundation of basic truths. In each case, each interpretation, fact, and description of how the context was set could have been otherwise.

> Otherwise could be other wise; one might imagine other ways of wisdoming, of knowing, of explaining the explainable. This interlude could be otherwise.

Chapters 2, 3, and 4 involve the narrative study of gendered relations. In Chapter 2, the focus turns to autobiographical storytelling. Differences between the ways men and women construct their life stories, especially with respect to their emphasis on professional achievements, are examined. The chapter is written with "ribbons" of text interspersing quotations from various authorities on biographical forms, the autobiographers themselves, and the author in order to highlight the possibility that other alternatives to the linear, progressive, and logically "tight" form of writing characteristic of academic prose can be created. The chapter serves as a critical wedge against the totalitarian force of traditional linear narratives in the generation of personal lives and scientific research findings.

Chapter 3 highlights questions related to the importance of storytelling in relation to the body: How is the body described through language? What kind of body "speaks" itself through language? What are the political consequences of speaking the body as woman or as man? In this chapter, we note how the foundations of biological givens are shaken and shaped via differing narrative imperatives for women and men.

Chapter 4 describes a research project that was designed to promote a social constructionist reinterpretation of the biomedical model of menopause. It centers on ways in which menopause, as it is currently framed within a medical discourse, plays a negative role in women's narratives of aging. The project, originating in a focus group, explored with participants how this medicalized version of menopause might be challenged.

Chapter 5 introduces the importance of self-dialogues in a constructionist account of personal life. To emphasize the dialogical character of such activities, the notion of "social ghost" is introduced to refer to the imaginal interlocutors with whom one converses. Within the social constructionist frame, even the seemingly private activity of introspection is given a relational turn that emphasizes the conversational quality of private thought. A survey research method served as the basis of this chapter.

The potential for investigating historical events to create new forms of psychological knowledge is examined in Chapter 6. The pivotal fulcrum of the chapter is the topic of the "male gaze" in relation to the female body. The formal design of this chapter is based on two "conflictual triangles," with two sides representing the interests of the "male gaze" and artistic freedom and the third representing an alternative, woman's point of view that questions these masculine prerogatives.

The final section of the book presents performative psychology. Chapter 7, "Woman as Spectacle," is created as a dramatic performance from a summary of diverse research studies describing the developmental trajectory of women in the later part of life. As such, the text serves as a form of emancipatory research, working to change the audience's perceptions of women in their mature years.

Chapter 8 is a dramatic soliloquy regarding the tensions between a feminist position and a nonfeminist postmodernism. The ultimate suggestion of the piece is that without a (nonfoundational) value position, in this case a feminist one, postmodern theoretics are lacking. Social constructionism may point the way to new modes of doing gender psychology, but without a feminist framework it is incomplete.

The conclusion wraps up the loose ends into an immediately unraveling narrative. An attempt is made to reach some temporary sanctuary within which the diverse modes of expression that have been presented in the earlier chapters can momentarily, at least, rest in equilibrium.

NOTES

1. Among the historical treatments of the development of the psychology of women are Alcoff (1988), Collins (1991), Farganis (1994), Morawski (1994), Nicholson (1990), and Russo and Dumont (1997).

2. The field of feminist psychology is also identified as the psychology of women, the psychology of gender, and the psychology of gender relations. Although each term

has important historical and semantic roots, I will look to their commonalities and use them synonymously in this book. I will say more about this later.

3. Although one may question the propriety of referring to all psychologists who work with gender issues as feminist psychologists, it is my experience that those who are deeply involved in the "psychology of women" or "psychology of gender" generally consider themselves to be feminists, which means primarily that they subscribe to a political agenda that strives for full equality for all women in every aspect of life. For example, the *Psychology of Women Quarterly*, the official journal of the American Psychology Association's Division 35, the Psychology of Women, defines itself as "a feminist journal that aims to encourage and develop a body of knowledge about the psychology of women." Despite the diversity of opinions about epistemologies, methods, and other questions of science and psychology, practitioners seem to be sufficiently in agreement on this stand that I will use *feminist psychology* as synonymous with *psychology of women* and *psychology of gender* throughout the book. Some feminist psychologists prefer to use *psychology of women* to emphasize the place of women in the man's world, whereas others prefer to use the term *psychology of gender* to stress the relational and socialized aspect of the field. I use both terms throughout this volume.

4. Attention to this question has resulted in various points of view, categorized as alpha and beta biases in a classic piece by Rachel Hare-Mustin and Jeanne Marecek (1990). An alpha bias emphasizes differences between women and men, whereas a beta bias serves to diminish them.

5. Multitudes of books have been written explaining the methods of doing proper scientific investigations, as well as defending logical positivist philosophy, which undergirds much of contemporary scientific activity. A few feminist writers who describe these practices from a critical stance are Bleier (1986), Farganis (1994), M. M. Gergen (1988), Harding (1986b), Hawksworth (1989), Hekman (1990), Hubbard (1982, 1988), Keller and Longino (1996), and Weedon (1987).

6. A certain ambiguity frames this conception, however, as psychologists are expected to use their mental faculties to gain objective knowledge, but the interiority of the subject is regarded as a realm of subjectivity.

7. *Feminism and Psychology* is published in Great Britain and is explicitly political in its founding principles. Its aims and scope include the following statement about research: "It publishes high-quality, original research and debates that acknowledge gender and other social inequalities and consider their psychological effects; studies of sex differences are published only when set in this critical context."

8. These two references are only a minute sample of the hundreds of articles published by feminist psychologists in this century criticizing empirical research that has supported sexist practices and promoted sexist findings regarding women. Unfortunately, sex difference research that is damaging to women's integrity as people continues to this day—for example, in research programs dedicated to finding brain and hormonal differences that cause men to be superior to women in mathematics (Tavris, 1992).

9. Among hundreds of contributors to this view are Bem (1974, 1993), Deaux and Major (1987), Eagly (1987), Grady (1981), Lott (1985), Sherif (1979), Spence and Helmreich (1978), and Weisstein (1993).

10. For those unfamiliar with the term, the major purpose of meta-analysis is to assess outcomes from multiple statistically based research sources. Findings from every

credible study published on a topic are combined and then analyzed in a statistically so-phisticated way to determine, on balance, if an overall effect has been found.

11. Psychology has become an academic home for many women over the past 15 years. In both graduate and undergraduate studies, women are now the majority (Howard et al., 1986). Yet according to a recent national review of arts and sciences cur-ricula initiated by the Association of American Colleges, scarce attention has been paid to the influx of women, and very little change over the past decades can be seen in the way the psychology curriculum has been structured (McGovern, Furumoto, Halpern, Kimble, & McKeachie, 1991). Addressing the issue of how to become more responsive to the needs and interests of nontraditional students, most psychologists surveyed indicated that "gender, ethnicity, culture, and class . . . should best be left to treatments determined by an instructor's sensitivities and commitments" but should not result in any general recommendations that would affect the traditional course of study (McGovern et al., 1991, p. 600). Though Howard et al. (1986) concluded that the dominance of women in psychology should be having a great impact on the field, no evidence for this could be found.

12. Critiques of empiricist psychology have flourished in Europe and Canada since the mid-1970s but have been ignored by and large in the United States (e.g., Buss, 1979; Harré & Secord, 1972; Henriques et al., 1984; Israel & Tajfel, 1972; Rommetveit, 1980; Strickland, Aboud, & Gergen, 1976). Alternatives to empiricism have taken many forms: "ethogenics" (Harré & Secord, 1972), ethnomethodology (Garfinkel, 1967), applied nonexperimental research (Israel & Tajfel, 1972), discourse analysis (Henriques et al., 1984), argumentation (Billig et al., 1988), cross-cultural approaches (Strickland, 1984), archival approaches (Morawski, 1988b), narrative approaches (K. J. Gergen & M. M. Gergen, 1988), critical analytical approaches (Rappoport, 1984), and others (Sampson, 1977, 1981, 1991). Feminist contributions to this movement are integrated within other parts of the chapter.

13. For example, the "crisis" in social psychology brought on by various critical voices within that specialty was declared at a national meeting of the Society for Experi-mental Social Psychology, and the audience cheered. Yet the claim that social psychol-ogy was historical—one of the main criticisms of the "crisis" group—became accepted as part of the ethos of social psychology, and discourse about discovering general, uni-versal laws of social behavior became muted. Business seemed to go on as usual; the change occurred and was unduly unnoted (Buss, 1979; Elms, 1975; K. J. Gergen, 1973).

14. The crisis in social psychology, in particular, spawned a plethora of critical texts related to the experimental method in the late 1970s. Feminist writers also joined in this attack (see K. J. Gergen, 1978; Harré & Secord, 1972; Israel & Tajfel, 1972; Reinharz, 1985; Roberts, 1981; Spender, 1980; Strickland et al., 1976).

15. In the past few years, the word *subject* has been replaced by *participant* in re-search articles to try to lessen the seeming disparity between researcher and researched and to imply that the participants have some independent contributions to make to the re-search endeavor. My view is that this word change is merely "window dressing" that has no value but to disguise the nature of the experimental task.

16. Several writers describing this position have also referred to it at times as cultural feminism (e.g., Tavris, 1992).

17. Although several different groups might be classified as standpoint feminists, this does not mean that they are harmonious or even similar in other aspects of their posi-

tioning. Often there are serious disagreements among various parties concerning political choices, strategies, and other value-laden preferences.

18. It is also the case that certain theorists place Marxist and socialist feminists in the empiricist camp because of their reliance on certain scientific methods in support of materialist claims. Naomi Black (1989), who advocated "social feminism," a standpoint position, wrote, "The belief systems conventionally labeled 'liberal,' 'Marxist,' and 'socialist' feminism are all varieties of equity feminism" (p. 1), which in Harding's framework is empiricist feminism.

19. Among the scholarly papers that might be cited are works by Apfelbaum (1993), Brown and Root (1990), Landrine (1995), LaFromboise and Plake (1984), Red Horse (1980), Reid (1993), and Wyatt (1992).

20. As of this writing, Mary Daly has agreed to terminate her courses at Boston College, spring semester, 1999, because of a conflict related to her refusal to allow two men to register for her feminist philosophy course, which she has opened only to women. The men are active in conservative politics on campus.

21. This one paragraph is devoted to deconstructionist ideas is designed to give a faint flavor of this extensively discussed and contested area of scholarship. Other references within the text will specify resources for a proper introduction to these ideas.

22. Kuhn was said to have been rather shocked to see how far his ideas were taken in terms of dismantling the respectability of science as an objective field of inquiry and tried to do damage control in his later works (Kuhn, 1977).

23. Harding's typology, as well as Rosemary Tong's (1989), refers only to the French feminists Cixous, Irigaray, and Kristeva when they describe the postmodern position.

24. These two constructionist groups are often able to form alliances concerning specific issues, but the latter group is regarded with some suspicion as lacking strict feminist principles, as being "relativist," and as including unreliable allies in political actions. In the remainder of the chapter, the differences between these two groups will not be examined, although it is important to recognize that there is much diversity and contention among those who are attempting to walk the social constructionist talk.

25. In support of this view, Jane Flax (1990), a psychoanalyst as well as a political scientist and postmodernist, suggested that "for all its shortcomings psychoanalysis presents the best and most promising theories of how a self that is simultaneously embodied, social, 'fictional,' and real comes to be, changes, and persists over time " (p. 16).

26. Recently, Lacanian analysts have begun to emphasize the postmodern features of their theorizing, in particular the impact of symbolic resources in various cultures on the development of psychic and social processes, and to deemphasize the individual's intrapsychic processes, in particular the Unconscious (D. Schnitman, personal communication, 1993).

27. Others have written on topics that are centered on the social construction of masculinity, gender relations, sexuality, femininity, and other features of contemporary social life, particularly Kimmel (1994), Kitzinger and Wilkinson (1994), Thorne (1990), Tiefer (1995), Walkerdine (1990), and Whatley (1991).

28. Another excellent example of a performative text is Patti Lather and Chris Smithies (1997).

Life Stories

Pieces of a Dream

> I have heard the mermaids singing, each to each.
>
> —T. S. Eliot (1963)

The songs of mermaids are not like other songs. Mermaids' voices sing beyond the human range—notes not heard, forms not tolerated, and each to each, not one to many, one above all. If we imagine the mermaids, we might almost hear them singing. Their voices blending, so that each, in its own special timbre, lends to the harmony of the whole. So it might be as one writes a voice in a choir at the threshold of sensibility. My voice shall be only one of many to be heard.

When you hear one voice, it is the voice of authority, the father's voice, the leader's voice. One voice belongs to an androcentric order. Will our singing mute the single voice before we drown? Or being mermaids, perhaps our burial grave is on the earth, not under the sea?

AUTHOR'S NOTE: Besides the many voices within the text, many others added their notes to this composition—in particular, my colleagues Carol Kessler, Professor of English at Pennsylvania State University, and Peter Mair, Walter Heinz, and Wojciech Sadurski, Professors at the Universities of Leiden, Bremen, and Sydney, respectively, and my hallmates at the Netherlands Institute for Advanced Study, who suggested readings and encouraged my writing. Representatives of both institutions were also very generous in granting me the support and time to work on the original piece. I wish to thank them, as well as George Rosenwald and Richard Ochberg, who were my first editors. Last, I wish to express my gratitude to Kenneth Gergen, my trusty dolphin, who saved me many times from floundering in this tide of words.

We need to learn how to see our theorizing projects as . . . "riffing" between and over the beats of patriarchal theories.

—Sandra Harding (1986a, p. 649)

This is an interwoven etude about life stories; it seeks to disrupt the usual narrative line, the rules of patriarchal form. Let us escape the culturally contoured modes of discourse. Be free of beginnings and denouements. Yet I too am mired in convention. I am captured by the contours of the commonplace. And danger lurks if I fling myself too far outside the normal curve. It is a conundrum. If I write in all the acceptable ways, I only recapitulate the patriarchal forms. Yet if I violate expectations too grievously, my words become nonsense. Still, the mermaids sing.

Finding voices authentic to women's experience is appallingly difficult. Not only are the languages and concepts we have . . . male oriented but historically women's experiences have been interpreted for us by men and male norms.

—Kathryn Rabuzzi (1988, p. 12)

We play at the shores of understanding. If you assent to the bending of traditional forms, then perhaps our collective act may jostle the sand castles of the ordered kingdom. We need each other, even if we do not always agree.

If we do our work well, "reality" will appear even more unstable, complex, and disorderly than it does now.

—Jane Flax (1987, p. 643)

THE PARADOX OF THE PRIVATE: OUR PUBLIC SECRETS

When we tell each other our deepest secrets, we use a public language. The nuances of consciousness, emotions both subtle and profound, inner yearnings, unconscious desires, the whispering of conscience—all of these are created in the matrix of this language. The words form and deform around us as we speak and listen. We swim in a sea of words. Only that which is public can be private. We dwell in a paradox.

Individual consciousness is a socio-ideological fact. If you cannot talk about an experience, at least to yourself, you did not have it.

—Caryl Emerson (1983, p. 260)

Our cultures provide models not only for the contents of what we say but also for the forms. We use these forms unwittingly; they create the means by which we interpret our lives. We know ourselves via the mediating forms of our cultures, through telling, and through listening.

What created humanity is narration.

—Pierre Janet (1928, p. 42)

"Know thyself," a seemingly timeless motto, loses clarity when we hold that our forms of self-understanding are the creation of the unknown multitudes who have gone before us. We have become, we are becoming, because "They" have set out the linguistic forestructures of intelligibility. What then does a personal identity amount to? Who is it that we might know?

Every text is an articulation of the relations between texts, a product of intertextuality, a weaving together of what has already been produced elsewhere in discontinuous form; every subject, every author, every self is the articulation of an intersubjectivity structured within and around the discourses available to it at any moment in time.

—Michael Sprinker (1980, p. 325)

If self-understanding is derived from our cultures, and the stories we can tell about ourselves are prototypically performed, what implications does this have for our life affairs? The reverberations of this question will ring in our ears.

Every version of an "other" . . . is also the construction of a "self."

—James Clifford (1986, p. 23)

> And, I add, "Every version of a self must be a construction of the other."

Our first mark of identity is by gender. We are called "boy" or "girl" in our first moment of life. Our personal identities are always genderized, so life stories must begin with this. I am concerned with the gendered nature of our life stories. What are Manstories and Womanstories? How do they differ? And what difference do these differences make?

The literary construction of gender is always artificial. . . . One can never unveil the "essence" of masculinity or femininity. Instead, all one exposes are other representations.

—Linda Kauffman (1986, p. 314)

This overture suggests the major themes. Countertones may resist articulation. You may not find what you want. The voices mingle and collide. Only in the confluence will the totality be fixed . . . temporarily.

Defining Powers: Doubts About the Structure

What do I mean by the narratives or stories of our lives? When we began our work on the narrative, Kenneth Gergen and I described it thus: The traditional narrative is composed of a valued end point; events relevant to this end point; the temporal ordering of these events toward the end point; and causal linkages between events (K. J. Gergen & M. M. Gergen, 1983, 1988; M. M. Gergen & K. J. Gergen, 1984).

Now I become uneasy. I wonder why this definition must be as it is. Doesn't a definition defend an order of discourse, an order of life? Whose lives are advantaged by this form, and whose disadvantaged? Should we ask?

What are the forms of our life stories? We recognize them as a comedy, a tragedy, a romance, a satire. We know them as they are told. Their plots are implicated in their structures. A climax is a matter of form as well as content. Though separating form and content may be desirable from an analytic point of view, it is also arbitrary. (What are the forms of a Womanstory and a Manstory? How do they differ?)

The dramatic structure of conversion . . . where the self is presented as the stage for a battle of opposing forces and where a climactic victory for one force, spirit defeating flesh, completes the drama of the self, simply does not accord with the deepest realities of women's experience and so is inappropriate as a model for women's life writing.

—Mary G. Mason (1980, p. 210)

Should we question the ways in which patriarchal authority has controlled the narrative forms? We would be in good company. Many feminist literary critics have expanded this perspective (see Benstock, 1988; DuPlessis, 1985; Smith, 1987). Writers such as Virginia Woolf (1929/1957) have also struggled with how male domination in literary forms has made some works great and others trivial, some worthy and some not. What has been judged by the authority figures as correct has been granted publication, critical acclaim, and respect; the rest has often been ignored or abused.

Both in life and in art, the values of a woman are not the values of a man. Thus, when a woman comes to write a novel, she will find that she is perpetually wishing to alter the established values to make serious what appears insignificant to a man and trivial what is to him important.

—Virginia Woolf (1958, p. 81)

Although androcentric control over literary forms is a serious matter, how much graver is the accusation that the forms of our personal narratives are also under such control? The relationship between one and the other is strong, but the more pervasive nature and consequence of male-dominated life stories is certainly more threatening, at least to me.

Narrative in the most general terms is a version of, or a special expression of, ideology: representations by which we construct and accept values and institutions.

—Rachel DuPlessis (1985, p. x)

I would add, "by which we construct and accept ourselves!"

Thus, I become increasingly skeptical of our classical definitions of the narrative. Judgments of what constitutes a proper telling are suspect on the grounds that what seem to be simple canons of good judgment, aesthetic taste, or even familiar custom may also be unquestioned expressions of patriarchal power. Under the seemingly innocent guise of telling a true story, one's life story validates the status quo.

Genderizing: Tenderizing the Monomyth

Myths have carried the form and content of narratives throughout the centuries. They tell us how great events occur, as well as how stories are made. Joseph Campbell (1956), a lover of ancient myths, proposes that there is one fundamental myth, the "monomyth." This myth begins with the hero, who is dedicated to a quest. To accomplish his goal, he ventures forth from the everyday world and goes into the region of the supernatural. Here he encounters strange, dangerous, and powerful forces, which he must vanquish. He struggles mightily and sacrifices much. Upon his eventual success, the victorious hero returns and is rewarded for his great deeds. The monomyth is the hero's myth, and the major Manstory. (I wonder, where is the woman in this story? She is to be found only as a snare, an obstacle, a magic power, or a prize.)

The whole ideology of representational significance is an ideology of power.

—Stephen Tyler (1986, p. 131)

This monomyth is not just an historical curiosity. It is the basic model for the stories of achievement in everyday lives. Life stories are often about quests; like the monomyth, they are stories of achievement. The story hangs on the end point. Will the goal be achieved or not? In such stories, all is subsumed by the goal. The heroic character must not allow anything to interfere with the quest.

Is a heroine the same as a hero? Some might say that narratives of heroes are equally available to women. I doubt that this is so. Cultural expectations about how the two genders should express their heroism are clearly divergent. Consider the central characters and the major plots of life stories codified in literature, history, or personal narrative; we could easily conclude that women do not belong, at least in the starring role. The adventures of the hero of the monomyth would make rather strange sense if he were a woman. If he is the subject of the story, she must be the object. In the system, opposites cannot occupy the same position. The hero is the knower. The woman represents the totality of what is to be known. She is life; he is the master of life. He is the main character; she is a supporting actress. He is the actor; she is the acted upon.

Although theoretically the hero was meant generically to stand for individuals of both sexes, actually, like so called "generic man," the hero is a thoroughly androcentric construction.

—Kathryn Rabuzzi (1988, p. 10)

In general, the cultural repertoire of heroic stories requires different qualities for each gender. The contrast of the ideal narrative line contrasts the autonomous, ego-enhancing hero, singlehandedly and singleheartedly progressing toward a goal, with the long-suffering, selfless, socially embedded heroine, being moved in many directions, lacking the tenacious focus demanded of a quest.

Culture is male; our literary myths are for heroes, not heroines.

—Joanna Russ (1972, p. 18)

The differences in our stories are not generally recognized in our culture. In a democratic society, we do not consider the absence of narrative lines as relevant to unequal representation of people in public positions of power. We do not turn to our biographies to help explain, for example, why we have so few women leading organizations, mountain-climbing expeditions, or math classes (or so few men serving as primary caretakers of children). Even when women are leaders in their professions, or are exceptional in some arena of life, it is difficult for them to tell their personal narratives according to the forms that would be suitable to their male colleagues. They are in a cultural hiatus, with a paucity of stories to tell. (How does one become when no story can be found?)

The emphasis by women on the personal, especially on other people, rather than on their work life, their professional success, or their connectedness to current political or intellectual history clearly contradicts the established criterion about the content of autobiography.

—Estelle Jelinek (1980, p. 10)

Feminist Theories and Gender Differences

Various feminist theorists have emphasized the underlying family dynamics that may sustain our gendered stories. As Nancy Chodorow (1978), Dorothy Dinnerstein (1976), Jane Flax (1983), Carol Gilligan (1982), Evelyn Fox Keller (1983), and others have suggested, boys and girls are raised to regard their life trajectories differently. As they have posited, all children have as their first love object their mothering figure. However, boys are reared to separate from their mothers; they learn to replace their attachment to mother with pride in masculine achievements and to derogate women and their relationships with them. Girls are not cut away from their mothers and are forced to reidentify themselves. They remain embedded in their relations and do not learn the solitary hero role. But they must bear the burden of shame that the androcentered culture assigns to their gender. Each man and woman acquires a repertoire of potential life stories relevant to his or her own gender, for personal use. Understanding one's past, interpreting one's actions, and evaluating future possibilities—each is filtered through these stories. Events "make sense" as they are placed in the proper story form. If certain story forms are absent, events cannot take on the same meaning as if they were there. We assume that life "produces" the autobiography as an act produces its consequence, but can we not suggest, with equal justice, that "the autobiography project may itself produce and determine life" (Paul de Man, 1979, p. 920)?

AUTOBIOGRAPHIES AS THE GENDERED STORIES OF LIVES

I have been studying the popular autobiographies of men and women. Of interest to me is not only what is there, in the story lines, but what is missing as well. What is it that each gender cannot talk about and thus cannot integrate into life stories and life plans? What can a Manstory tell that a Womanstory cannot, and vice versa?

What appears as "real" in history, the social sciences, the arts, even in common sense, is always analyzable as a restrictive and expressive set of social codes and conventions.

—James Clifford (1986, p. 10)

In critical works concerning autobiography, women's narratives have been almost totally neglected (see Olney, 1980; Sayre, 1980; Smith, 1974). Women's writings have usually been exempted because they did not fit the proper formal mold (Lieblich, Tuval-Mashiach, & Zilber, 1998). Their work has been more fragmentary, multidimensional, understated, and temporally disjunctive. "Insignificant" has been the predominant critical judgment toward women's autobiographies (and their lives) (Jelinek, 1980).

When a woman writes or speaks herself into existence, she is forced to speak in something like a foreign tongue.

—Carolyn Burke (1978, p. 844)

Interpreting the Stories

I look into autobiographies to discover the forms we use to tell a Manstory, a Womanstory. What story can I tell?

Autobiography reveals the impossibility of its own dream: what begins on the presumption of self knowledge ends in the creation of a fiction that covers over the premises of its construction.

—Shari Benstock (1988, p. 11)

My materials are taken from many autobiographies. This chapter concentrates on but a few. In this way, a sense of life may perhaps be felt. The quotations I have drawn from these texts are hardly proof of my conclusions; they are better viewed as illustrations to vivify my interpretations. Other interpretations can and should be made by me and by others.

The Quest

Traditional narratives demand an end point, a goal. Concentrating on the goal, moving toward the point, putting events in a sequence, building the case (no tangents, please)—these rhetorical moves are required by custom. Classical autobiographies delineate the life of cultural heroes, those who have achieved greatness through their accomplishments. We expect that those who write their biographies will be such heroes.

Men tend to idealize their lives or to cast them into heroic molds to project their universal import.

—Estelle Jelinek (1980, p. 14)

How singleminded are these heroes in pursuit of their goals? How committed are the women who write their biographies? Do their stories also fit the classic mold? Listen to some of their voices. Lee Iacocca's (1984) best-selling autobiography focuses on his automotive career. His family life, in contrast, receives scant attention. Iacocca's wife, Mary, was a diabetic. Her condition worsened over the years; after two heart attacks, one in 1978 and the other in 1980, she died, in 1983, at the age of 57. According to Iacocca, each of the heart attacks came following a crisis period in his career at Ford or at Chrysler. Iacocca writes, "Above all, a person with diabetes has to avoid stress. Unfortunately, with the path I had chosen to follow, this was virtually impossible" (p. 301). Obviously, his description of his wife's death is not intended to expose his cruelty. It is, I think, a conventional narrative report appropriate to his gender. The book (and his life) are dedicated to his career. It appears that Iacocca would have found it unimaginable that he should have ended or altered his career to improve his wife's health. As a Manstory, the passage is not condemning; however, read in reverse, as a wife's description of the death of her husband or child, it would appear callous, to say the least. A woman who would do such a thing would not be considered an outstanding folk hero, as Iacocca has been for many people. She might instead be scorned or worse.

Yeager is the autobiography of the quintessential American hero, the pilot with the "right stuff." His story is intensively focused on his career in the Air Force. His four children, born in quick succession, provided a highly stressful challenge for his wife, who became gravely ill during her last pregnancy. Nothing stopped him from flying, however. Constantly moving around the globe, always seeking out the most dangerous missions, he openly states, "Whenever Glennis needed me over the years, I was usually off in the wild blue yonder" (Yeager & Janos, 1985, p. 103). America's favorite hero would be considered an abusive parent were his story regendered.

Richard Feynman (1986), autobiographer and Nobel prize-winning physicist, was married to a woman who had been stricken with tuberculosis for 7 years. During the war years, he moved out to Los Alamos to work on the Manhattan Project (developing the atomic bomb), and she was several hours away in a hospital in Albuquerque. The day she was dying, he borrowed a car to go to her bedside. He reports: "When I got back (yet another tire went flat on the way), they asked me what happened. 'She's dead. And how's the program going?' They caught on right away that I didn't want to moon over it" (p. 113).

Manstories tend to follow the traditional narrative pattern: men becoming their own heroes, facing crises, following their quests, and ultimately achieving victory. Their careers provide them their central lines of narrative structuring, and personal commitments, external to their careers, are relegated to insignificant subplots.

What does one find among women authors?

There is virtually only one occupation for a female protagonist—love, of course—which our culture uses to absorb all possible "Bildung," success/ failure, learning, education, and transition to adulthood.

—Rachel DuPlessis (1985, p. 182)

Beverly Sills, who became a star performer at the New York City Opera, all but gave up her singing career for 2 years to live in Cleveland because this was where her husband had his job. She describes her thoughts:

> Peter had spent all of his professional life working for the *Plain Dealer,* and he had every intention of eventually becoming the newspaper's editor-in-chief. I was just going to have to get used to Cleveland. My only alternative was to ask Peter to scuttle the goal he'd been working toward for almost twenty-five years. If I did that, I didn't deserve to be his wife. Not coincidentally, I began reevaluating whether or not I truly wanted a career as an opera singer. I decided I didn't. . . . I was twenty-eight years old, and I wanted to have a baby. (Sills & Linderman, 1987, p. 120)

The only businesswoman in my sample, Sydney Biddle Barrows, also known by her autobiography's title, the *Mayflower Madam* (1987), has second thoughts about maintaining a then extremely successful business when it clashes with private goals:

> By early 1984, . . . I realized that I couldn't spend the rest of my life in the escort business. I was now in my early thirties and starting to think more practically about my future which would, I hoped, include marriage. As much as I loved my job, I had to acknowledge that the kind of man I was likely to fall in love with would never marry the owner of an escort service. . . If I didn't want to remain single forever, I would sooner or later have to return to a more conventional line of work. (p. 205)

Martina Navratilova (1985) discusses her feelings about going skiing after many years of forgoing this dangerous sport:

> I made a decision in my teens to not risk my tennis career on the slopes, but in recent years I've wanted to feel the wind on my face again. . . . I wasn't willing to wait God knows how many years to stop playing and start living. (p. 320)

Nien Cheng's *Life and Death in Shanghai* (1986) details her survival during years of imprisonment in China. Though her own survival might be seen as the major goal of her story, this focus is deeply compromised by her concerns with her daughter's welfare: "I hoped my removal to the detention house would free her from any further pressure to denounce me. If that were indeed the case . . . I would be prepared to put up with anything" (p. 132). Discovering that her daughter is dead greatly disturbs her own will to go on: "Now there was nothing left. It would have been less painful if I had died in prison and never known that Meiping was dead. My struggle to keep alive . . . suddenly seemed meaningless" (p. 360).

For these women, the career line is important, but it is not an ultimate end point. Whereas the men seem to sacrifice their lives to careers, the women seem to tell the story in reverse. This is not to say that women avoid the achievement of goals. They too yearn for the joy of success. But men and women do not describe their feelings in the same way. Let us listen.

Lee Iacocca (1984):
My years as general manager of the Ford Division were the happiest period of my life. For my colleagues and me, this was fire in the belly time. We were high from smoking our own brand—a combination of hard work and big dreams. (p. 65)

Chuck Yeager:
I don't recommend going to war as a way of testing character, but by the time our tour ended we felt damned good about ourselves and what we had accomplished. Whatever the future held, we knew our skills as pilots, our ability to handle stress and danger, and our reliability in tight spots. It was the difference between thinking you're pretty good, and proving it. (Yeager & Janos, 1985, p. 88)

Edward Koch (1984):
I am the Mayor of a city that has more Jews than live in Jerusalem, more Italians than live in Rome ... and more Puerto Ricans than live in San Juan. ... It is a tremendous responsibility, but there is no other job in the world that compares with it. ... Every day has the possibility of accomplishing some major success. (p. 359)

When John Paul Getty drilled his first great oil well, he was overjoyed: "The sense of elation and triumph was and is always there. It stems from knowing that one has beaten nature's incalculable odds by finding and capturing a most elusive (and often a dangerous and malevolent) prey" (Getty, 1986, p. 28).

The tone of the male voices often has an element of hostility, aggression, or domination in it. Their celebration of achievement seems to be the result of what is fundamentally an antagonistic encounter between themselves and other people or nature itself. The ways that women's voices speak of achievements take a rather different tone.

Martina Navratilova (1985):
For the first time I was a Wimbledon champion, fulfilling the dream of my father many years before. ... I could feel Chris [Evert] patting me on the back, smiling and congratulating me. Four days later, the Women's Tennis Association computer ranked me Number 1 in the world, breaking Chris's four year domination. I felt I was on top of the world. (p. 190)

Beverly Sills:
I think "Se Pieta" was the single more extraordinary piece of singing I ever did. I know I had never heard myself sing that way before. ... The curtain began coming down very slowly ... and then a roar went through that house the likes of which

I'd never heard. I was a little stunned by it: the audience wouldn't stop applauding. (Sills & Linderman, 1987, p. 172)

Sydney Biddle Barrows (1987):
   I was motivated by the challenge of doing something better than everyone else. . . . I was determined to create a business that would appeal to . . . men, who constituted the high end of the market. . . . I was sure that we could turn our agency into one hell of an operation—successful, elegant, honest, and fun. (pp. 48-49)

In the Womanstories, the love of the audience response, the affection of the opponent, and the satisfaction of customers are the significant factors in their descriptions. The achievement is described in relational terms, with more stress on mutuality than supremacy. The Womanstory emphasizes continuity with other's goals, not opposition to them. In fact, it is possible for one's opponent to be seen as a necessary part of one's own success. As Martina Navratilova (1985) says,

You're totally out for yourself, to win a match, yet you're dependent on your opponent to some degree for the type of match it is and how well you play. You need the opponent; without her you do not exist. (p. 162)

Emotional Interdependence

What do these stories tell about emotional interdependency—that is, the desire to be with others and to engage in reciprocal affection? Here, the Manstory appears to be rather thin. Sticking to the narrative line may cut short their affective lives, at least in print. But this is too black and white a message. Men have their buddies, sidekicks, intimate rivals, and compatriots. Perhaps the difference is that together they look outward, rather than at each other. Let us look at how Manstories allow for the expression of relatedness and emotionality.

Ed Koch (1984), reporting a conversation:
   I've been Mayor for close to three years. . . . I get involved in a lot of controversies and I make a lot of people mad at me, and so maybe at the end of these four years they'll say, "He's too controversial and we don't want him!" And maybe they'll throw me out. That's okay with me. I'll get a better job, and you won't get a better mayor. (p. 227)

Chuck Yeager:
   Often at the end of a hard day, the choice was going home to a wife who really didn't understand what you were talking about . . . or gathering around the bar with guys who had also spent the day in a cockpit. Talking flying was the next best thing to flying itself. And after we had a few drinks in us, we'd get happy or belligerent and raise some hell. Flying and hell raising—one fueled the other. (Yeager & Janos, 1985, p. 173)

John Paul Getty (1986):

> For some reason, I have always been much freer in recording my emotions and feelings in my diaries. . . . Taken as a whole, they might serve to provide insight into a father's true feeling about his sons.

1939

> Los Angeles, California: May 20: Saw George, a remarkable boy, rapidly becoming a man. He is 5'9" tall and weighs 145 pounds.

> Geneva, Switzerland: July 8: Ronny is well, happy and likes his school. His teachers give him a good report. He is intelligent and has good character, they say. Took Ronny and Fini to the Bergues Hotel for lunch and then to Chamonix.

> Los Angeles, December 10: Went to Ann's house [Ann Rork, my fourth wife, who divorced me in 1935] and saw Pabby and Gordon, bless them. They are both fine boys. (p. 11)

Manstories seem to celebrate the song of the self. Emotional ties are mentioned as "facts" where necessary, but the author does not try to recreate in the reader empathic emotional responses. Getty's descriptions of his interactions with his sons, for example, are very meager in emotional feelings, despite his claim that the diary entries show his depth of caring. The willingness to play the role of the "bastard" is also seen in Manstories, as, for example, in Koch's remarks above.

What about our heroines? What do their stories tell about their emotional interdependencies? How important are relationships to their life courses? Is there a Womanstory too?

Let us listen.

Beverly Sills reminisces that "one of the things I always loved best about being an opera singer was the chance to make new friends every time I went into a new production" (Sills & Linderman, 1987, p. 229). She writes when she and Carol Burnett were doing a television show together, they cried when the show was over: "We knew we'd have nobody to play with the next day. After that we telephoned each other three times a day" (p. 280).

Martina Navratilova (1985) writes that "I've never been able to treat my opponent as the enemy, particularly Pam Shriver, my doubles partner and one of my best friends" (p. 167).

Sydney Biddle Barrows (1987) emphasizes in her book her ladylike upbringing, her sensitive manners, and her appreciation of the finer things of life. Her lifestyle is obviously besmirched when she is arrested by the police and thrown in jail. She writes that on leaving a group of streetwalking prostitutes with whom she has been jailed,

> As I left the cell, everybody started shouting and cheering me on. "Go get 'em, girlfren!" I left with mixed emotions. These girls had been so nice to me, and so

open and interesting, that my brief experience in jail was far more positive than I could have imagined. (p. 284)

The necessity of relating to others in a Womanstory is especially crucial in Nien Cheng's (1986) narrative about solitary confinement. To contend with the long and bitter loneliness, she adopted a small spider as a friend. She describes her concern for this spider:

My small friend seemed rather weak. It stumbled and stopped every few steps. Could a spider get sick, or was it merely cold? . . . It made a tiny web on the toilet edge . . . forming something rather like a cocoon. . . . When I had to use the toilet, I carefully sat well to one side so that I did not disturb it. (p. 155)

Though many other examples might be given, these illustrate the major differences I have found between the relatively more profound emotional interdependency and intimacy requirements of women in the telling of their stories and those of men. In general, the important aspects of women's autobiographies depend heavily on their affiliative relationships with others. They seem to focus on these ties without drawing strong demarcations between their work world and their "private" life. Their stories highlight the interdependent nature of their involvements much more vividly than do the stories of the men. The centrality of emotional well-being to all facets of life is found there much more frequently than in the men's stories.

VOICES AS VERSES: FORMS AND FOAM

As stories are told, forms are recreated. The content belongs to the forms, and the forms control the content. Let us look at the forms more closely.

Individuals have characteristic ways of navigating their lives. What is characteristic, the signature we read across episodes, exists at the level of narrative structure. We can analyze the structure of a life plot as symbolic in its own right.

—Richard Ochberg (1988, p. 172)

Popular autobiographies of men are very similar in form. Their narrative lines tend to be linear (that is, strongly related to an explicit goal state, the career or quest) and progressive (the action moves toward this goal). Manstories also tend to be characterized by one or two major climaxes, usually related to career trajectories. The emphasis of a Manstory on the single narrative line is evident from the beginning of the book. Edward Koch's autobiography, *Mayor,* for example, is totally devoted to his political career, especially as it "mirrors" the life of New York City from the mayor's office. Chapter 1, entitled "A Child of the City," begins not with a biological childhood but with his political youth: "In March of 1975, when I was a U.S. Congressman from New York. . . ." Koch begins at a crisis point for the book's long-suffering heroine—not a flesh-and-blood woman, but New York City. Chuck Yeager's book about his life as a pilot begins with a crash landing. Getty (1986) initiates his book with a sentence indicating that he was born in 1892 and has been "an active businessman since 1914" (p. vii). Physicist Feynman (1986) starts, "When I was about eleven or twelve I set up a lab in my house" (p. 3). Iacocca (1984) states, "You're about to read the history of a man who's had more than his share of successes" (p. xiv). The origin of the life story is at the beginning of one's professional career.

The autobiographer confronts personally her culture's stories of male and female desire, insinuating the lines of her story through the lines of the patriarchal story that has been autobiography.

—Sidonie Smith (1987, p. 19)

Womanstories also contain a progressive theme related to achievement goals, but often the text emphasizes another facet of personal identity and deviates from one clear narrative line associated with career. Beverly Sills's first chapter recalls the last night she sang at the New York City opera house at a gala charity performance. The event is presented not as a career triumph but rather as an emotionally significant "swan song" (Sills & Linderman, 1987). Sydney Biddle Barrows's (1987) book commences with a description of the annual meeting of the Society of Mayflower Descendants of which she is a member, thus foregrounding the question of how, as a member of such an elitist social group, she became the owner of an escort service. Nien Cheng (1986) recalls her old home in Shanghai, her daughter asleep in her room. The importance of her daughter's activities plays a strong counterpoint to her own issues of existence. "Apple Trees" is the title of Martina Navratilova's (1985) first chapter; she begins, "I was three years old when my mother and father divorced" (p. 1). For female authors, the story forms available are much fuller (and more multiple in perspective) than for the men. Career successes and failures are mingled with other issues of great personal importance. Thus, the story line becomes less clearly demarcated. The narrative threads are more complexly woven for the women tellers. The story is about a person who is embedded in a variety of relationships, all of which have some priority in the telling of the life. Ambiguities about any outcome make more complex the task of giving value to any particular event.

Can Stories/Lives Be Changed?

Throughout this chapter, I have illustrated how personal identities are construed through the gendered stories of lives. Autobiographies exemplify the repertoire of life story forms by which "significant" members of a culture define themselves. Less important people, those who merely tell their stories to themselves and their private audiences, also use these forms. We all know ourselves, we define our pasts, and we project our futures as they fit into the acculturated story forms. But the forms for each gender are restrictive, and in many critical areas, such as achievement strivings and intimate relationships, men and women are inhibited from formulating selves that would allow for a different range of expressions and actions. Neither a man nor a woman can easily swap roles without the loss of social approval.

The structure of autobiography, a story that is at once by and about the same individual, echoes and reinforces a structure already implicit in our language, a structure that is also (not accidentally) very like what we usually take to be the structure of self-consciousness itself: the capacity to know and simultaneously be that which one knows.

—Elizabeth W. Bruss (1980, p. 301)

I began this work with a special sensitivity to the losses that women have endured because they have been absent from the public sphere. I saw that because the story lines that lead a woman from childhood to maturity did not show the path by which strong achievement strivings could be satisfied without great personal sacrifice, women could not become all they had the potential to be. As I read the autobiographies of our "great" men, I confronted anew what many social critics, especially feminists, have frequently claimed: that the goals, values, and methods that sustain men's lives are antagonistic to other significant social values, those associated with women's narratives and lives. Particularly in revisioning these stories, I saw the basic values of each clustering around themes of power versus themes of love. Increasingly, as I read, it seemed to me that what most needed change was not women's narratives, to become more like men's, but the reverse. Men, perhaps even more than women, needed new story lines, lines that were more multiplex, relational, and "messy." Both seemed imprisoned by their stories; both bound to separate pieces of the world that, if somehow put together, would create new possibilities—ones in which each could share the other's dreams. But how can we escape our story lines, our prisons made of words?

Plots are dramatic embodiments of what a culture believes to be true. . . . Of all the possible actions people can do in fiction, very few can be done by women.

—Joanna Russ (1972, p. 4)

LANGUAGE: SOURCE AND SORCERESS

Language seems almost magical. Only through its powers to name can we identify our experiences and our persons. There are no social structures that bear upon us beyond this linguistic order. All that exists is within it. If we want to change our lives, we need to change our patterns of discourse. The "language games" constitute what there is to change. Can we lift ourselves by our bootstraps?

Individuals construct themselves as subjects through language, but individual subjects rather than being the source of their own self generated and self expressive meaning adopt positions available within the language at a given moment.

—Felicity Nussbaum (1988, p. 149)

Our narrative forms, our metaphors, our ways of communicating do not emerge from nothingness. They are embedded in the foundations of society. Stories and their structural instantiations reverberate against and with each other. Are we prisoners of our father tongue? Yes—mostly—maybe—sometimes—no. Perhaps we can, at least, wiggle a bit.

In altering the images and narrative structures through which we compose the stories of our lives, we may hope to alter the very experiences of those lives as well.

—Annette Kolodny (1980, p. 258)

Many voices singing different tunes can sound noisy. Do you feel drowned out? We must sing like mermaids and hope that a melody or two will be carried on the wind.

Subversively, she rearranges the dominant discourse and the dominant ideology of gender, seizing the language and its power to turn cultural fictions into her very own story.

—Sidonie Smith (1987, p. 175)

How do we rearrange the melodies of talk? I will suggest some ways. Let us listen carefully as our words divide us and emphasize power differences among us. Let us resist these discordant tunes. (This will be less appealing at first to those whose words have been on everyone's lips.) Let us note, for example, that we call ourselves for some man long since dead. In a sense we belong to him. Let our names hang lightly in the air, or let us blow them away if we wish.

For a symbolic order that equates the idea(l) of the author with a phallic pen transmitted from father to son places the female writer in contradiction to the dominant definition of woman and casts her as the usurper of male prerogatives.

—Domna Stanton (1984, p. 13)

Let us listen to the metaphors we carry with us. Let us choose them carefully. Do we mimic our brothers who scoff at "soft" sciences and who love "hard" data? Do we feel the grasp of "sexual politics" at our throats?

To change a story signals a dissent from social norms as well as narrative forms.

—Rachel Duplessis (1985, p. 20)

Let us play with story lines. Let us not always conform to androcentric styles. Let us demur. Maybe stories don't need lines. Perhaps they need to step out of the queue and refuse to march in orderly progression. Let us not stick to the point. Let us improvise!

The construction is nothing more than an improvisation.

—George Rosenwald (1988, p. 256)

Let us claim the tentative and fuzzy nature of all our linguistic formulations. Let us shake the tree of knowledge, unashamed. Let us eat the apple to the core, and spit out "truth." Let us grant ourselves the pleasures of making languages, and changing them, as they transform us. Let us sing songs that will free us from the past and hum sweet dirges for androcentric systems as they drown.

3

Gendered Narratives
Bodies Under Construction

A body "is not the juicy mortal flesh itself, but a linguistic sign for a complex structure of belief and practice through which I and many of my fellow citizens organize a great deal of life.

—Donna Haraway (1997, p. 217)

The body is among our cultural artifacts rather than our natural objects. . . . Bodily inscriptions . . .[are] the corporealization of culture.

—Katharine Young (1993, p. 5)

I am truly distinct from my body, and . . . I can exist without it.

—Rene Descartes, Sixth Meditation
(quoted in Keller, 1992, p. 148)

I'm just a material girl.

—Madonna

How shall the Body be brought into this conversation? There are many controversies about this question. Though critics of social constructionism agree that social categories such as status, educational level, or social class are constructed, they are often adamant that material things, such as death, rocks, furniture, and bodies, cannot be.[1] For them, the body exists before classification, an essential part of the nature of the universe. Social constructionists, on the other hand, resist drawing a line between the given and the constructed, contending that all categories, without exception, are constructed. Because the body is the prime signifier of gender and sex differences, it becomes a critical topic for discussion in the context of this book. Within this chapter, the assumption that social practices create the body is expanded through a study of the popular autobiography in an approach similar to that taken in Chapter 2. Rather than concentrating on the nature of female and male bodies over the life span, we attend to the ways in which the gendered body is "spoken" over the life span by various well-known people. The project began with a curiosity concerning how men and women might tell their bodily experiences differently. From these excerpts, we might speculate on how such differences create gaps between us, insulating us from each other's cares, reducing communication, and leading to different interpretations of how men and women experience the world.

In this chapter, as well as in Chapter 2, we engage the gendered body from the narrative position. In Chapter 7, it will be revisited in the form of a performative psychology piece, a soliloquy dedicated to the plight of the aging female. Each of these forms designates special facets of a postmodern positioning on the nature of embodiment. Through the focus on the body, the sometimes subtle distinctions among the various theoretical positions in feminism, as outlined in Chapter 1, are also made clearer.

CREATING THE GENDERED BODY IN NARRATIVE

The female/male distinction, a powerful constituent of everyday and scientific life, is also a basic building block of our ways of talking. Within many languages, every word is marked by gender. Upon this binary pair many other linguistic distinctions have been built (Bohan, 1993; Hekman, 1990). In accordance with historical traditions, philosophical arguments, religious doctrines, and prevalent social stereotypes across many cultural boundaries, maleness has been associated with culture, mind, rationality, abstractness, and order, and femaleness with the opposite side of the pairs: nature, body, emotionality, concreteness, and chaos. So, for example, we speak in English of "Mother Nature" and "Father Time"; we worry about men's lack of emotional expressiveness and women's PMS; we give men credit for their logical abilities and women for their intuition. Men's bodies, especially their sexual aspects, are considered externalized, apparent, and pure, whereas women's are internalized, secret, and potentially polluted (Douglas, 1980). The dichotomies that are created in language by virtue of these two major categories have implications for how we shape our apparently given material worlds. Within the narrative forms by which we tell our stories of ourselves, these powerful gendered differences can make segregated selves very "real."

Almost without exception, people are socialized into their gendered caste. Boys are turned into men who are expected to live very different lives from girls who are turned into women. The prime cultural difference is the expectation that girls will grow up to become wives and mothers and thus more oriented to reproductive and familial relations and that boys will become oriented to the marketplace, where they will specialize in earning money and gaining public recognition. A variety of cultural forms prepares the way for these transformations: fairy tales and children's stories, family histories, television and movie stories, advertising, and the like. As these examples illustrate, the narrative is the central means by which people learn to endow their lives with meaning across time (Bruss, 1980; Rabuzzi, 1988; Russ, 1972; Sprinker, 1980). As we indicated in Chapter 2, as people are exposed to the popular stories within the culture, they learn how to "know" themselves, how to make themselves intelligible to others, and how to act. This perspective reverses the more traditional notion that the story is fashioned from the raw materials of life. Instead, one can argue, the story produces the life. To the extent that narratives are gendered, furnishing different structures of meaning for men and women, so do they contribute to cultural patterns that differentiate between the genders and prescribe what is likely and unlikely, desirable and undesirable during a lifetime.

Also as noted in Chapter 2, the autobiography has become extremely popular among the reading public, and how the body is inscribed or invested with meaning has become a topic of central concern for feminist scholars.[2] Thus, as men and women tell the stories of their bodies—what they are, what they mean, and how they should be regarded—they place themselves within other dialogues, those that affect the course of their relationships with others, their career potentials, and their life satisfactions. If the stories of embodiment of men and women differ importantly, they may also generate estrangements. To live in a story of the body that is different from another's can render an impasse of understanding. Male and female actions toward each other may be misunderstood, and relationships may become alienated.

NARRATIVES OF EMBODIMENT OVER THE LIFE SPAN

To explore these issues, I studied a popular narrative form—the autobiography. The choice of this medium was fashioned by the need to find published sources that are easily acceptable to the general reading public. The forms of these volumes are shaped to seem as close to "true" reports of life stories as possible. The authors and their ghost writers are engaged by editors to expose their stories without obfuscating literary accouterments. Thus, these narratives are in the mainstream of accessible prose, not at the cultural fringes where conventional narratives might be challenged or destroyed through either rare forms of writing or esoteric life events. For this study I analyzed 24 books, whose authors were equally divided between women and men. I drew from these autobiographies all of the passages in which the authors described their bodies over the life span. By dividing their narratives into youth, adulthood, and maturity, we may better discover when and how divergencies in stories of embodiment occur. For example, we might investigate whether the stories of young girls and boys are more similar in terms of attention to bodily descriptions than those of adolescents and whether older people tell more similar stories of embodiment than younger adults do.

Although the full complexity of these accounts cannot be conveyed within this chapter, illustrative quotations are included to emphasize the ways in which the stories of embodiment over the life span differ for women and men, as well as how they are similar.

Bodily Inscription From Childhood to Puberty

Remarkable differences between men's and women's accounts of their bodies begin to emerge from their earliest reminiscences of childhood. The sharpest distinction, and the most persistent, is the consistent inclusion of bodily references by girls in their stories and the absence of "body" talk by boys.

A typical example of the "indifferent" male author, with almost nothing to say about his body, is Thomas J. Watson, Jr., who followed in his father's footsteps to become the powerful boss of IBM. Describing a homemade film of himself in his first-grade class, Watson reports one sentence: "I'm the tallest, long boned and ungainly" (Watson & Petre, 1990, p. 4). A more poignant childhood self-description, at least to the reader, if not to the writer, is photographer Ansel Adams's (1985) account of how he acquired his "parabolic" nose:

> On the day of the San Francisco earthquake [April 17, 1906] . . . I tumbled against a low brick garden wall, my nose making violent contact with quite a bloody effect. When the family doctor could be reached, he advised that my nose be left alone until I matured; it could then be repaired with greater aesthetic quality. Apparently I never matured, as I have yet to see a surgeon about it. (pp. 7-8)

For Adams, the contorted nose that punctuated his face simply became irrelevant to his life (or at least became a good story about his indifference to the aesthetics of his own facial countenance, which fortunately did not extend to his sensitivity to the physical beauty of his photographic subjects).

For women, the tribulations associated with their physical nature in childhood are often central to their narratives of growing up. These issues are given strong and deep emotional significance and sometimes continue to be important to them many years after. Their feelings of present-day self-worth seem strongly conditioned by the physical nature of the person they once were. For example, comedienne Joan Rivers (1986), who has maintained a Barbie doll look-alike quality through the best cosmetic miracles that can be achieved, has made a career out of comic references to her misbegotten self. Describing a family photograph, she says,

> When I make jokes . . . about being fat, people often think it is just my neurotic imagination. Well, on the right, with her mother and sister during a vacation trip to Williamsburg, Virginia, is the . . . fat pig, wishing she could teach her arms and hips to inhale and hold their breath. (p. 183)

Fat also plagued the prima ballerina, Gelsey Kirkland (1986), who writes of her dancing debut at camp as a form of self-defense for her misshapen body:

> The other children taunted me about the disproportions of my body. I never let them know how much I was stung by their disparagements. . . . I turned my abdominal bulge to advantage by performing a belly dance to amuse those in my cabin. (p. 10)

Tennis star Martina Navratilova (1985) had the reverse problem—being too small:

> I was tiny, not an ounce of fat on me—nothing but muscle and bone—just sheer energy. In school I was kind of embarrassed about being so small, but on the tennis court it didn't really matter that much. (p. 24)

Two facets of difference bear particular notice in these autobiographies. In general, men disregard their physical beings except to note how effective their bodies were in attaining their goals, especially in athletic contests. Second, men display little emotion when making these descriptions. They do not rue their fates, whether it is to be lanky or short, sickly or well. No male autobiographers admitted to being a chubby-child, perhaps because this physical attribute, associated with femaleness, would compromise their masculine image too greatly. In general, the body is virtually absent in their reminiscences. Women's stories tend to be far more centered on their embodiment. Beginning in childhood, women include greater detail in the descriptions of the body, and they are often emotional in describing their embodied lives.

The impact of physiognomy is often intensified in puberty. Chuck Yeager, the man with the "right stuff," looks back with pleasure at his body's capacities: "By the time I reached high school, I excelled at anything that demanded dexterity. . . . In sports, I was terrific at pool and pingpong, good in basketball and football" (Yeager & Janos, 1985, p. 11). Having an athletic body also helped ease a racially tense social scene for footballer Amad Rashad (1988), as well as contributing to his self-esteem: "If you lived in my neighborhood . . . you tended not to go to Eastside—they would kick your ass over there. Because of my . . . athletic ability, the law of the street didn't apply to me" (p. 47). T. Boone Pickens, Jr. (1987), the billionaire "takeover" tycoon, says of himself, "Fortunately, I was well coordinated. . . . Only five feet nine inches tall, . . . but a basketball player" (p. 17). In effect, being short was a threat to adolescent identity; being coordinated was a fortunate compensation. Donald Trump (1987), New York's bad boy builder, avoids any physical description of himself as a youth except to relate that he was physically aggressive to the point of giving a music teacher a black eye when he was in second grade "because he didn't know anything" (p. 71).

Lee Iacocca (1984) turns the story of his youthful illness into gains in the realms of gambling and sex:

> I came down with rheumatic fever. The first time I had a palpitation of the heart, I almost passed out—from fear. I thought my heart was popping out of my chest. . . . But I was lucky. Although I lost about forty pounds and stayed in bed for six months, I eventually made a full recovery. (p. 16)

While convalescing, he started playing poker and reading books: "All I could remember about the book [*Appointment in Samarra*] was that it got me interested in sex" (pp. 16-17). Iacocca's single reference to a budding interest in sex is unique among these American heroes whose autobiographies I read. An occasional mention of sexual conquest is the only other form in which this topic is raised.

An exception to the bravado and self-assuredness of the vast majority of auto-biographers is Watson's portrayal of himself as unathletic: "While I was skinny and taller than most other kids, I was no athlete. My eye-hand coordination was terrible, so I hated baseball" (Watson & Petre, 1990, p. 34). Late in his life, he proved himself physically by going sailing in dangerous waters away from medical supports, in part to overcome his fears of dying following a heart attack. A theme of overcoming his bodily and psychological defects is a stronger undercurrent in his book than in others. His success in mastering himself is illustrated, however.

For men in contemporary Western culture, the adolescent challenge largely takes place within the arena of athletics. For these males, body and identity are more closely linked in this period than at any other time in the life span. In adulthood, the body does not figure in men's stories; only in late adulthood do we see its "ugly" head emerge once again, as an enemy within.

For the adolescent girl, character is made not so much on the playing fields as in private chambers. As Navratilova (1985) comments,

> The girls started to fill out in the sixth or seventh grade, but I didn't wear a brassiere until I was fourteen—and God knows I didn't need one then. I was more than a little upset about developing so late. (p. 24)

Folksinger Joan Baez (1987) recounts her entry into junior high school as marked by rejection, which stemmed from her physical appearance. Without much pathos, she describes her image: "Joanie Boney, an awkward stringbean, fifteen pounds underweight, my hair a bunch of black straw whacked off just below my ears, the hated cowlick on my hairline forcing a lock of bangs straight up over my right eye" (p. 30). In high school, her self-evaluation reflects a degree of self-confidence mixed with doubt: "On the one hand I thought I was pretty hot stuff, but on the other, I was still terribly self-conscious about my extremely flat chest and dark skin" (p. 43). Beverly Sills, the great opera singer and director of the New York City Opera, describes her reactions to puberty:

> I developed breasts earlier than any of my classmates, and that was a great source of anguish for me. . . . When it became obvious in gym class that I was the only girl who needed a bra, I didn't just become miserable, I became *hysterical.* I was so

unhappy with the sheer size of me that my mother bought me a garter belt, which was about seven inches wide, and I wore it around my chest. (Sills & Linderman, 1987, p. 17)

Because girls seem more fully identified with their bodies, bodily changes at puberty become an enormous issue for identity formation. For women's stories, one's beauty is a critical integer in the kind of story one can tell of one's accomplishments in many facets of life. Men's stories are silent about bodily concerns. They write as though it does not matter very much how they look. To the extent that athletic activities are important to their sense of identity, this aspect of life is inscribed. However, the body is not described as just an object of aesthetic or social appeal; men do not include how handsome or sexually mature they were in adolescence. (I have yet to read one passage in the thousands of pages I've covered about a man's insecurities about the size or shape of his penis!) This is not to claim that men don't have any anxiety about their physical appearance but rather that these fears are not an acceptable part of their life stories.

The Adult Years: Living Within and Beyond the Body

The tendency for men telling their life stories to distance themselves from their bodies intensifies in adulthood. The language used to describe "it" is coldly instrumental. It would seem that the male author regards his body as merely a necessary "machine" for living. For example, this is how Yeager describes his body:

Being in our early twenties, we were in good physical shape and at the height of our recuperative powers—which we had to be to survive those nights. That was our Golden Age of flying and fun. By the time we reached thirty, our bodies forced moderation on us. (Yeager & Janos, 1985, p. 180)

In effect, according to Yeager's narrative, one simply goes on until the machine begins to break down.

Should one's body come under scrutiny from others, it can be unexpected and unappreciated. Donald Trump (1987), commenting on his efforts as a young man to join a prestigious Manhattan club, is shocked to find his body is a consideration in membership selection: "Because I was young and good-looking, and because some of the older members of the club were married to beautiful young women, [the officer of the club] was worried that I might be tempted to try to steal their wives" (p. 96). Having a "good-looking" body can thus be a career impediment. It can also cause other troubles, especially for the man who takes too much pride in it. Consider J. P. Getty's (1986) attempt to pass himself off as a boxer in order to impress some women he is interested in seducing. Enticing his friend the professional boxer Jack Dempsey to spar with him, he finds himself in difficulty:

A few moments after we began to spar, I realized that Jack was pulling his punches. My *macho* was taking all the punishment, for there were two or three very attractive young women friends watching at ringside. I wanted not only to test my ability as a boxer but also to prove myself. . . . "Damn it, Jack, treat me just as you would any professional sparring partner." . . . I swung my lefts and rights as hard as I could. Jack . . . moved back a pace or two.

"Okay, Paul," he said, "If you insist. . . ."

The first punch was hard. Jack swung again—and connected. That was that. . . . I picked myself up off the canvas, fully and finally convinced that I would thenceforth stick to the oil business. (pp. 276-277)

One might also note from this little tale that Getty was willing to subject his body to a Dempsey punch in order to satisfy his "macho" needs.

Because the body as an asset is taken for granted—much like the beating of a heart—only its potential for failure must be confronted. The male reaction is expressed in two major ways: *anxiety* and *denial*. Among autobiographers, overtly expressed fear of dysfunction is predominant among men whose career success is closely linked to physical condition. Thus, Rashad (1988) comments, "Injuries are the ultimate reality for a pro athlete—they throw a shadow over your days. . . . Football is not just a job, it's an adventure—until it comes time to get killed" (pp. 118-119).

However, by far the more common reaction to the threat of dysfunction is denial of the impact of bodily events on the character of the man. Chuck Yeager gives an account of his emergency exit from a crashing plane. Yeager's parachute catches on fire as ejects himself from the cockpit. Upon hitting the ground, he wanders toward a passerby who has seen him land.

My face was charred meat. I asked him if he had a knife. He took out a small penknife . . . and handed it to me. I said to him, "I've gotta do something about my hand. I can't stand it anymore." I used his knife to cut the rubber lined glove, and part of two burned fingers came out with it. The guy got sick. (Yeager & Janos, 1985, p. 360)

Yeager himself registers no reaction. He's obviously made of the "right stuff."

The major plot in adult male autobiographies is focused on career success, which is typically defined independently from the body. The discourse of career tends toward the transcendent—emphasizing ideals, goals, values, and aspirations as opposed to organicity. The body, if mentioned at all, tends to be characterized as servant to the master's plans and purposes, whether for career or pleasure. Only on occasion does the body enter the register of meaning, and that is when it serves as an asset or a liability to ends that lie beyond.

Women's accounts of embodiment in the adult years stand in marked contrast to men's. Consider the detail in which Joan Baez (1987) describes her preparations for a major performance:

By three o'clock I have finally ironed a yellow parachute skirt and cobalt blue blouse, dug out the belt with the big silver circles and the necklace made of spoon ladles linked together, and the nineteen-dollar black sandals bedecked with rhinestones. I spend an extra twenty minutes hunting down my half slip. . . . They escort me to the green room. All the saliva in my mouth evaporates on the way. I have to go to the bathroom desperately, but it's too far and won't do any good anyway, so I sit tight, sip water, and ask Mary not to let anyone talk to me. (pp. 355-357)

What is so womanly about this passage is the focus on embodied details. As Baez's autobiography reveals, she pays great attention to her clothing, describing in minute detail the outfit she decides to wear for this very important performance. Not only do these details give a picture of her stage dress, they also reveal her emotional state. Her nervousness over the event is played out not in general expressions of why she is fearful but in how she obsesses over her appearance. The intimate bodily detail of wanting to urinate concretizes her general anxiety in a vivid manner. The body is the register of emotional experience. This level of detail is characteristic of the women's autobiographies, and countless other examples are found in the women's books, but not in the men's.

Although women's bodies seem to be the sign of who they are, women also speak of their bodies as instruments of achievement. For women, appearance constitutes an integral part of every story they tell; they are often keenly aware of the impact of their appearance on others and of shaping their bodies for ulterior ends. In her dramatic tale of survival in a Chinese detention prison during the era of the Cultural Revolution, Nien Cheng (1986) describes the beginning of her long ordeal with the Red Guard. Two men arrive unannounced at her home to take her to her "trial." As she prepares herself to go downstairs to her demise, she considers how best to preserve herself. In this tense situation, her first thought is directed at how to contrive her physical appearance. She wants to confound the image of rich, Western-influenced capitalist with her dress.

I put on a white cotton shirt, a pair of gray slacks, and black sandals, the clothes Chinese women wore in public places to avoid being conspicuous. . . . Then I walked slowly, deliberately creating the impression of composure as I confronted them. (p. 8)

Although as readers we confront the heavy emphasis on appearance in women's autobiographies without notice, it would seem odd indeed for us to read a male author describing how he picked out his wardrobe and walked down the stairs as his arresting party awaited him.

Effects of appearance on career goals continue to be especially relevant to women in the public eye. Comments by Linda Ellerbee (1986), a television journalist, are telling:

I was told to lose weight if I wished ever to anchor again at NBC News. I wonder if anyone's ever said that to Charles Kuralt. . . . Regarding my hair—I have lots of hair—I've paid attention to commands to tie it back, bring it forward, put it up, take it down, cut it, let it grow, curl it, straighten it, tame it—and I stopped doing so before someone asked me to shave it off. . . . Maybe I'd just gotten older, not mellower, or maybe I'd had it up to here with men telling me to do something about my hair. (p. 119)

Because women describe themselves as deeply embodied, they are more often candid than men about the discomforts and threats to their bodies. A typical example is furnished by Beverly Sills as she describes her bout with ovarian cancer at the age of 45: "I was lucky. I had a tumor the size of a grapefruit, but the doctor removed it entirely" (Sills & Linderman, 1987, p. 264). Then she adds a gratuitous aside from a medical or biographical standpoint, but one that obviously has special importance to her: "After my operation, I probably weighed about 125 pounds. I don't think I'd weighed 125 pounds since I was four years old" (p. 264). Returning to the stage very quickly, she mentions the pain she suffered. "To be blunt about it, I was in agony. . . . The pain was almost unbelievable. The plain truth is that if I had canceled, I would have worried that I was dying" (p. 267).

The terror of being held prisoner in solitary confinement is inscribed by Nien Cheng (1986) in terms of intimate bodily experiences. Her description is rich with details of her illnesses, suffering, and her deteriorating condition: "After some time, hunger became a permanent state, no longer a sensation but an ever present hollowness. The flesh on my body slowly melted away, my eyesight deteriorated, and simple activities such as washing clothes exhausted my strength" (p. 185).

Given women's close identification with their bodies, it is also possible to appreciate why violations of the body are so unsettling for the woman: they represent invasive negations of one's identity. Consider Sidney Biddle Barrows's (1987) account of how nude photos taken of her were published in national newspapers. Her downfall began on a trip to Amsterdam with a boyfriend:

We went to the houseboat and sampled our new friend's excellent hashish. After a while, [the friend] tactfully disappeared, leaving us together in the shimmering afternoon sun. . . . I was delighted to have him snap some shots of me in my skimpy summer clothes. Pretty soon, he started flattering me: I looked so terrific, the light was just right, so why didn't I take off my clothes and let him shoot some nude photographs? (p. 22)

Later, when Barrows was arrested for running a high-class escort service, her former boyfriend sold the photos to the *New York Post*:

I was devastated. I could live with being called the Mayflower Madam, and I could even tolerate having my real name known. But now nude photographs of me were being splashed across two of the largest newspapers in the country! I couldn't believe that Rozansky had so shamelessly betrayed me, and I was disgusted that I had ever given him the time of day. (p. 290)

Other intimacies of the body that involved challenges to identity were shared by Ellerbee (1986) in her description of her illegal abortion:

> I'd been one of those women . . . who'd gotten pregnant, then gotten the name of someone through a friend of a friend, paid six hundred dollars cash, and waited, terrified, at my apartment until midnight when a pimply-faced man showed up, exchanged code words with me, and came in, bringing cutting tools, bandages and Sodium Pentothal—but no medical license I could see. I was lucky. I did not bleed uncontrollably. I did not die. I recovered. I was no longer pregnant. But I wasn't the same, either. No woman is. (p. 96)

From the standpoint of the unity of mind and body, it is also possible to understand why women's stories—and seldom men's—often contain instances of bodily alteration, mutilation, or destruction. When a woman is unhappy with her identity—feeling like a failure, wishing for a change—the frequent result is some form of bodily obliteration. Ballerina Kirkland (1986) describes a period of despair: "I wanted to lose my identity. . . . [At night, sleeping,] I was able to dream my way into somebody else's body. I was no longer Gelsey" (p. 205). At another point, she writes of a painful separation from her lover (Mikhail Baryshnikov) and the manner in which she involves her body in the loss: "I went through another round of cosmetic surgery. I had my earlobes snipped off. I had silicone injected into my ankles and lips" (p. 126). This self-alteration and in some cases mutilation is evident in various passages as women describe ways they mark their psychological distress on their bodies. Joan Rivers (1986) turns suicidal thoughts into something more bearable, even perhaps comedic. Her efforts at a symbolic self-mutilation are described:

> That winter, in fact, suicide become one of my options; a way to strike back at all the people who did not appreciate me, a way to make them pay attention and be sorry. . . . I wanted to do something terrible to myself, expend my powerless rage on my body, so I went into the bathroom and with a pair of scissors crudely chopped off my hair. (p. 249)

The woman's sense of identity remains closely tied to her physical condition. It is not so much that the body is used instrumentally—as a means to some other end outside the body. Rather, to be in a certain bodily condition is to "be oneself." Or to be who one is to be in the unified totality of one's self-in-body.

The general trend for the narratives of embodiment for the adult years suggests narratives running in reverse, with a man's bodily self fading evermore into the background as career involvement expands, and with women typically remaining intensely identified with their bodies regardless of their career involvements. In their identification with their bodies, self and bodily activities are one. This unity is supported by the social worlds in which they have careers, as well as private lives. In addition, regardless of whether the woman is an athlete, journalist, executive, or performing artist, her appearance is an element in the success she experiences at work. If her body begins to show signs of aging or unattractiveness, her career potential is also blunted. No matter what career she is in, her talent is seen as correlated with her appearance.[3]

Embodiment in the Later Years

Especially for men, the story line of an autobiography is a coherent progressive, linear form, with the writer describing early events in such a way that later outcomes are clearly previewed. As noted in Chapter 2, the climb up the ladder of success in whatever domain they are involved is the central plot of the book, and extraneous details are generally eliminated. Among the omitted details are the personal costs sustained in these endeavors, especially as they impinge on private (nonwork) lives, reveal personal limitations, or signal psychological distress. Doubts about the value of masculine pursuits, escapist fantasies, or examples of poor judgment are generally suppressed. Only if it is a matter of public record, necessary for the telling of the next stage of the success story, or a means of creating a more sympathetic character, are personal details such as these described. In most cases, the embodied state of the protagonist is irrelevant. As the central character ages, the chance that significant attention must be paid to the body also increases. As health threats impinge on the body, it cannot be safely ignored any longer. For the older male authors, three primary reactions to their bodily states tend to be found. First, there is a *self-congratulatory* theme. If one's body has remained in reasonably good health, one may offer it (as separated from "I, myself") some form of congratulations. Like a motor car that has outlasted those of one's friends, it is a machine of which one may feel proud to be the owner. This orientation flavors John Paul Getty's (1986) commentary on how well he is doing, except for some minor limits of aging: "I am eighty-three. . . . I can't lift weights or swim for hours or walk five miles at the brisk pace I did ten years ago. . . . Luckily, I can afford the best medical care available" (p. 275). With a "touch" of the "chronic," Getty appears to celebrate his 73-year-old self and indirectly claims to be holding on quite well 10 years later. Also in this vein, creating a mininarrative of achievement, Boone Pickens (1987) describes getting out of shape, "which is easy to do in your late thirties or early forties," and then, after his second marriage, how he begins to work to get back into shape: "I jogged and took up racquetball seriously. Today, I may be the best fifty-eight-year-old racquetball player in America." At least he has the modesty to add, "(There aren't many players my age)" (p. 279).

Among those writers who are not so fortunate as Getty and Pickens, two other orientations are taken toward the body. One is *begrudging admission* that one has a body and that it must be given its due. This approach is taken by Chuck Yeager: "My concession to aging is to take better care of myself than I did when I was younger. . . . I'm definitely not a rocking-chair type. I can't just sit around, watch television, drink beer, get fat, and fade out" (Yeager & Janos, 1985, pp. 422-

423). Interestingly, Yeager treats his alcohol consumption as a part of the "boys will be boys" syndrome in his younger years. As an older man, alcohol, without it ever having appeared to be a problem in his life story, disappears. The begrudging interruption of the heroic narrative is more dramatically illustrated in Ansel Adams's (1985) revelations of his chronic and increasingly disabling problems: "As I cleared the decks for future projects, I found an ever-present complicating factor: Health. My mind is as active as ever, but my body was falling farther and farther behind" (p. 365). (One may note that the "real" Adams is the mental form and that the body is a recalcitrant fellow traveler who is lagging behind.) Without any prior warning to the reader that he has struggled with circulatory problems over many years, Adams describes having heart surgery (a triple bypass and valve replacement). An interesting aspect of Adams's story line is that his annoyance with his bodily ailments is based on the social limitations of his heart problems. He has plans to effect that failing health may interrupt. The notion that this problem may suggest death, or the fear of mortality, is not insinuated into the text.

A third orientation to the aging body is often encountered in the male autobiography, essentially a *trauma of broken defenses*. If the ravages to the body in the later years become of overwhelming importance to one's public activities, the picture of the self during the middle years—detached from biological anchors—can no longer be maintained. With the disruptive sense of being the victim of a "dirty trick," the male at last confronts the possibility of finitude. Watson's description of his heart attack is illustrative:

> That night I woke up with a pain in my chest. It wasn't very intense but it wouldn't go away. Olive was in the Caribbean with friends, so I drove myself to the emergency room at Greenwich Hospital . . . having a heart attack. (Watson & Petre, 1990, p. 392)

Employing the metaphor of the body as the serviceable machine, Watson also reveals his sense of vulnerability: "When you have a heart attack, you realize how fragile your body is. I felt that mine had let me down, damn near entirely, and for several months I had very volatile reactions to insignificant things" (p. 394). Although the emotional reaction of anger seems rather inappropriate, it is more rational if one presumes that the rage is directed externally, and not to a breakdown that has occurred in oneself. It is strange, from my standpoint, to be enraged by a body that has had a heart attack. But it makes more sense if one segregates one's mind from one's body.

It would be useful to make broad comparisons between autobiographies written by older men and older women. Unfortunately, there are few popular autobiographies written by women who are over 60. Women's reputations tend to result from achievements of young adulthood, and this is when their stories are written. For those older women who do write autobiographies, the body continues to figure importantly in two ways. First, although one might anticipate a drawing away from bodily identification as it becomes more problematic, this does not seem to be the case. Instead, the writers continue to "live their bodies," despite transformations. Beverly Sills's account of her body's reaction to her chores in the management of the opera company after her retirement as a diva is illustrative:

> I was working like a horse, my blood pressure was way up, and I was eating six meals a day. . . . I came into my job as general director weighing 150 pounds; on June 16, 1984, when I visited the endocrinologist, I weighed 220 pounds. (Sills & Linderman, 1987, p. 345)

Again, one can gather that the stress of her occupation is measured out in pounds of accumulated weight. Emotional life is registered in bodily distress.

There is a second theme located in the accounts of women, including those in later years, which is far more subtle in its manifestation, but pervasive and profound. This is the notion of relational being—that is, the idea that one's identity is commingled with others. Language that suggests the intermingling of one's own corporeal boundaries with others is more noticeable in women's than in men's stories. Nien Cheng's (1986) autobiography is a continuous conjoining of her life with that of her daughter, who was killed by the Red Guard. After the memorial service for her daughter, she describes a night without sleep.

> Lying in the darkened room, I remembered the years that had gone by, and I saw my daughter in various stages of her growth from a chubby-cheeked baby . . . to a beautiful young woman in Shanghai. . . . I blamed myself for her death because I had brought her back to Shanghai. (p. 495)

Because the woman's body is so closely identified with the self, one's bodily relations with others essentially extend the self. In the same way that violations of the body are defacements of identity, so are investments of the body in others' modes of unifying self and other. Thus, violations of a loved one's body deface one's own identity. In pondering the preceding years and the meaning of one's life, women's stories are more given over to ruminations about children, lovers, and parents—those with whom bodies have been intimately shared—and others, such as friends, who are now part of oneself.

This recounting of significant connection is not wholly reserved for old age, however. Even when the younger women think back on their lives, their reflections tend to center on those related through extensions of the body. For example, Joan Baez (1987) writes an epilogue in which she describes those who have been important in her life. In the final pages, she talks of going to a party in Paris with her son. When she returns home,

> Mom will have a fire going in the kitchen and perhaps a Brahms trio on the stereo. Gabe will fall into bed, and I will sit in front of the fire, dressed like a Spanish prin-

cess, telling Mom how the sun rose, piercing through the mist over the lake . . . and how there was peace all around as the castle finally slept. (pp. 377-378)

For men, rumination about the significance of intimates plays but a minor role in their stories. When one is on the grand highway to heroics, it is important to travel light. Thus, Yeager and Getty speak only in passing of deaths and illnesses within the family; Trump describes himself, his family members, and his wife, Ivana, as "rocks." For Trump, rocks are hard, sturdy, and without emotional excesses. In general, the major exception to this disregard is the death of a father, which often receives considerable attention, given the general tendency to avoid sentimentality, family revelations, and details about one's own vulnerabilities and private sorrows. The importance of the father's death can be traced to the threat it may symbolize to the male portrayals of invulnerability. Because one can see within the father's death the possibility of one's own finitude, added attention is needed to keeping the psychological defenses strong against such powerful feelings. Watson writes in great detail about his father's death: "I can't characterize anybody's grief but my own, but I felt as if a very big piece of my life was being pulled away. He was the foundation on which I had been standing for forty-two years" (Watson & Petre, 1990, p. 275). Interestingly, in making the funeral arrangements, he integrates an achievement motif into the expression of filial obligation: "Dick and I agreed that the greatest tribute we could give him was to make the funeral as well run as any IBM meeting during his life" (p. 276).

Even in describing father's death, the male autobiographer focuses on the abstract, even spiritual, quality of the attachment, not on the embodied connection. It would be unlikely that one would write as Nien Cheng (1986) does when she is finally allowed to leave China. Continuing her embodied discourse, she describes her physical state as she leaves Shanghai on a passenger ship. She recalls the feeling of the heavy rain, her lack of umbrella or raincoat, her "staggering up the slippery gangway . . . , the wind whipping my hair while I watched the coastline of China receding." She ponders her daughter's fate: "I felt guilty for being the one who was alive. I wished it were Meiping standing on the deck of this ship, going away to make a new life for herself" (pp. 534-535).

CONSEQUENCES OF EMBODIED STORIES OVER THE LIFE SPAN

As the present analysis indicates, autobiographies differ dramatically in the meanings they impart to gendered bodies over the life span. The male autobiographer suggests that the man should be "above bodily concerns," more invested in culture than nature, more in rationalities and goals than in the corporeal.[4] To be fixated on one's body in a Manstory would be narcissistic and demeaning. To put matters of corporeality aside is also highly functional for the male in terms of career aspirations. More hours can be devoted to achievement, and with fewer complaints. It is only in the later years that the male autobiographer admits an important relationship between self and body, and it is often an admission of shock, fear, and sorrow. The grand story is being brought to a close by a secret villain, and that villain dwells within.

Female autobiographers present a life story in which body and self are more unified. To be a woman is to be embodied; to fail in attending to one's corporeality would be to ignore the culturally defined essential core of being. But the body offers its travails. As Adrienne Rich (1977) has put it, "I know no woman—virgin, mother, lesbian, married, celibate—whether she earns her keep as a housewife, a cocktail waitress, or a scanner of brain waves—for whom her body is not a fundamental problem" (p. 14). Perhaps *problem* is too narrow a category. It can also be one's joy and one's pride. This embodiment seems to lend itself to a far greater sense of unity with others, particularly with those who have shared the flesh, than disembodiment can. To be embodied in this way is thus to be in significant relationship with others. The body can be a clearinghouse for joy and fulfillment. At the same time, the discourse of embodiment sets the stage for deep unsettlement during puberty, for self-mutilation during periods of disappointment, and for a more profound sense of aging in the later years.

Inevitably, an analysis such as this raises questions of cultural good. For if one lives the life course within frameworks of meaning, and if these meanings invite and constrain, celebrate and suppress, then one may ask whether it might be otherwise. If we could alter the forms of meaning—whether in autobiography or elsewhere—should we do so? From the female standpoint, there is much to reject in the male narratives of life and the practices that they favor. The male life course seems a constricted "out-of-body" experience, one that devalues potentially significant aspects of human life. For the male, the female's mode of indexing life seems often irrelevant to the tasks at hand, lends itself to emotional instability, and aligns itself more easily with the recognition of the arch-enemy of the striver—death.

It is amazing, from this perspective, that heterosexual relationships are achieved, given how differently popular narratives position embodied experiences. Giving one's body in a sexual relationship is often a very integrative experience to a woman, whereas it might be regarded as an impersonal exchange by a man, whose focus might be elsewhere. From this perspective, the coherence of same-sex relationships, their forms and modes of satisfaction, can be better understood. For lesbian lovers, sexual expressions mingle with other forms of human connectedness. For homosexual men, sex may well be a segregated activity, with no implications for other facets of identity or purposiveness. Casual sex in a public washroom, with unidentified strangers, may be coherent for men who are looking for a "quick fix" to their mechanistic desire for sexual repair; it would be much less likely to fit into feminine stories of embodied identities. Of course, other stories can also be told that would connect men to their emotional sides and women to their sexual drives as separated from their emotions. These stories just don't get repeated in the autobiographies of famous women and men.

However, rather than defining themselves as participants in "the longest war," perhaps women and men might benefit more from developing syntheses that would expand life story options for all. At the same time, however, further attention is needed to the cultural patterns in which these discourses are embedded. As long as the power relationships between men and women appear to favor the male versions of reality and value, as long as the workplace makes little allowance for embodied selves, and as long as relationships are treated in a utilitarian manner, new stories of a more embodied nature may not be able to survive.

Clearly, the autobiographical form today supports the traditional binary oppositions of male versus female, with its supporting polarities of natural versus cultural, emotional versus rational, weak versus strong, and so forth. This logical pattern entails support for the more general hierarchical patterns of the social order. As a result, I suggest, men fear becoming women and thus lead more barren emotional lives and die younger. Women are prevented from full access to male forms of power and regard themselves as objects for male pleasure instead of as persons. Both sides lose. Yet one might hope that within dialogues, through reciprocal and reflexive endeavors, and via political and social changes, new stories with emancipatory potential might emerge. These stories would be in violation of the installed practices and the binary oppositions that sustain them. Women and men might temporize their commitments to their traditional roles, engaging in career activities without forsaking their bodily states and taking pleasure in physicality without being totalized by physical limitations. The possibility of deconstructing gender as a biologically based class of difference that regulates life in its most minute detail is set in motion.

NOTES

1. See Jonathan Potter (1996), who refutes this suggestion.

2. Scholars who have shaped the issues in this arena include Butler (1990, 1993), Fine (1997), Flax (1993a, 1993b), Fuss (1989), Gallop (1988), Griffith and Griffith (1994), Grosz (1994), Irigaray (1985a, 1985b), Vance (1984), and Williams (1989).

3. It is interesting to note how much more attractive women who reach high-level positions in politics become as they settle into their new roles. It is as if their capacities to govern are considered to be directly related to their appearance. In addition, one must presume that personal coaches are employed to create this makeover. Evidence for this transformational trend can be seen in the careers of Margaret Thatcher and Madeline Albright. Other female leaders in Asia (e.g., Bhutto, Gandhi, Marcus) have also been known as attractive public figures. An exception to this trend was Golda Meir, who made a career of being a grandmotherly figure.

4. It should be emphasized that the subject of concern here is how embodiment is described in autobiographies. It is possible that in private spheres men express their embodiment involvements much as women do in print. At times this distinction becomes muted, perhaps because the alienation apparent in the texts seems so pervasive that it is hard not to imagine that conversations in everyday life bear strong resemblances to these trends.

Talking About Menopause
A Dialogue

Other: This chapter is constructed as a coauthored conversation with two voices marked "Other" and "MG." Perhaps the readers might like to know about who this "Other" you have invented is. We can all guess who MG is.

MG: The Other is the alterity, or better still, alterities, voices that are "not-me-as-writer." You, as the Other, are the "free-floating" signifier, who never stays in one place for long. Sometimes you are the various shadow voices speaking to me as though reading over my shoulder. Your otherness at times speaks for a reader. And sometimes you become the uncontrollable other. I don't know where you come from or are going in moments like those.

Other: Why have you invented this Other?

MG: There is no one answer to this question. You exist to demonstrate that writers are constructors of the real and use their powers to persuade others what the real is. We writers work to seal over cracks that might appear in our arguments. We strive for coherence, to make our narratives seamless. Your presence as Other serves to reveal the arti-facts. You can expose the gap between my unexamined assumptions.

Other: I am the de-constructor of your constructions? An interesting task, if we can trust you. But aren't you worried about using such an artificial means to make this piece polyvocal?

MG: Frankly, yes. Your presence at times may seem overly contrived. Yet this rhetorical form gives me a sense of engaging with my readers, my respondents, and my own multiple selves. We can soften the boundaries between the writer and the reader, and the analyzer and the analyzed. You help me to be reflexive. There is also a feminist strategy in creating a dialogue. Though I cannot fully escape the "manmade" linguistic traditions that allow us to communicate, I can write to undermine a posture of total authority. That's another role for you, as Other, and one I don't always appreciate.

Other: So by undermining your authority at times, I actually serve a political purpose, at some cost, of course, to your personal pride at being Number One Author.

MG: That's one of the side effects of this conversation, which I am arranging, sometimes despite my better judgment.

Other: But enough about us. Let's turn our attentions to the focus of our dialogue—which, as the title suggests, is something about menopause.

MG: The chapter involves the description of a research project in which a group of women came together—as a focus group, one might say—to discuss the meaning of menopause in their lives.

Other: A focus group, a term I associate with market research. Are you selling a product?

MG: In a sense, that meaning of the term is apt. But I was suggesting that the group came together for the purpose of a discussion, as peers with a focus, if you will, on a common interest—in this case, the so-called "change of life."

Other: So you really weren't so interested in the individuals as psychic entities as with their conversation. The nature of discourse possibilities, would you say?

MG: Yes to your ideas. It is helpful to see it that way. It is stunning to realize that when the name *focus group* gets appended to this "happening," new interpretations of what we were doing emerge.

Other: The form of the chapter as conversation also seems to echo the style that was central to the research itself.

MG: Yes, a conversation about a conversation. One purpose of this form is to invite readers into the dialogue as well. They have their own conversations as they read ours.

Other: This inclusivity brings to mind the notion of action research that many feminists have written about and worked to achieve (see Fals-Borda & Rahman, 1991; Fine, Weis, Powell, & Wong,

1997; Maguire, 1987; McIntyre & Lykes, 1998; Reinharz, 1992; Stam, 1996; Weitz, 1998).

MG: Some might call it that. I had in mind an engagement with my participants such that within their conversations certain changes might occur in their views on menopause, especially as it relates to their own lives. As for the readers, entering into the conversation, even if after the fact, they might come to question their own suppositions about menopause, as well as the ways the scientific and therapeutic communities present this event.

Other: A double-barreled action research volley, so to speak. Challenging the meaning of menopause prevalent in society among both actual participants and the reader. This must be where your feminist rubber meets your methodological road.

MG: Yes, my own form of liberation methodology, the goal of which is to encourage women, and men as well, to resist the ways society has organized their lives along, shall we say, "blood lines."

Other: Including those who write about menopause, such as medical experts and feminist authorities?

MG: Writing a conversation has an exciting aspect I hadn't anticipated. I feel a bit out of control of this material because I never know what you are going to say. Fiction writers often marvel at how their characters develop a life of their own, those that cannot be totally regulated once they are brought to life on paper. I'm beginning to have that feeling about you, Other.

Other: It's not about me, really, but about the polyvocality of the piece. We are doing this together, don't forget.

MG: Dialogic writing, just like conversation, can sometimes create highly unpredictable outcomes.

Other: This endeavor is getting a bit complicated. You are writing about a research project with you and me in an imaginary dialogue, which we acknowledge is refracted through the reader's gaze. Front-back-side views, like a three-way mirror in a clothing store. With careful arrangements, we can set up an infinite regress of possibilities. But where do we find the real, the substantial, the proper point of view in such a complex array?

MG: That's a very pertinent question, especially for those of us interested in philosophical issues. The "real" has receded. We have only each other—you(s), me(s), and them(s)—each partaking in and transforming our separate contributions. This dilemma of not knowing exactly where to look or what image to accept, as you suggest, leaves us filled with questions and doubts. And given the indeterminacy of the real and the impossibility of producing actions to create it, we do all find ourselves in a permanent "house of mirrors."

Other: And without much to laugh about. Given these multidimensional complexities, what do you hope will evolve?

MG: We touch on many issues in which psychology has a stake: women's lives in middle age and older; and that so-called "change of life"—menopause. My hope is that we challenge both the silence and the noise in psychology.

Other: This is enigmatic; can there be both silence and noise?

MG: The resounding silence that has left women's lives, except for their reproductive aspects, unexamined in their adulthoods; and the deafening roar of biodescriptors that threaten to parse us into microscopic pieces as well.

Other: You sound quite negative about psychology's contributions to adult development. Surely, with so much research in progress, that can't be true today.

MG: Psychology has had little to say about middle age generally, and even less about women in adulthood (M. M. Gergen, 1992a). Take a look in any textbook; weigh the pages devoted to the first decade of life compared to that last six. Once the excitement of childhood and puberty are over, women become more and more invisible as objects of research concern. Menopause offers the only flicker of interest in what seems to be a journey to oblivion. It is usually inscribed as the beginning of the end, where osteoporosis, widowhood, Alzheimer's, dependency, and death are the liveliest topics that follow.

Other: The "change of life" then is from a life of meaning to a life of loss. No wonder women don't want to talk about it!

MG: It's the Humpty Dumpty slide down the far side of the life span slope. And there is rarely a word spoken against this story.

Other: Like Humpty Dumpty, I guess you can never get (your eggs) put back together again.

MG: There is a biological resonance to your metaphor that fits this story rather well.

Other: In other words, there is no return from this ending, no repair or replacement, is there?

MG: Well, there is replacement, estrogen replacement, but that is an issue we are not going to tackle here.[1] Our main focus is on the way psychology has inscribed women of a certain age.

Other: Old men probably don't get much attention in life span development literature either. Middle age and old age never were popular research topics. For one thing, you can't use college sophomores for research. Check the newsstands as well. To look at the
magazine covers, you'd think no one lives past 30 in America.
Perhaps you are taking this aging woman problem too personally. Aging is everybody's dirty little secret.

MG: There is a personal side to this research as well as a professional
critique; isn't that almost always the case when psychologists
take up a particular topic? As a woman in her 40s when I began
this project, I had a negative reaction to going peacefully into the
menopausal mists. I wanted a new and more radiant figure of
mature women, as they are and can be, sketched into the picture
of human development.

Other: A real Leonarda da Vinci, but you cannot just sketch in anything
you want, can you?

MG: No, much as I'd like to, I can't. As social constructionists
remind us all, making meaning always requires the supplements
of others.

Other: It takes two to tango, so to speak.

MG: It is a difficult task to challenge such a fixture of human development as the notion of the "change of life." Clearly, women
have "bought" a vision of menopause that the medical profession
and its supporters have constructed. Women reaching the end of
their childbearing years continue to assimilate the vision of themselves that the field of psychology, directly or indirectly, has provided for them since their teens. Just look at the self-help book
section in bookstores. With all of the ammunition provided by
the other side, my efforts and those of others like me are not, by
any means, going to destroy the conventional wisdom. I just hope
they will enlarge the spectrum of possibilities a small degree.[2]

Other: Your humility is well placed, given my reading of what has been
happening in the field of menopause in the last decade. It has, to
borrow a metaphor, come out of the closet, and in a terrifying
outfit, I might add.

MG: Since I began this work, notions of menopause have grown in
their power to reduce women to pitiable creatures, overwhelmed
by chemical imbalances (Martin, 1987). The medicalization of
menopause has succeeded in turning all women nearing the age
of 50, and afterwards, into patients (Leng, 1997).

Other: It seems that you are throwing stones at armored vehicles waving the flags of the AMA and the APA (both Psychology and Psychiatry).

MG: I fear this is a losing war; even the victims rally to the cause (Gannon, 1985, 1990).

Other: Before we get too involved in personal history, and militaristic fantasies, could you say something about the methods you employed in this research project? We know you held a focus group, and they discussed menopause. But then what?

MG: Two aspects of dialogic methods were important in this research. The first was how the semistructured dialogue among participants as the research method within the encounter was constructed. The second was the form my interpretation takes. It is important for me, as analyst, to remember that the outcome of a conversation is a shared creation, something that could not have existed without the particular contributions of each party to it. Also, dialogue takes place within a particular place and time. Its meaning is connected to this tissue of intersecting events.[3]

Other: It all sounds pretty seamless to me. Isn't that one of the dangers I'm supposed to call out?

MG: Yes, you are right. But sometimes seamless is sublime. In fact, when we disrupt the seamless flow of conversation to analyze it, we are in danger of destroying what we set out to reveal.

Other: Like taking apart a clock to see what makes it tick, I suppose.

MG: Because of this inextricable web of persons, context, and talk, analysis is always, to some extent, a violation of that connective tissue. In this sense, analyses are always and inevitably disruptive and incomplete. To reproduce a transcription of a segment of dialogue between participants is a very delicate task. It is only through the good will and trust shared between readers and writer that any interpretation is possible. Within the chapter, we document in a selective way the flow of a conversation within the research setting, analyze this discourse, and offer counterpoints through the Other's voice.

Other: You and I are quite the jugglers here, with many balls in the air: the conversation between us; the conversations of the participants; the interpretations you make of the dialogues; and finally, the ongoing conversations of readers and this text. Let's hope no one drops the ball before this is over.

MG: You are right to emphasize these complexities. Each element is a support in the construction of a particular reality. By pointing this out, you also create distances among us. This chapter is in some ways like a Brechtian play, in which the playwright reminds the audience that it is, after all, a play and should be critically viewed.

Other: Brecht was looking for political action, not bourgeois tears. Where is the political activism in your aspirations?

MG: I have no precise political agenda. Yet I do wish to influence others to reject the claims of medicine and psychiatry that women suffer from the disease of menopause and must be cured.

Other: We can be clear about your bias anyway. This is the product the focus group was asked to evaluate. And your interpretations relate to how the group reacted to your efforts. Sounds pretty unorthodox to me.

MG: This design is not unique, however. Despite the rigid method-ological requirements prevailing within much of experimental psychology, at the fringes of the field some innovative projects along these lines have been forthcoming. This is especially the case within disciplinary enclaves such as queer studies, minority studies, men's studies, and, most of all, women's studies.[4]

Other: Why do you think these researchers have been more likely to break ranks with the mainstream views?

MG: I think these psychologists are in the forefront of those challeng-ing the mainstream, or at least are open to exploring alternative forms of research methods, because of their own histories within the field (Bohan, 1993; Morawski & Bayer, 1995). The belief that certain groups of people have been oppressed has led to an alienation from the traditions within the field, even if the subver-sion has been subtle (Fine, 1992; hooks, 1990; Lopes, 1991; Reid & Comas-Diaz, 1990).

Other: Although there are others who have used these forms, I imagine there are many more who would like to if they knew more about how to do it. Could you be more specific about how you devel-oped your analysis of the conversation in this project?

MG: Let me distinguish three ways in which I approached the inter-pretation of the conversation. I call them psychological, performative, and generative. There are differences among them, but the similarities are also apparent.

Other: So how can conversations be analyzed from these three different positions?

MG: Perhaps the most familiar is the psychological framework, in which the discourse is presumed to be a surface manifestation of an individual's underlying psychological dynamics. Words, sentences, and expressive acts within a conversation are interpreted as evidence of the cognitive, emotional, and motivational states of the individual throughout the conversation. Many therapists, for example, are trained to interpret linguistic activity as surface emanations of internal psychic phenomena.

Other: That approach seems rather sensible to me, unless of course, I start hearing about my castration anxieties or penis envy.

MG: It will be one or the other, I assure you.

The second form of analysis is one I call performative. Here the analysis results in suggestions about the processes within the group by which its reality is socially constructed. In this sense, the dialogue among participants is performative—that is, through conversational performances, "reality" is produced (Potter & Wetherell, 1987). This type of analysis has been foreshadowed by sociologists of science, who have investigated the ways in which natural scientists working in laboratories generate the realities of their research findings through their dialogic interactions.[5]

Other: So in acting together, the scientists create the science, and they are greatly influenced by such nonscientific things as grant funding requirements, equipment access, graduate student availability, theoretical preferences, traditions of the particular laboratory team, and historical precedents, to say a mouthful.

MG: But this is the case in all human interactions, from architecture to zoo management. The scientists make the most interesting case, one might say, because they are the most likely to deny that social factors have had a hand in their scientific activities.

Other: Performative analysis is different from psychological analysis in that talk is not regarded as an epiphenomenon of another realm, the invisible interiority of the individual, but as a phenomenon to be studied in its own right, right? People use language to perform, create, and do things. Linguistic "moves" within a dialogue can have an impact on subsequent actions of the participants. From a performative stance, the researcher might regard the conversation as a "game."

MG: That is a good analog. One might note how the speaker is located as a player within a conversational segment. How much does she get to play? How often is she sitting on the bench? Do her comments shape the conversation, or do they count for nothing?

Other: So a comment is similar to a pass thrown by a quarterback. Is it caught or not? Is it intercepted? Is the quarterback sacked?

MG: Questions such as what was accomplished with a particular remark, how it fit with other preceding and concurrent remarks, and what kind of relational ties such comments enhanced or suppressed are all relevant.

Other: The performative analysis is very different from the psychological one because it is involved with what is on the surface. No digging for buried treasures here.

MG: But interesting in its own right. And perhaps more useful in understanding how people make meaning together.

Other: How do people play their game of words? What are the rules, and how good are they at playing? Whoever gets the most meanings wins?

MG: That's one way to put it. Philosopher Ludwig Wittgenstein described language games before we did, of course, and it is now a popular phrase in many circles.

Other: I like that expression. It reminds me of times when I've turned down the sound on a television show—you can still see that people are coordinated with one another. It looks like a choreographed dance.

MG: This is why the expression "It takes two to tango" is so apt. There are many metaphors we might tap in addition to games and dance. Some social constructionists have emphasized the notion of drama in describing language games. A drama is rather like a dance, without music.

Other: But with plenty of words.

MG: Many theorists use the idea of scripts or scenarios when describing language games from a performative stance. These analysts think of people as playing out already established social scripts.[6] One cannot just say anything at all once a familiar scene is initiated. A brief example: If one person says, "Hello, how are you?" then you have a limited number of things to say in return. You cannot pass the salt. You must say something like "Fine, and you?" or "Could be better." On the other hand, if someone asks for the salt, you are rather obliged to pass it or explain why not. "Fine, and you?" would be inappropriate, as would most responses besides passing the salt shaker.

It is this type of performative analysis that is central to my work here.

Other: That's a rather big mouthful to swallow. Perhaps an example might help to clarify the distinction between the psychological and performative ways of using dialogic methods. Otherwise, readers may be tempted to take all of this with a grain of salt.

MG: Let me explain with an example from the focus group. (Later I will introduce you more formally to the group. Please be patient.)[7]

During the first portion of the discussion, the participants avoided any mention of the negative psychological impact of menopause. However, as the discussion proceeded, the following conversation took place:

Marla: *There's one person now . . . whose periods are very irregular and she's feeling unstable. Now maybe these other people who I talked to—who feel so good now—didn't feel so good before they went through menopause.* [Loud general talking among the group; comments of agreement with the last statement]

Sandra: *They're not talking about how they felt before!* [Loud laughter and inaudible comments follow from the group]

MG: Within a psychological interpretation, we might say that Marla brings up her fear that women often become emotionally unstable during the process of menopause. One might interpret her comment as revealing her own inner doubts about who she is and whether she is going to suffer emotional instability, despite the assurance of postmenopausal women that all is well. Other possible thoughts, emotions, and motives could also be attributed to Marla as a result of her comment. Perhaps she has had feelings of emotional instability or anxiety already and wonders if she is entering menopause, or she may be unhappy about something in her life unrelated to menopause, which leads her to thinking about emotional instability.

From a performative analysis angle, one might describe her reaction as a "move" to produce solidarity among the group as nonmenopausal women versus menopausal ones. This is done by directing the attention of the group to the ways in which postmenopausal women talk to premenopausal ones. She may be suggesting that older women are lying to the younger ones by not giving them all the gory details associated with menopause, such as losing one's mind. The effect of Marla's statement might be considered as creating a platform for conversation among the premenopausal women in the group about becoming emotionally unstable as one goes through menopause. The reiteration of Sandra, which is an almost identical reframing of Marla's remark, supplements Marla's response and indicates to Marla that her position has been affirmed by the group.

Additional material for the performative analysis comes from Suzanne's remarks that follow immediately after Marla and Sandra's statements. Suzanne speaks of the feeling of loss that comes from knowing you can never have children again.

Suzanne: *When you say goodbye to a part of your life there has to be some little thing you feel, to be honest.*

MG: From a performative stance, Suzanne's words "to be honest" again open up the option for the group to address the issue of whether they are being deceived by the older women, as well as enhancing the group's solidarity in their identity as premenopausal women. The admonition "to be honest" also encourages the women to be honest with one another rather than to be so guarded in their opinions. It suggests that they can dare to speak more openly, especially with words of "loss."

In contrast to this view, a psychological analysis might suggest that Suzanne's comments express a longing to be pregnant and deep personal concerns about her fertility and the finality of menopause.

Other: You mentioned earlier that there were three ways in which you might analyze the group discourse. The first was the psychological, in which you interpret words as representative of individual psychic worlds; the second, the analysis of how language is used performatively, to create events and entities in the world. You defined the third form as generative. How is this different from the others?

MG: Interpreting from the generative stance refers to the practice of looking at the discourse in order to construe the ways in which it has allowed for the production of new outcomes. The notion of the generative suggests the new, the created, that which could only come into being through some synthesis of preexisting elements combined in new ways. Generativity stresses transformation in a sought-after direction. Specifically, conversations can create changes among participants (including the researcher) through their mutual interactions. This orientation is an outgrowth of feminism as expressed through political action—in this case, action within a context of doing research (Fine, 1992; Fine & Gordon, 1991; Fine et al., 1997).

Other: I doubt that one must be a feminist to do transformative research. Anthropologists (whom I might not call feminists) have long been associated with this type of endeavor (Clifford & Marcus, 1986; Crapanzano, 1980; Favret-Saada, 1980).

MG: I agree, one need not be a feminist. However, my hope was that through this dialogic project an emancipatory feminist goal would be achieved, in which participants could talk themselves into an alternative discourse of womanhood that would be more resistant to the notions of infirmity associated with menopause.

Other: You mentioned overlap before. Do these types of psychological, performative, and generative analysis have any commonalities?

MG: The major overlap I see is in the sense that one must acknowledge that all interpretations are constructions. No matter how one chooses to interpret the discourse, it is important to be sensitive to the one's own "hand" in the process of analysis. This sensitivity, or self-reflexivity, has been described by many social scientists, including sociologists of science, ethnographers, and cultural anthropologists. Unlike paradigmatic experimental psychologists, who put forward their findings as "just the facts," these analysts tend to be open about the nature of their own cultural biases and personal investments in the production of their research activities. As Roy Wagner (1975) has described it, ethnographers participate in the subject culture not as pure outsiders, nor as natives, but as those simultaneously enveloped in their own world of meaning and that of the people under study. Investigators such as James Clifford (1983) claim that the accounts anthropologists make are joint productions of respondents and researchers. By implication, such analysts recognize that their accounts are partial, not settled once and for all, and are constantly open to new interpretations within the flux of the descriptive moment.

Other: The kind of researcher you are describing sounds more like an artist than a scientist to me. What rules govern this artist? It seems that this artist/researcher has a great deal of freedom in presenting the so-called facts of any matter. The scientist in me gets nervous. Scientists always seem to me to be so uncomplicated when it comes to analyzing their data. They more or less tell it like it is. At least, that is what they tell me.

MG: The analog of analyst and artist is apt, I think. And scientists are often more artistic in their interpretations and analyses than they admit. Some theorists argue that the line between the two forms is becoming increasingly fuzzy. Ethical considerations, relations among participants and researchers, community standards, and the critical judgments of the readers are very significant in determining what counts as proper criteria in any discipline (Garratt & Hodkinson, 1998; Lincoln, 1995).

Other: But there will be no end to this dialogue, I predict. How do you defend the criteria by which you have chosen your words?

MG: It is hard to defend the choices I have made. The tape recording of a conversation with eight people, one and a half hours long, especially when everybody talks at the same time, is a challenging task to make sense of. Not every line of the transcript of the formal discussion is of equal interest to me, although I can well imagine that each line might be fascinating from some particular framework or another. The major question I am asking within this text is whether my efforts to change the way these women talk about the consequences of going through menopause occurred within the discussion and, if so, what dialogic moves the members of the group went through to reconstruct their languages of menopause to avoid becoming "patients at 50," or, in other words, to see menopause as a more positive or uneventful occurrence and less of a medical problem in their lives.

Other: I am curious—once you knew you wanted to study menopause, how did you decide what shape the actual research event would take?

MG: My involvement with this project was an outgrowth of a desire to create a method for studying lives that would not violate ideals of research that I had come to accept. I asked myself what would happen if I were to do a research project in light of my own critique of mainstream methods. This led me to establishing that the project would have to be *intersubjective, participatory,* and *emancipatory.*

Other: That sounds like a noble endeavor, but how did you translate these phrases into practice? How was the research "intersubjective," for example?

MG: First, I decided that I would recognize in all phases of the study the interdependence and mutual involvement of the participants and me, and as a consequence I decided to maximize the possibilities for relating that prior acquaintance allows. I took this decision to the point of inviting as my participants a small group of friends. In addition, I called myself a participant. I filled out forms, paid myself a subject fee, and signed a receipt.

Other: So if nothing else, you got $15 and a free lunch from the occasion. This does get rather tricky, doesn't it?

MG: But I also had to do the dishes. It certainly is a violation of the usual standards of normal science, where the events under study are cut away, as much as possible, from entangling outside influences. My goal was to avoid decontextualizing the research. Instead, I tried to design an event that was quite conventional: a luncheon among friendly acquaintances. Participants were invited to come to my home; there we sat at a table on the back porch, having first a group discussion and then lunch. Though we had never been together at my house as a group, we had all been at informal luncheons before. Having a tape recorder on the table and being invited to discuss menopause and women's lifestyles between the ages of 40 and 60 was not a typical event at a lunch, but it was not out of the question that this group of eight women would find themselves discussing women's issues and personal concerns at such gatherings.

Other: Tell me something about your group.

MG: We all know each other from playing tennis at a nearby club in a suburban Philadelphia neighborhood. We ranged in age from 41 to 48; all of us were college educated; Suzanne has a master's degree in social work, and I have a Ph.D. At the time we were all married, living in our own homes, with children, most of whom were teenagers or older. Suzanne (an owner of a real estate agency) and I were the only ones with full-time careers, although Bonnie had started up her own craft business. The rest had worked in the past, were seeking part-time jobs, or worked a few hours a week. Debra was in the United States on leave from Australia with her husband, an executive with a multinational firm. Other husbands were involved in business careers or in professions. All of the participants were premenopausal except Terry, who, as it turned out, had had a hysterectomy.

Other: You also described the ideal research event as participatory. What to you mean by "participatory" research, and in what ways did you try to achieve this goal? And while I have the floor, isn't it a contradiction in terms to talk about achieving participation, something like saying, "I made us all do exactly what each wanted to do?"

MG: The goal of participatory research is to eliminate, insofar as possible, any hierarchical or authoritarian aspects. Such a goal must be considered an ideal to be approximated rather than a practical achievement. Once I had decided that I wanted to arrange this project, I had taken one step down the road to authority. When I chose the problem, the method, the participants, the fees, the time, the space, and the structure of the occasion, I had taken many giant steps toward authority. A more fully participatory project would be less unilateral in these facets of development, and if I had it to do over again, I would involve myself more deeply in structuring a participatory approach in which we all formulated the nature of the event.

Other: Sounds like science by democratic means, but not very systematic.

MG: Though I would emphasize the desirability, even the necessity, of a participatory approach, I am also opposed to a position that denies the right of a social scientist to have special talents and expertise, special investments in projects, and the capacity to explore issues that are not identified as important by the affected population. After all, no one knew they wanted a "Walkman" until they were on the market.

Other: Given that you planned most dimensions of the day, how did you give away your power to create a more participatory event?

MG: Within the discussion itself, I kept a low profile. I strove for equality among participants' contributions so that everyone had a chance to express her opinions freely. In the first half of the hour's discussion, I said very little, limiting myself to facilitating the discussion of the other seven participants. In the second portion of the discussion, I introduced my ideas about menopause. In particular, I challenged the notion of the medical model and advanced the idea that menopause was socially constructed— that is, it could be erased from our vocabularies, made to seem a positive event in our lives, or otherwise redefined by women themselves. This was the form of my major intervention into the dialogue. I was hoping that the seed I planted within the conversation would bear fruit as the dialogue progressed.

Other: A rather pregnant metaphor, don't you think? You mentioned three aspects of your study: intersubjective, participatory, and emancipatory. Did you, as host, succeed in liberating your hostages?

MG: Your punnish reflection is not far off the mark, in my view. But aren't we all, including you, whatever your identity, hostages to social conventions? To break out or at least shake the bars of our confinement was one critical aspect of my emancipatory goal.

Other: Touché. But you must admit that doing research that claims to be emancipatory defies the customary positivist version of science, which requires a neutral or "value-free" approach to a problem.

MG: Yes, ordinarily research projects do not attempt to introduce change into the lives of the participants for their benefit directly. The usual goal is for the benefit of "Science," with a big S, the research project itself, or "humankind." Those are the only kinds of value statements that creep into the sacred circle of scientific descriptions.

Other: So you've really put your foot into it, scientifically speaking.

MG: Putting the shoe on the other foot, I'd agree with Shulamit Reinharz's (1985, 1992) view that researchers not only should declare their "values" relevant to a particular domain but should openly foster them in their work. My criteria for emancipatory feminist research are (a) to acknowledge my research goals and to advance them, (b) to create an effective opportunity for change for participants in the research endeavor, and (c) to be personally open to change in unanticipated ways as a result of the commingling of influences of all participants.

Other: I like this idea. It contrasts strongly with the vague promises scientists often make to "help mankind" (just as they give some poor sap the sugar pill). In this view, the researcher is committed to the immediate well-being of the coparticipants.

MG: The sharpest contrast between this feminist approach and all others is that the one-way influence effects are negated; researcher and participants are both vulnerable to change. This openness can result in dynamic and possibly chaotic moments in the research process. The valuing of unplanned outcomes highlights the discrepancies between this approach and the conventional research arrangement, where the last thing one would want is the potential for chaos.

Other: Should I say, "Vive la différence," or is it too early to celebrate? Go on with your chaos-inducing event. Why did you decide to concentrate on middle-aged women in your emancipatory research strategy? You might have applied it to many other areas.

MG: True, but what group might be most in need of a little liberating? I was 45 years old when I began this project, and I was beginning the countdown to 50. As I mentioned earlier, what psychology stood for in terms of women's development stirred me from my daily routines. The accepted facts that menopausal women will lose just about everything that is meaningful in their lives— their primary biological function of childbearing; their physical attractiveness, which is a source of esteem and power for most women; and their vocational function as mothers when their children grow up (leaving them with the well-publicized "empty nests")—aroused my combative spirits greatly.

Other: It sounds like a midlife crisis to me.

MG: The famous midlife crisis, emphasized by Levinson (1978) and others, may occur early in middle age for men, during which time they are prone to buying red sports cars or getting a mistress to compensate for their fears of waning potency. But they usually are able to return to some higher state of integration when it is resolved. No equivalent possibility is forecasted for women. The notion that men have greater transitional potential seems to extend over the life span. Freud's descriptions of these different trajectories is apposite. A 30-year-old woman is viewed as rigidly finalized and a man of the same age as youthfully resilient (Freud, 1933). Psychologists, too, tend to view men more than women in terms other than chronological or reproductive age.

Other: Despite many claims to have discovered the change in life in men, none of them seems to have stuck. Men don't get older, they just get better, it seems.

MG: At least until their untimely demises. Yet despite all this negative publicity coming from all directions about the dire straits of women at 50, when I looked around at my own life, at the lives of my friends and colleagues, and at women in public life, the news of our decline seemed premature and exaggerated. Well-known women, such as Jane Fonda and Gloria Steinem, had not donned the sackcloth and ashes and given up on life once past 40. Some, such as Barbara Walters, had grown not only in stature but in beauty as well. Certain contemporary perceptions of middle-aged women thus struck me as being at great variance with the tales of gloom fostered by the "science industry." Yet psychological wisdom is reflexive in a culture. Thus, women who might normally be enjoying their new freedoms, liberated from "the curse" and their children, might question themselves, looking for the signs of depression, loss, aimlessness, illness, and aging that are predicted for them. And normally, if one looks long enough and hard enough, compelling evidence will be forthcoming.

My aim was to create a forum for rebuttal to the bleak notion of what it is to be a "middle-aged" woman in America.

Other: I understand your motives, both self-interested and, on your terms, liberatory. Though it is admirable to try to change women's images of "middle age," you can't deny that women do go through physiological changes. Menopause is a fact of life, and possibly a medical issue, isn't it? How do you propose to deal with these facts?

MG: From the social constructionist standpoint, nothing stands by itself as a social fact. Menopause exists with all its attributes and associations by virtue of cultural agreements to package it in this particular way. Note that a similar notion, the climacterium, has also been formulated as a biological event in the lives of men, but so far it has not made the top of the medical charts. It is faltering, perhaps, because it does not serve men's social needs to emphasize an end to their sexual potency. On the other hand, the climacterium may not be totally useless as a "biological event" for men because it could help to explain poor sexual performance. We shall have to wait to see which function is more strongly supported over the coming years. The recent popularity of medical interventions in promoting strong, long-lasting erections attests to men's preferences (Tiefer, 1995). That thousands of men chose gene-altering medications and penile implants, painful injections into their penises before sex, in order to guarantee a 2-hour "hard-on," suggests that the climacterium is definitely not being accepted lying down. The immediate success of Viagra, introduced in 1998, suggests that more men than one might have imagined wish to improve their sagging sexual performances.

Other: And egos. It does emphasize the extent to which men as well as women want to resist attributes of aging and decline for themselves, not to mention "bad" sex.

MG: What I am focusing on, however, is the extent to which a biological event is singled out, popularized, and signified according to other important social meanings in the culture. Menstruation and menopause are both important constructs in most societies because they are used to signal the delimits of a significant social function: reproduction. (Why societies care who can and cannot become pregnant is a very deep question of religious and economic as well as social significance that is beyond the scope of this chapter, but the paternalistic power patterns infecting it are not far from sight.)

Other: How does the social constructionist framework play out in your research?

MG: I assumed that the participants already would be influenced by the popular culture to accept the social construction of menopause as an indicator of the loss of youth, beauty, and maternal functions. I was not certain, however, of their individual experiences with menopause. (My own personal history was that at that time I had had one "hot flash" and one 10-minute discussion with my closest friend from adolescence, who told me that she had begun taking supplementary estrogen.)

Other: In other words, you took your words about accepting uncertainty pretty seriously. It is hard to plan in uncertainty, though, isn't it?

MG: I left space for the group to take over the conversation. My plan was to insert my views into that mainstream. Though this seems to have overtones of big sister superiority, I did consider deeply the dialectic aspects of the discussion. I did not see myself as involved in coercively persuading the participants of what I believed and expecting them suddenly to become disciples of my words. For one thing, as tennis players and friends, they were not interested in suddenly viewing me as an authority figure. (My serve and volley were not that good.) I did, however, want to create conditions within the dialogue that would yield up a new form of meaning to apply within their lives. I hoped they would reframe the "medical model of menopause" to a more positive image of adult women in general and themselves particularly. I thought it would do us all good.

Other: What happened as a result of your interventions into the discussion?

MG: I used pre and post measures of attitude change to supplement my analyses of the conversation. I wanted to isolate the possible effects of the discussion on individual attitudes toward menopausal issues as indicated by paper-and-pencil measures. When the participants arrived at my home, they were individually given a group of three short questionnaires to complete. Then after the session they were given a similar packet to take home with them to fill out the following day. These materials were then mailed back to me. One questionnaire, called "Opinions About Menopause," was filled out on both days. This instrument was designed to tap agreement with traditional medical and psychiatric views about menopause.

Other: Your dirty word for this chapter seems to be *medical model,* so perhaps you could say more about this phrase.

MG: Simply put, the medical model implies that during menopause a woman's hormonal level changes, which creates other physical changes that lead to a worsening condition of the body and in addition produce diverse psychological problems, many of them stemming from the realization that the woman can no longer become pregnant. In sum, menopause is an illness.

Other: So to test how much the women in your group were buying into this model, you gave them questionnaires about it, right?

MG: Indeed, a short one of seven questions about the medical model of menopause. For example, I asked whether they agreed with the following statement: "Menopause is basically a medical problem." The participants could indicate agreement or disagreement on a 7-point scale. A second scale, also taken twice, was called "Images of Woman." This one was designed to assess changes in self-image at 20, 35, and as projected to age 50. (Menopause is usually in process by age 50.) The participants rated themselves on 20 paired adjectives, such as *calm* versus *nervous* and *happy* versus *sad,* at each of the three ages. I anticipated that the impact of the discussion group would decrease group agreement with the medical model of menopause and increase the positivity of rating of self-image at 50, as compared to their prediscussion ratings.

Other: Sounds rather individualistic, and not very dialogic to me.

MG: My feelings about this aspect of my research have wavered over time. At first, I did it so that I would have something "solid" to report besides my analysis of the tape recording. Later, I thought of discarding the questionnaire responses and only using qualitative analysis of the discourse. Now I consider the responses also as a form of dialogue, with me as the silent interlocutor with each of the respondents. The answers they gave served as a form of self-presentation in that context with me.

Other: This suggests that any researchers might describe any results from a pencil-and-paper scale as a form of interactive discourse sample as long as they reminded themselves and the audience for the research that the outcomes were contextualized and dependent in part on the researcher's questions. Of course, researchers would have to give up the Big T game and be willing to renounce Objectivity—a risky shift in any science game, I'd say.

MG: You see why a social constructionist position is not an easy position to maintain.

Other: This might be a good place to report what you found using these methods.

MG: There is something so clean and well defined about working with numbers. There was "hard" evidence that participants became less committed to the medical model after the discussion, but with eight discussants, no statistical analyses would be useful. After the discussion, participants more strongly disagreed that most women "would rather continue to menstruate than not," "feel negative about their loss of fertility," "keep menopause a secret, as something shameful," "become less attractive after menopause," "get emotionally more unstable after menopause," and "become less interested in sex." These represented a majority of the questions asked, and I think the responses indicate that the antiwoman medical model views were rejected by the women as strongly or more strongly after the discussion than before it.

Other: Did you have such encouraging results with the self-image scale?

MG: To complicate matters, I encountered a ceiling effect. That is, the participants rated their self-images at the outset very positively; therefore, there was not much room for improvement after the discussion. Before the discussion, they saw themselves as very competent and satisfied people at 20 and at 50 years of age. Interestingly, many indicated that they had been less satisfied with life at 35 than they had been at 20 or thought they would be at 50. (The discussion brought out comments about how hard life had been at 35.)

Other: I suppose your participants at 35 were what we call the "soccer moms" today.

MG: You have it right about that. Yet there were some differences before and after the encounter. Afterwards, the areas of noticeable enhancement in self-image were in the traits of *stability* and *strength*. Participants tended to see themselves as more stable and stronger at 50 after the intervening discussion than before it. These increases provided support for my expectation that the nature of the conversation would have the effect of changing the image of the older woman in a positive direction.

Other: These results, though positive, were not very sensitive to the changes in meaning that you might perceive on a more holistic level. What about analysis of the dialogue itself? Did the conversation in which these participants engaged create new forms of meaning about these issues of aging?

MG: I cannot analyze the entire text of the discussion in detail here. But I would like to provide one analysis, which is primarily performative, to indicate how the conversation allowed the group to achieve three forms of tasks: bringing itself into being

as a group; confronting the challenge I brought to the group concerning the discussion of menopause; and resolving the tension
between the members' ordinary discourses of life, including
menopause, and my intervention regarding the harmful consequences of accepting current social views of menopause and
aging.

To give an overview, I perceived the discussion as dividing
into three sequential forms of discourse on menopause: *denial
and resistance, cohesion and containment,* and *review and
restoration.*

Other: This sounds very theatrical—a three-act play. I'm curious about
the analysis you will provide to convince us of your views.

MG: Here is a preview of my analysis.[8] The first stage of the discussion focused on denying and dismissing the topic. According to
the participants, menopause was shameful or boring to speak
about and/or irrelevant to their interests. The group's dilemma
was: How would they maintain their usual friendly and casual
relationships in the context of a "psychological experiment"
about a taboo topic? In the second stage, more details related to
menopause were explored, and the group groped for a means of
developing cohesiveness as they confronted the topic. This stage
displayed an uncomfortable negativity surrounding talk about
menopause and also aging. Menopause was something that happened to others. Then, slowly, personal details began to be
revealed, and the discussion became more open and intense.
Fears that were denied in the discourse of indifference about
menopause were described. By this time, I had interjected some
ideas critical of the medical model of menopause and had suggested that menopause could be interpreted in different, more
positive, ways. In the third stage, review and restoration, the
group began to review the evidence and, with some security
about the solidarity of the group, to restore their original confidence in themselves and their group ties. They also came up
with a generative solution to the "problem of menopause."

The creative outcome of their conversation was the construction of a relatively comfortable life that they projected for themselves at 50. This lifestyle was contrasted to their earlier one as
struggling housewives and mothers of dependent children. They
engaged in fantasy talk about the joys of living in their "empty
nests." The only disruptive element mentioned was husbands,
whom they had some misgivings about in terms of their capacities as transitional items in the dream. Finally, the discussants
developed the solution to the challenge of age: They were going

to beat the system. As relatively well-to-do, well-educated, and active women, they described availing themselves of the best in information, health care, and personal services in order to extend their youth indefinitely. In so doing, of course, they would re-define the social construction of what it means for a woman to be "50."

Other: A happy ending. What a relief. Would you have it any other way? Knowing you, I doubt it. You remind me of the child in the joke that ends "There must be a pony in here somewhere." Going back to the discussion, why do you describe the first state of the discussion as one of denial and resistance?

MG: The initial remarks of the participants formed my first impression that this was going to be a long afternoon.

Bonnie: *I thought one of your questions was interesting, that it's [menopause] something to be ashamed of, . . . and I think that . . . not that it's something to be ashamed of. But I don't know of anybody that has even spoken to me about it.*

Debra: *It's an age branding, isn't it?*

Bonnie: *Yes, I mean in this age of youth you certainly aren't going to go around and admit that you are involved in this process . . .*

MG: Bonnie's remarks served to open the question as to whether this was an atmosphere in which this possibly shameful topic could be discussed. I had asked them to talk about something that might put them in an awkward social position. Bonnie seemed to be testing whether this was a good idea, due to its seemingly taboo nature. I say *seemingly* because later remarks indicated that menopause was discussed but only seemed never to be discussed. Debra then zeroed in on one significant aspect of the concern, being branded as old. Branding as a metaphor is significant because it suggests that something is irreversible, visible, and ugly. To talk about menopause is to brand oneself, a rather foolish thing to do.

The group then began to declare that they were too young to concern themselves personally with the topic. They positioned themselves as cooperative but uninterested participants.

Other: You must admit that the group discussion got off to a pretty dismal beginning. It must have been worrisome, to say the least.

MG: Yes, but fortunately we all stuck with it. The original stance of the group seemed to be that they would cooperate with me in being a part of this "experiment," but they wanted to make it clear that this was not their idea and that the topic was not of their choice or interest. The function of the dialogue served to separate themselves from issues of menopause and thereby allowed them to maintain their "youthful" status within the group.

Sandy: *I'm 41 and I don't really . . . Listen, it's not something you're going to sit around and discuss unless you have to. I mean, I wouldn't think of it as a particularly interesting topic of conversation.*

Suzanne: *[Mentions a friend who is 56 and seems to be still menstruating] We don't discuss intimate things like that. Not that we don't discuss it, but as she [Sandy] said, its not all that fascinating; we're going to get another 10 years. [Very strong laughter follows]*

Marla: *I don't really think about it because it's too far away. I don't have to think about it yet. [Marla is the oldest person in the group at 48]*

MG: The denial tactics shifted somewhat when Debra, one of the youngest and most attractive group members, "admitted" that she was beginning the process.

Debra: *Well, I think I'm going through it right now. I'm 41. [She describes her symptoms] . . . And my mother was exactly the same. It doesn't worry me in the slightest.*

MG: Debra took a swift plunge into the topic of the day with this admission. She was able to do this because she was extremely popular within the group, young, and known for speaking her mind. Her comments served as a dare to all the older group members to be more forthright. At the same time, she denied that these bodily changes concerned her. Then she contradicted herself.

Debra: *That's incorrect. It does bother me. I will go to a doctor, just to be sure. . . . It's just that thing in the back of the mind . . . you want it checked.*

Other: What impact do you think Debra's remark had on the group's conversation? Did it serve as a transition from denial and resistance to the second stage that you described as cohesion and containment?

MG: Although things do not run smoothly in actual conversations, I think her comments were important to reshaping the talk. After her revelation, the group members began to speak more freely about menopause as an event of consequence in their lives. Testing the waters of trust, they carefully kept the dialogue primarily focused on others.

Other: Is that what you mean by containment? They kept the conversation revolving around other people?

MG: Yes, and as they talked they congealed into a more unified group.

Marla: *The most concerned I ever was, really and truthfully, about menopause, was when I was a freshman in college and my roommate's mother was going through menopause at that time, and she went off her rocker. She was boiling dishrags for dinner. Hadn't slept with her husband in who knows how long.*

[*Group responds with ohs, ahs*]

Marla: *This girl was telling me these tales. . . . God, at that point I was wondering if everyone did that sort of thing. . . .*

Suzanne: *I think there is a lot of association to things we expect to be there; of getting older, of getting forgetful. . . .*

Bonnie: [*Talking of her mother*] *In the back of my head, I thought, "Oh, she must be going through menopause, she's really crabby, why does she have to be like this?"*

After this, the group shifted to the topic of menstruation, emphasizing its negative properties. By complaining about the trials of menstruating, they built a platform from which menopause might again be discussed. A logical form was created as well:

If menstruation is a negative event, then getting it over with should be a positive one.

Group cohesiveness and trust were building, and a less negative tone was placed on the topic of menopause by the group as a whole; however, one group member, Terry, seemed to derail this process by continuing to concentrate on negative topics. After several comments about the perils of menopause, the group walled her off, refusing to supplement her comments, almost as if she had not spoken. Part of the group's rejection of her as a deviant may be traced to the fact that she had had a hysterectomy, although she still had one remaining ovary, as she described it to the group.

Terry: *Everybody I talked to said that if you don't have hormones you do age. . . . They've talked about the wrinkles and, the way, the one girl said, the vagina dries up.* [*Group murmurs and mutters in mixed tones, some of agreement*]

Terry: *The dryness of the vagina, that's how the doctor could tell she had aged. It was lack of hormones. . . . Oh, and the other thing was osteoporosis from the lack of hormones. So all this scared me, and I thought . . . I think I'll go to the doctor. I think I'll get hormones. Among my friends that are going through menopause, that's a big discussion.*

MG: The group, after serious, measured discussion of the question of hormone replacement, finally laughed and joked in response to Terry, who mentioned the hot flashes one friend had been experiencing.

It seemed that the group could not tolerate any more problematic symptoms from Terry and looked for an opportunity to "lighten up." Suddenly, Debra began clowning around.

Debra: *The favorite joke around the club now [she holds her hands at her waist, pantomimes bobbling heavy breasts and makes gestures about pulling up on them], if you're not doing this . . . [Laughter and remarks from the group blot out the rest of the sentence]*

Debra: *They joke about old age. When you get older, they start to hang. . . . I guess as you get older there's a close relation between tragedy and comedy.*

Suzanne: *Things are so tragic you have to laugh.*

MG: In this segment of the discussion, the ills associated with menopause were being laid out. Suzanne's last remark highlights a group strategy, using humor to shift the conversation when it got too negative. The general approach of the group was to probe the questions put forth, often by me, generate related comments, and then confine it, mostly through quips, jokes, and sudden laughter, before grimness set in.

Following Suzanne's remark, Sandy began to weave a second aspect of the eventual solution to the problem of how to live with menopause: She emphasized how much better off the group was now than older women once were.

Sandy: *We just look so much better than past generations. [Group agrees vigorously]. I mean . . . we are such a healthy generation. . . . I think it is just tremendous. I see more less trim people in their 20s. . . . I think that's really sloppy. I think, why do you look like that when there's no reason for it? You know you can really do something with yourself. Now look at this group. . . . I think we are a good-looking, healthy generation, and I don't think that menopause is going to affect us like it did past generations. [Group agrees] We're healthier, we feel better, and we're going to be able to play through it, tennis, golf, whatever. . . .*

Pat: *If you stay home and brood, then I think you're going to make more of it than maybe there is.*

MG: The group had reached a state where they comfortably owned up to the fact that they were coming into the menopausal zone of life. They had reached concurrence that menopause would be easier on them because of their physical state than it was for their mothers' generation. Sandy's metaphor of "playing through it" seemed very apt, given that the group played tennis. Her comments stressed the idea that despite the minor inconvenience of menopause, the active, healthy lifestyles we led would stave off problems. The worst thing to be done would be to sit home and worry about it.

    I wanted to pursue other avenues of concern besides physical symptoms and conditioning with them. In so doing, I stressed the fabric of trust and cohesiveness the group had achieved.

Mary: *What about the emotional side to menopause? Some think menopause symbolizes that you've come to the end of a certain lifestyle.*

Sandy: *I think most people when they go through menopause are also going through having their kids leave. Maybe it has nothing to do with menopause. . . . Maybe it has to do with everyone going here and going there.*

Marla: *Another thing that concerns me is . . . how bitchy we've become. . . . It's got to be connected with menopause. There has to be some kind of result on our mental well-being because of the physical changes in menopause. . . . While we're going through it, it's got to do something mentally to us, I would think. Make us more sensitive, more unstable.*

Suzanne: *How could I get much more?* [*Group laughs*]

MG: Sandy had exposed the "empty nest" question, and Marla responded with a personal concern of being more emotionally unstable and negative. These are two pertinent traits often associated with menopausal women. Suzanne humorously deflected the argument that women get unstable emotionally when they reach menopause by admitting that she had always been extremely "emotional." Sandy again came up with a method of solving emotional problems concurrent with this age. She had raised one of the threatening problems, and she took the responsibility for solving it.

Sandy: *I think that if you can talk it out . . . the older I get, the more I appreciate my girlfriends . . . and rely on them so much. I have a terrific relationship with my husband, . . . but boy, there's nothing like a good girlfriend to sit and chat and cry with and laugh with, and let your hair down, it makes things much easier. If you keep things inside of you they tend to grow and be more serious than maybe they are.*

MG: Sandy's comments cut both ways in this moment in the dialogue. She was telling the group that it was good, even necessary, to talk to girlfriends about these issues. And at the same time she was indicating that there might be things to worry and cry about. Yet she may have also been drawing a line between this group and a one-on-one talk with a good girlfriend. She may have been telling me and the other members that this was not the context for that form of sharing. She would not cry and reveal her worries with us. Her move in the conversation did facilitate a certain level of "girl talk" among these interlocutors.

Pat: *I know that's true. When I think about my friends, we're all about the same age, and I know we're all going to hit it together.* [*Group breaks into chatter, laughter*]

Suzanne: *I think this generation talks a lot more than our mothers did. . . . I think they thought it was something to be ashamed of.*

MG: Suzanne's comments also suggested that it was permissible for this group to talk about menopause and that it was not something for only very close friends to share. The ability to admit to negative feelings and to share these feelings with friends was resolved within this portion of the dialogue. The group continued to explore the negative aspects surrounding menopause. Periodically, threads of optimism were strung through the gloom. Throughout much of discussion, I brought up problems that have traditionally been associated with menopause: sexual abandonment, loss of love, and aging. The group parried my concerns using various strategies described above. They managed to maintain the group facade and their own sense of self-esteem, but with greater self-disclosure.

The group members also defended against any challenges to their status as attractive, vital women.

Suzanne: [*Speaking of going through menopause*] *It's not like you're walking through the airport, and you put your stuff through and you come out and and you're another person* [*Voices all rise in agreement*] *. . . and you can look at someone and say* *aha! [Laughter has reached the level of hysteria] You've gone through menopause, haven't you?*

MG: The group seemed to agree that although others cannot tell from the outside if you have gone through menopause, internal factors may indicate your change. Interestingly, Suzanne, who had just strongly argued that you cannot tell if menopause has occurred, was the one to mention a negative indicator and then to counter it almost in the same breath.

Suzanne: *I've had people say to me . . . that you sort of dry up, that your juices aren't as flowing. [She speaks of the differences between young and old animals and people, and she mentions that young people may avoid older people because they do not have this vital quality] I think there is a "juices flowing" kind of thing here. But I know plenty of gals who are past menopause who are full of it, and I find that very encouraging.*

MG: Though Suzanne brought up a negative commentary on menopausal women, she was reluctant to hold this position for long and countered her own remarks about the juiciness of some of her women friends who had passed menopause.

Other: Judging from your analysis, the group discussion seems to have come a long way from its rather desultory beginnings. The discourse evolved through the group process from something dull and dreary to a conversation that was very lively, emotionally rich, and also humorous. Earlier, you characterized the last portion of the discussion as a period of review and restoration. What did you mean by this description?

MG: As the discussion proceeded, the various socially sustained "goblins" of menopause were brought out for discussion and then put away again. It was as if the group oscillated over each topic and, with each return visit, dealt with it more completely. Within the review and restoration segment, the group, with its boundaries intact and its viability established, concentrated on resolving how to best proceed with facing menopause personally. I use the terms *review* and *restoration* to indicate that material that had been discussed was reintroduced and that negative elements were recast more positively.

Marla: *When I think now of the women I know who have been through menopause, not one of them is not happy about it. They are all happy about having gone through it. Having their period finished. They've given me a very positive feeling about it. I haven't heard any complaints.*

Sandy: *I'm much more confident now. . . . And I don't know why, to tell you the truth. I feel like I could conquer the world. And I'm simply biding my time right now, and my future is all ahead of me.*

Debra: *We were living in Sydney; he asked me how I'd feel if we didn't stay there very long. It really hit me. Now when he says we are moving, I say great. I have much more confidence in myself. The difference really hit me. I don't know if that's a sign of aging or what.*

MG: Not everyone felt so rosy, but within the context of the group it was allowed.

Pat: *I have difficulty projecting myself into the future. . . . Len is fairly . . . , what's the word I want to use? Give me a polite word [Laughter] Independent. Very macho oriented. The woman does this, the man does that. . . . When I see older people . . . wives have become mothers to these men. . . . I think, oh God, I don't want to end up like that. Old married couple fighting with each other.*

Other: You mentioned that you tried to present a view of how women might envision themselves in a more positive way after menopause. You planned to introduce them to the view that menopause was a social construction. What happened as a result?

MG: In the latter portion of the discussion, I did try to interject my view that menopause is a social construction given meaning and value by the language community that we all share. It is a meaning that often conveys a strong negative message to women about their social value. I hoped that women would not accept this definition and that they would form new images of adult women beyond their childbearing and rearing days. I wanted our discussion group to lend itself to this goal.

Other: How was this idea received by the group?

MG: It was not a brilliant success, in the way I had envisioned it, but other consequences of the dialogue were gratifying. First of all, I discovered that my participants were fairly committed to "naive realism." They were not very interested in thinking about biological events as social constructions. They were not willing to give up on the "reality" of menopause. In this sense, I failed to accomplish my goal.

Other: Did you learn something by engaging in this participatory framework of research that you might have missed otherwise?

MG: Glad you asked. Yes. As a member of the group, I was looked upon as an equal participant by the others most of the time. And in terms of life experiences with menopause, it was the case. What I realized as we talked was that among us we had developed an alternative solution to reconceptualizing the event as a non-event, an outcome that I had gone into the research desiring as emancipatory. Instead of deemphasizing menopause as a significant life event, which is how some research suggests older women view it, the outcome was that we might overcome the limits of the event through healthy warfare. We would fight with our generation's superior weapons of exercise, diet, good health practices, medical assistance, including hormones perhaps, and the social support of our friends and families.

Other: This is a cautionary tale in that it suggests that one cannot manufacture social constructionist views on a one-trial basis. And another limit illustrated is how difficult it is to be truly a participant if one is a researcher as well. It seems that there were many aspects in which you were the conductor and the others the musicians of this concert.

MG: Through this analysis, I "discovered" that by organizing the event and creating the means to attempt certain goals, I separated myself from the group in significant ways. Many of the participants' comments, I believe, were directed at the group problem of handling my intrusion as a psychologist into a very loosely knit group of friendly tennis players.

Other: Did you find the operations of the group satisfying, given your other feminist research goals?

MG: Yes, and I would state it like this: The discourse provided the women with linguistic resources for presenting themselves as more optimistic and self-confident women. The social constructions they produced in interaction together provided the option for each to alter and expand her social role as a mature woman in a manner that did not exist before this research encounter began. As one of my goals was to benefit my actual subjects, rather than "humankind" in the next decade or so, I was satisfied in that respect.

The dialogue also helped form a viable group, one that could function to work out the issue of what to say about the topic of menopause within this setting. At least within this protective shell of group membership, statements were made that supported my notice of what image women should have of their menopausal lives.

From a social constructionist perspective, I also felt some joy about the success of the endeavor. As I have already mentioned, I failed to "teach" the notion of social constructionism to the participants, yet they seemed to create a solution to the problem by actually planning to transform the image of the older woman through action rather than through words. Though no one was willing to discard the reality of menopause as a biological event, they were eager as individuals to act and feel about themselves in a manner that challenged the older-woman image. Through their behaviors, they would remake what it means to be "50" and beyond. It would be the work of others in the society to readjust the stereotype.

Other: A decade has passed since your group met. Do you know what has happened to them since this conversation?

MG: Good taste and brevity prevent me from giving a complete recital of their personal narratives (as I know them). I visited Debra in Australia, where she seemed to be continuing her active and upbeat life. Careers begun at about this time have flourished (Sandra was hired by Suzanne and has become a highly success-ful real estate salesperson; I'm now a full professor instead of an assistant and am enjoying life immensely); businesses have been expanded (Bonnie is now a well-known designer in her field, as well as a joyful grandmother; Pat continues to help her husband in his work). Suzanne sold her agency at a tidy profit in order to retire to the beach, where she plays tennis every day. Most of the rest of us still play as well. All of the marriages seem to be doing well, except for two of the group members (Marla and Terry), who have divorced. I spoke to Suzanne once about this project. She said she wished we'd have this conversation again, now that we are all older and wiser. I also asked Bonnie what she recalled of this gathering. She said she remembered what a good time everyone had. I suppose there are worse ways to remember being involved in a psychology investigation than that.

NOTES

1. An exception is *Reinterpreting Menopause: Cultural and Philsophical Issues,* ed-ited by Paul Komesaroff, Philipa Rothfield, and Jeanne Daly (1997), which is an explica-tion of this trend and some vital resistances.

2. I am not the only investigator who has suspected that menopause has been con-strued as a detrimental factor in women's lives. A study comparing attitudes about meno-pause indicated that women did not view menopause as negatively as members of the medical professions did (Cowan, Warren, & Young, 1985). Gannon and Ekstrom (1993) found that among 581 women and men, views of menopause depended greatly on how

menopause was defined: as a medical problem, as a life transition, or as a symbol of aging, with the medical context eliciting the most negative attitudes. Attitudes became more positive with age and experience with menopause. Bernice Neugarten (1979) reported that among 100 women ages 45 to 55, menstrual cycle was an unimportant predictor of psychological well-being: only 4% thought menopause was an important worry, and 96% were able to mention positive aspects of menopause. Yet an underlying ambivalence toward menopause was indicated, as most women rated themselves more favorably than they rated "women in menopause." In my own research, the modal response to the question of what was the happiest time of life from women between 63 and 93 was 55. The major reasons were related to having a healthy husband, extra time and money, and freedom from children. Not 1 of 50 woman indicated that menopause had been a problem worth mentioning in her life.

Cross-cultural studies also indicate that attitudes toward menopause are not universal. In Asia, for example, menopause is viewed as liberating women from pregnancy, thus increasing their personal freedom (Maoz, Dowty, Antonovsky, & Wijsenbeck, 1970). Among menopausal women, depression, the principal psychological syndrome related to menopause, is found only in cultures where women's status decreases after menopause (Bart, 1971; Datan, 1997). Menopausal depression seems to be the result of cultural appraisals in which women are valued only for their maternal role (Becker, 1964). Depression is not simply a matter of hormones, or their lack, but rather of lack of alternative life options.

3. Even though certain ideas may be synthesized by given individuals, the currency of any idea must be given value by the community surrounding those individuals, or it will fail. In this process, changes occur that are the result of the dialogue within which ideas are set (Gadamer, 1976; Wortham, 1986). Giving ownership to ideas—that is, seeing ideas as private property—is symptomatic of patriarchy, in which everything, including the seas and outer space, is "owned." Feminist often call into question this concept of ownership (Owens, 1983).

4. A special issue of *Psychology of Women Quarterly* spanning two volumes, sponsored by the American Psychological Association and edited by Mary Crawford and Ellen Kimmel (1999), for example, highlights innovative projects within feminist psychology. Many other innovations have been noted in other chapters of this book.

5. Among such investigations are those by Gilbert and Mulkay (1984), Kuhn (1972), Latour and Woolgar (1979), Mitroff (1974), and Woolgar (1987, 1988).

6. Theoretical notions of social scripts are developed in the work of Gagnon and Simon (1973), K. J. Gergen and M. M. Gergen (1983), Goffman (1959), Simon (1996), and Simon and Gagnon (1986), among others.

7. Except for my own, the names of the discussants have been changed.

8. Although I was one of the group in some sense, as the organizer of the experience, I was also part of the "problem" that the group had to confront. Thus, I prefer to use the third-person pronouns to describe the discussion among the seven other members of the group.

5

Social Ghosts
Opening Inquiry on Imaginal Relationships

Your own elders sing inside you like a cicada:
Talking to a ghost is the best way to greet yourself.

—Craig Williamson[1]

As I have emphasized throughout the book, feminist psychology has been characterized by a greater openness to diverse topics and methods than many other areas in psychology. The previous chapters have pursued these indulgences by emphasizing theoretical and critical pursuits, narrative projects, and discourse analysis of a discussion group. This chapter fleshes out a topic that has rarely received attention in any area of psychology, and as such it is a highly speculative constructionist effort on my part. The chapter involves bringing together diverse linguistic strands to birth a new discursive entity—in this case, what I have called *social ghosts*. At the same time, the methods used to investigate this topic are highly conventional. Although there is less to contest about the mode of doing the research, it is my hope that the subject of the research will invoke interest among readers and prompt other researchers, therapists, and teachers to continue to develop this overly ripe apple of my eye.

Traditionally, psychologists have approached the study of interpersonal relations by observing and analyzing aspects of face-to-face interactions. Although much has been learned through this emphasis on "real-time" observable interchange, the orientation has also neglected certain other important social relations. One area of particular interest for me has been that of imaginal relationships—

AUTHOR'S NOTE: I wish to thank Sharon Younkin for her personal involvement and valuable assistance with many facets of the project discussed in this chapter.

that is, relations with others who are not (or may never have been) in one's immediate social context. In these relationships, private conversations, usually but not always produced in silence, are held in which the other interlocutor is someone absent who exists or who has existed or who is imagined. This other has died, is otherwise removed in time and/or space from the conversation taking place, or may take the form of a spiritual existence, such as God. As a fictional character, the social ghost might be an imaginary friend, a comic strip character, or any of a host of other possible entities with whom one might "interact" in an imaginal sense. It is also interesting to extend this notion of social ghosts to include alterities from within—that is, other aspects of the self that are segregated as "Other" during an internal conversation.[2] In the scope of contemporary psychology, little attention has been paid to these "dialogues" in personal life, yet they may often make significant contributions to one's ways of living and life satisfactions. Though it is clear that there is much rich territory to be explored in this realm, it is also the case, as the renowned cultural critic Joshua Meyrowitz (1994) has said in describing his work with "media friends," that "as a culture, we are still lacking in the terminology and conceptual frameworks to analyze fully these strange bonds" (p. 52).

Interestingly, from a social constructionist stance, a focus on this type of interaction serves not only to elucidate an underdeveloped topic in psychology but also to construct the very phenomenon itself. That is, in a very important sense I am contributing to the generation of such a reality by studying it. Once this commitment is made, questions of the value inherent in such a study come to mind. These will be addressed in the concluding portions of this chapter. However, an early recognition of the value orientation of this study is in keeping with a feminist stance, which includes acknowledging that all forms of study are, at base, connected to the pursuit of certain social values and the neglect or denunciation of others.

DEFINING THE SOCIAL GHOST IN DAILY LIFE

Attention to the possibilities of this new realm of study originally came from reflecting on my own activity. I am frequently engaged in internal dialogue with others who are not within range of my voice. I envision others watching me as I go about my daily affairs. I am in imaginal contact with others as I am reminded of their preferences and antipathies. I see how my children have grown up, and I "hear" my mother's voice cautioning me to enjoy their childhoods because they grow so quickly. Watching the football scores, I "exchange views" with my father about how the Vikings are doing. Sometimes, I try to "advise" the president, as well as his advisors, on matters of public policy. I commend them when they do what I think is right. Putting mayonnaise on white bread, I "hear" my Jewish lover laugh at my "goyish" ways of making a sandwich. If I am troubled about a personal decision, I bring in my therapist for a consultation on the private sofa of my inner chambers. When I prepare to have a difficult interchange with a colleague, I speak to her in advance to soften my words before they have a chance to land. These are just a smattering of details from the welter of imagined interactions with what I call my "social ghosts."

Once I considered how important these imaginal interactions might be in the course of ordinary human life, I became curious about how they might be written about as forms of cultural life. I began to engage more fully in the possibilities of describing who these social ghosts are, where they come from, when they are likely to be most present, and what functions they may serve in people's lives. Until I began this project, I had never discussed my "social ghosts" with others, and I had never heard others speak of their imaginal relations either. Yet I suspected that if I am frequently involved in imaginal interactions with others, especially when I am otherwise alone, then perhaps such phenomena could become realized in discourses with others as well.[3] "Imaginal conversations" might become constructed as part of all human experience and might even take on some greater import within individuals' lives. Through expanding our dialogues with social ghosts, we might be better able to create changes in our ongoing relationships with "real-time" others, changes that would be beneficial to others as well as ourselves. This possibility opens space for applications in the vast world of psychological theorizing, therapy, counseling, and spiritual practices.

Frank Farra [is one of my social ghosts]. . . . He taught me to respect myself, my mind and my body. He showed me that when the two are working together there is nothing that I could not accomplish. His inspiration and determination in everything he attempted helped to guide me to finish my college career. I think of him a lot when things aren't going exactly the way I would like them to be. And the thought of him telling me to be the best I can helps me to make the best of any situation.[4]

Why Ghosts Are Social

When I first began to shape this study, I needed a name for the partner in these imaginal encounters. It didn't seem that there was any label that was suitable at that time. Children were often described as having imaginary friends, but I thought that promoting the idea that we all have imaginary friends would be a highly limiting theoretical move, given the diversity of imagined others I wanted to name. I chose to call them social ghosts for several reasons. First, I wanted to emphasize the social aspect of this phenomenon. I wanted to indicate that these interactional partners were the result of prior social experiences with other people, fictional and flesh and blood, and that relationships with them were also social—that is, the imaginal relationships paralleled those of embodied social life in many ways.[5] The dialogic relationship, although carried on alone, involves familiar scenarios of interchange. To talk, laugh, and wonder, to be surprised, upset, hurt, angry, and amused, and to engage in other physical acts could all be a part of imaginal interactions. The provocation of the word *ghosts* intrigued me. A ghost can be defined as a form of spirit; a ghost can visit, but it is not present in a conventional sense. Also, ghosts can have qualities of creatures who have lived, yet their status is different. Ghosts can also haunt one. They are not always at our beck and call. Sometimes social ghosts are not welcome in one's life. They may remind us of things we would rather forget. At other times they take us back to moments that are intensely significant in our lives, and we feel almost forced to relive those moments through the powerful interventions of our ghosts. Together, the two words *social* and *ghost* remind us of our embedded existence in the social realm but also our existence beyond the immediate context, in historical moments, as well as in the present. In all our present relationships, we carry the essences of the past.

Background of the
Social Ghost Phenomenon

Whereas the social sciences, especially psychology, have been sparse and sporadic in mentions of such fictive figures and interactions, literary sources have been rich with accounts of imagined relationships. Significant roles are frequently played by social ghosts in novels, poems, plays, and other dramatic forms, as well as in the production of action in the plot. Great importance is often placed on characters' fantasies, remembrances, emotional attachments, and imagined constructions of others from the past. Relations with ancestors, ancient heroes and heroines, lovers, parents, companions, and enemies, as well as supernatural figures such as angels, phantoms, and witches, play powerful roles in many fictional works. Ghosts often visit earthly characters to frighten, advise, entertain, and admonish them. We remember Shakespeare's Hamlet as a man tormented by his "social ghosts," as are Lord and Lady Macbeth. Edgar Allen Poe's poems and short stories are dominated by imaginal dialogues, including the famous raven saying "Nevermore." Harvey, the imaginary rabbit, entertained generations of filmgoers, and the Disney empire rests on thousands of imagined stars. However, despite the dependency of diverse literary forms on imaginal dialogues, one may argue that there is a significant bifurcation between the "real world" and the imaginary one. To what extent can one trust literary accounts as keys to unlock the mysteries of everyday life? Should "social ghosts" be treated as literary devices for enhancing drama only, or should they be viewed as having a significant role to play in normal lives as well? Should we think of them as poetic symbols? Or shall we consider them as aspects of normal human thought processes?

A social ghost for me is Don D. I saw Don, a former friend, change in a lot of ways the more he used drugs. He changed from someone who was really nice and outgoing to a more bizarre individual. . . . One reason I never go near any drugs is I've seen what it did to Don.

THEORETICAL BACKGROUND OF THE STUDY

Although the origin of my interest in social ghosts was personal experience supported by literary accounts, I also wanted to connect the study of imaginal relationships to psychological issues. To the extent that people do experience interactions with social ghosts, many interesting questions emerge regarding the psychic state of such individuals. As a psychologist, one might look for ways in which imagined interactions might affect one's mental health, emotional stability, or social relations. Could they herald or be symptomatic of mental illnesses? One might ask, for example, whether such experiences are generally limited to special groups, such as the emotionally disturbed, as some clinical psychologists would suggest, or young children, as some developmental psychologists would believe. When do these interactions occur in people's lives, and does this tendency increase or decrease with age? Is my claim that I often have experiences with my social ghosts a sign of that I am entering early stages of dementia? Or, if not signs of diminished cognitive capacity, are these imaginal encounters stress related? Is it only when I am feeling overwhelmed with everyday life that I escape to my imaginary world? Or not? Might a psychoanalyst see in the characteristics of the social ghosts aspects of neurotic attachment or sublimated desire? Can basic motives and needs be explored through analyses of these interactions? Can cognitive maturity or stages of moral thought be determined by examining these mental personifications? Do social ghosts have effects on our attitudes and feelings about ourselves or other people and events in the world? Do they have an impact on our behavior? Is there any relationship between theories giving accounts of imaginal encounters and stereotypes of gender identity? It is to such concerns and questions that the present study was directed.

I was curious how other theorists had dealt with this process. As a result, I searched through many scholarly works, looking for some mention of this phenomenon. A brief overview of the theoretical accounts that I found most closely associated to an exposition of imagined interactions may help to expand the relevance of this topic for readers, as well as affirm their own knowledge in an area I have always found intriguing and underappreciated.

Cognitive Theories of Development and the Social Ghost

In general, my study suggested that most of the theories of relevance hold that imaginal relationships are symptomatic of emotional instability, intellectual immaturity, or mental illness. For example, theories of the renowned developmentalists Lev Vygotsky and Jean Piaget consider imaginary interactions a cardinal feature of childlike thinking and, for various reasons, a form of cognitive activity that almost disappears in favor of more mature forms of intellectual processing in adulthood. As characterized by Vygotsky (1962), children develop internal dialogue as a result of having achieved a certain competence in speaking with others. For him, the social world prepares individuals for self-communications. Vygotsky considered the major function of internal speech to be self-regulation. He did not emphasize the social nature of interiorized language but concentrated on the monologic characteristics of this form of talk. Egocentric speech in young children, in which imagined dialogue could be discerned, was regarded by Vygotsky as an inferior form of talk compared to the sophisticated and elaborate monologue that eventually developed. Vygotsky neglected to acknowledge any positive and prolonged value of imagined dialogic talk in adulthood.

Piaget (1955) designated two forms of talk: egocentric and socialized speech. Egocentric speech, in which the child does not take account of a listener's perspective, is described as primitive and infantile. Though some pleasure and satisfaction may be gained by the child in the practice of egocentric speech, it fails to achieve a communicative function and was thus seen by Piaget as a type of speech that should give way to a more adaptive form. Piaget (1960) also saw intellectual development as a process in which one is increasingly able to operate at an abstract level. According to him, young children live in a concrete world of things. They personify natural forces and objects and see independent forces as interactive and intentional. Older children do not do this. In discussing moral thought, Piaget also posited increasing levels of abstraction. Whereas a young child might think of moral issues in terms of imagining a parent giving praise or punishment, for example, older children should be able to think more in terms of rules or principles rather than personifications. In terms of decision making, generally, the more mature and competent individual would weigh alternatives without needing to imagine conversations in which various people offered differing opinions. From this perspective, those who imagined interactions would be considered less cognitively mature (Piaget, 1955). Generalizing from these cognitive psychologists, one might conclude that the immature thinker is one who clings to concrete personifications of ideas, whereas the mature thinker is inclined to use symbols, abstract logical processes, and derivations from principles and rules to engage in cognitive activity. The work on moral development by Lawrence Kohlberg (1981), derived from Piaget's notions of cognitive development, and emphasizing the progressive stages of moral decision making from the concrete, as in authority judgments (such as "Father told me so") through conventional stages, in which concerns for others' opinions and social customs are central (such as "This pleases my friends") to higher levels at which the application of abstract principles is stressed, is an expansion of this valuing of the monologic. The critical response to this argument in Carol Gilligan's classic volume *In a Different Voice* (1982) emphasized the way in which Kohlberg's system denigrated the notion of care as opposed to justice in the creation of moral choices; Gilligan associated this preference for abstract universal principles to hegemonic masculine stereotypes. Drawing from her distinctions, it is possible to speculate that the silence surrounding dialogic thought may involve gender distinctions as well as other historical exigencies. Maintaining a relational form of thinking may be too strongly tied to stereotypic feminine forms and as such may be regarded as less highly evolved.

Elsewhere, it is difficult to find cognitive/developmental psychologists who have supported dialogic forms of development. Most have not discussed imaginal discourse, and those who have tend to minimize its importance as children age. An exception is Brian Sutton-Smith (1971), who has been interested in studying play and children's imaginary companions. Sutton-Smith's theoretical views are exceptional among developmentalists in that they do support symbolic play as children's ways of constructing social reality and not as indicative of their inability to accommodate to external reality or their failure to overcome the limits of egocentrism. However, in general, an emphasis on the importance of such activities is almost nonexistent in the repertoire of psychological concepts of development in most academic disciplines today.

An important social ghost for me is Eddy Cheever, a famous F1 driver. After watching many races with him many times lose and sometimes win, I became very interested in auto racing. Actually he has a major influence in my leading up to being a mechanic.

Most contemporary cognitive social psychologists have studied the notion of social ghosts under the rubric of "person memory" in laboratory settings. These researchers are primarily engaged in experimentally manipulating factors that enhance, retard, or "distort" the ability to remember certain aspects of laboratory-induced others, who may be real or fictitious. Generally, this research is aimed at contributing to the literature in cognitive specialities such as person memory and coping strategies.[6] Although these various empirical investigations are important for tracking cognitive processing, they do not focus on the spontaneous experience of individuals relating to people in memory or on the functions of such imaginary interactions in subjects' lives. The imaginal dialogue is unwieldy for experimentalists to work with and, does not enhance existing cognitive research paradigms—as a result it does not generally attract researchers' interest now and is unlikely to attract it in the future.

Social Ghosts From a Therapeutic Perspective

Social ghosts have had a livelier existence among therapists than among research scholars. From the point of view of many clinical psychologists and psychiatrists, imagined interactions are maladaptive. In descriptions of mental illness or emotional instability, "hearing voices," engaging in imaginary conversations, or seeing or being seen by an imaginal figure, absent or fictional, is symptomatic of severe problems. Bleuler (1912/1951), a well-known authority on mental illness, referred to fantasizing as "autistic thought." Descriptions of schizophrenia also include such imaginal activities among the symptoms (American Psychiatric Association, 1994). From a Freudian perspective, social ghosts may be construed as representatives of lost "objects,"—that is, persons with whom one has had an important affective relationships, real or imagined, that can no longer be sustained. Fantasy serves as an escape from reality, from coping with the past, or from facing an uncertain or unpleasant future. Roy Schafer (1992), a prominent psychoanalytic writer, referred to one category of "primary process presences" as "introjects." These introjects are similar to social ghosts as he described their form and functions: They serve to guide the individual, to offer support, and to provide identification figures. Schafer also referred to the capacity of introjects to give the persona a greater sense of power and to serve as objects for emotional outlets. He argued that despite these apparently useful functions, introjects should be given up, and the person should instead learn to treat these personifications as unadorned perspectives, thoughts, or feelings. In this view, he was consonant with developmental psychologists, such as Piaget, who opt for abstract rational thought as a superior form of intellectual activity.

Despite the generally negative evaluation given these imagined interactions in much therapeutic work, certain clinical psychologists have taken a more positive stance (Griffith & Griffith, 1994). The most noted defender of this position is Mary Watkins (1986), who has explored the ways in which therapy can utilize "invisible guests" through the development of imaginal dialogues. She has criticized psychologists for reducing the import and value of these dialogues and has instead insisted that they may be viewed as a source of significant enrichment within adult life.

> Psychotherapy may continue to help reflect and perpetuate the sociocultural bias against imaginal dialogues by continuing to mislabel experiences of the imaginal, assigning many of them a pathological status, discouraging the reporting of thought's many conversations. . . . But we will continue to dream. We will continue to fantasize. . . . We will continue to take on others' voices and intonations, and we will continue at times to act and speak in ways that surprise us—as though for the moment we have given over our place to another. (pp. 171-172)

Within her therapeutic work, Watkins encourages people to learn to dialogue with their other social selves rather than to be immersed within them or torn apart by them. In teaching her clients about their capacities to dialogue imaginally, Watkins argues that they gain new strengths, demand less consistency from themselves, and move from a "literal to psychological and metaphorical modes of understanding" (p. 169). By experiencing the self as "a collection of voices, organized through dialogue" (p. 169), the client becomes free of many traumatic involvements that formerly constrained him or her within specific self-modes. Watkins cites many examples from her clients' lives in which successful outcomes resulted from approaching them in this manner.

Clint Eastwood influences me especially when I'm angry or playing a sport. I'll put on my dark sunglasses, and suddenly I'm in control because I think of Clint, as Dirty Harry, as my sidekick.

Work by Paul Rosenblatt and Cynthia Meyer (Rosenblatt, 1990; Rosenblatt & Meyer, 1986) on imagined interactions has suggested that imaginal interactions can be helpful to therapeutic goals and individual adjustment in family therapy. Rosenblatt and Meyer (1986) stated that "even though relationships may ordinarily benefit by face-to-face interaction, perhaps particularly about sensitive issues, implicit versions of such interactions may be beneficial" (p. 324). When clients are unable to face others about certain problems, creating imaginal dialogues can allow for outcomes similar to those produced via actual interactions. In the past decade, family therapists who specialize in forms of narrative therapy have created innovative methods of using imaginal dialogue to assist people in breaking through barriers of communication created through absence or indifference (Anderson, 1997). Peggy Penn and Marilyn Frankfurt (1994) of the Ackerman Institute, for example, have aided clients in facilitating relations with social ghosts by writing letters to them, which may never be sent. In some instances, clients create dialogues with their social ghosts that allow them to take the role of the other, which may result in a greatly altered understanding of this person. Michael White of the Dulwich Centre in Adelaide, Australia, and David Epston from the Family Therapy Centre in Auckland, New Zealand, have developed many experimental modes that use imaginal social activities to help therapeutic clients improve (White & Epston, 1990). For example, in the treatment of eating disorders, Epston has developed the notion that anorexia is a social ghost, which he helps his patients to regard as the enemy within. He assists them in creating conversations between the person and the enemy to stave off anorexia's overtaking of the body. Other therapists use forms of narrative reconstruction to help clients change their lives with others (Anderson, 1997; Goolishian & Anderson, 1987). Sallyann Roth and Richard Chasin of the Cambridge Institute in the Boston area engage clients in dramatic scenarios, which they begin by imagining a scene from an unremembered past (Roth & Chasin, 1994). These therapists anticipate that when these scenes are played out, with imagined characters mingling with those present, new forms of relating, new understandings, and new resolutions can occur. In one such case, a man who had been unable to interact comfortably with his father learned new skills through role-playing a scene invented by the therapists that suggested that he had been warm and open with his father as a much younger man. The violence research team of the Ackerman Institute, led by Virginia Goldner (Goldner, Penn, Sheinberg, & Walker, 1990), has also used imaginal dialogues to facilitate relations between couples involved in abusive relationships. Describing a violent man's imaginal dialogues, in which he repeated what his father's advice to him was, they wrote, " 'You must never be a wimp or feel afraid, but watch out for women. They can do you in. For every Sampson there is a Delilah with scissors' " (p. 351). The recall of this imaginal dialogue allowed the therapeutic team to enlarge the couple's understandings of their violent interchanges and to create ways to undermine and defuse them. Although these examples stress the positive outcomes of using forms of encounters with social ghosts in therapy, my review of the literature suggests that clinical psychologists in general have paid little attention to spontaneous imaginal relationships as a significant aspect of a therapeutic relationship.

An area that has seen a shift to a greater acceptance of "social ghosts" has been work with trauma and grief. Over the past decade, James Pennebaker and his colleagues have been involved with a research program on the effects of confiding traumatic events on conditions of health (Pennebaker, 1990). Using a technique in which subjects write detailed memories of either traumatic or nontraumatic events, these researchers have tracked the relationship between such activities and subsequent health status through observing visits of the participants to the university clinic. Although those who write extensively about past negative events do seem to be healthier following the writing exercise, the theoretical reasons for why this should be so are not clear. Pennebaker (1988) has speculated:

> These findings suggest that people write or talk about traumas to an imaginary or symbolic other. . . . Future studies must examine the nature of the symbolic other in far greater detail. For example, addressing an earlier trauma, with the imagined audience being one's parents, therapist, minister, friend, political leader, or God, would undoubtedly result in different interpretations of the same event. (p. 681)

And, I might suggest, it would result in different outcomes for the person's well-being or emotional satisfaction.

Until very recently, the general theoretical leaning of most therapists dealing with reactions to personal loss has been toward breaking or giving up ties to the deceased. The bereaved have been counseled to reestablish life without the lost person and told that the sooner this is accomplished, the faster healing will occur. Of late, other indicators support the notion that maintaining emotional ties to the lost person may be helpful to them. Surveys of surviving spouses indicate that maintaining ties via imaginal interactions can be as satisfying and supportive of a balanced life as cutting off communicative ties (Stroebe, Gergen, Gergen, & Stroebe, 1992). The Tubingen research group, which conducted interviews with bereaved marital partners, found that widows and widowers who maintained strong emotional ties with the deceased described various forms of emotional, psychological, and practical supports derived from their imaginal contacts with the lost spouse (Stroebe & Stroebe, 1988). Studies of aged widows who live alone have found them to be remarkably healthy, independent, and satisfied with life, more so than similarly aged married women. Researchers speculate that one of the reasons for this surprising outcome is that their homes help to keep alive memories of—perhaps we might say imaginal relationships with—"social ghosts," deceased spouses and other family members who are no longer in the house (O'Bryant & Nocera, 1985). Their single status may also lend itself to a selective form of relating over which they have a great deal of control. They can fashion their relationship with their spouses to suit their needs, without the interference of an actual living person, who might not maintain the standards of conduct that their imaginal relating can achieve.

My father, deceased, is a social ghost in my life. I will usually try and decide if he would object or permit me to do what I am considering doing, or figure out what he would do in a certain situation. (Unfortunately, I usually will do it anyway.)

Social Ghosts From Sociological/Anthropological Perspectives

Theorists from other disciplines besides psychology, in particular symbolic interactionists within sociology, are also less pessimistic about the effects of engaging in imagined interactions than many of those cited above in psychology and psychiatry. In George Herbert Mead's self theory (1934), for example, imagined dialogues are necessary preformulations for the development of a mature self-concept. Mead identified the creation of the Generalized Other, a composite internalized figure that represents the values and the norms of the broadest community of which the person has been a part, as the necessary consequence of normal development. For Mead, the ability of individuals to consider the effects of the self on others and then to internalize the observing presences as a Generalized Other is necessary for the formation of the self and for effective social interactions in the external world. The inner world, as described by Mead (1934), "is a field, a sort of inner forum, in which we are the only spectators and the only actors. In that field each one of us confers with himself" (p. 401). Although the ability to forge imaginary relationships with social ghosts might be construed by Mead as a necessary preliminary step to the creation of a Generalized Other, his theoretical position suggests that this is a temporary process only; the truly mature individual would give up these diverse connections and merge separate voices of the self into one. Mead would most likely have been critical of the permanent fragmentation of voices into disparate parts. He also reflected primarily on the social control function of the Generalized Other and did not focus on any emotional or expressive functions that internal dialogues might offer.

Many self theorists from both sociological and psychological backgrounds have followed Mead in looking to the significance of the social and how it is internalized to create the person's self-concept. Especially important to self theorists has been the idea of the development of the Generalized Other in relationship to the self (Gordon & Gergen, 1968; Lynch, Norem-Hebeisen, & Gergen, 1981; Suls, 1982). Although each of these self theories has emphasized imaginal dialogue, which creates a sense of splitting within the speaker, the partners in conversation are often seen as stable, identifiable, and unitary elements of the exchange. However, recent theoretical work on imaginal dialogues supports the notion of the self as multiple and, as such, allows for dialogic processes occurring between different voices within one person as a normal process, as suggested above.[7]

When I'm playing basketball, I like to do some monster Jams. [Charles] Barkley [formerly of the 76ers] and me are one.

In *Imaginary Social Worlds,* anthropologist John Caughey (1984) examined the culturally constructed nature of various forms of mental life: dreams, fantasies, memories, and hallucinations. He argued, along with Vygotsky and Piaget, that our imaginal dialogues prepare us for actual social life. Our imaginal social worlds allow us to associate ourselves with various cultural conventions and values, such as being famous or sexually attractive to others; they also allow us to escape from oppressive cultural conditions to become masters and mistresses of our fates; and they let us dream of ways of innovating and revitalizing cultural norms. As an ethnographer, Caughey has studied two non-Western societies, Micronesia and Pakistan, as well as American psychiatric wards. In his major work, however, he interviewed over 500 noninstitutionalized people in all walks of life in the United States and found that forms of imaginary social relationships are everyday occurrences within diverse social groups. From his perspective, such seemingly antisocial activities as John Hinckley's attempt to assassinate President Reagan to gain the favor of his fantasy-girlfriend, the actress Jody Foster, are not unfathomable mysteries, as some might conclude, but rather are similar to ordinary social behaviors in that they are outgrowths of culturally formed dialogic thought. (In this case, one acts heroically to impress one's reluctant girlfriend with one's virtues and thereby "win" her.)

Social Ghosts From a Bakhtinian Perspective:
A Note on the Superaddressee

Another framework for discussing the process of dialogic thought is offered by the Russian psychologist and literary theorist Michael Bakhtin (1986), who suggested the notion of a Superaddressee, or third presence, that accompanies every conversation, including all of those with others. Though we may speak to a living other, we simultaneously address this imagined social ghost, "whose absolutely just responsive understanding is presumed" (p. 126). In expanding this notion of the third presence, the communications scholar John Shotter (1995) has written:

> It is as if at each moment a third invisible agent, another voice, created by the dialogue or conversation itself, emerges from the background between the dialogue partners, to decree the options open to them or the limitations upon them. (p. 50)

In a similar fashion, Perelman and Olbrechts-Tyteca (1969) posited a "universal audience" imagined by the speaker, a listening post that is presumably able to fairly judge the adequacy of all arguments.

How imagined interactions are to be defined, with whom they might be carried out, and how they function in social life are as yet unanswered questions. Whether interactions with social ghosts are of positive or negative value in terms of human functioning also remains controversial. Is this activity a symptom of mental illness, maladjustment, or poor coping skills, or is it a normal human process with positive aspects and potential benefits? Might these dialogues be harmful as well as helpful? The present investigation enlarges inquiry into these and related questions.

INVESTIGATING SOCIAL GHOSTS WITH OTHERS

When I began this research project, there were no models for me to imitate. Thus, I wondered how I might enter into dialogue with others about these "social ghosts." I wanted to develop ways of exploring this unknown, or perhaps I should say "invented," territory with others. The inquiry became the basis of a research-oriented project, of which this chapter is an outcome.

It is difficult to frame a question that has never before been asked. Inventing a term, such as *social ghosts,* requires some introduction so that others may be able to give a meaningful response. To gain some appreciation for how others might respond to inquiry about "social ghosts," I created a simple and fairly unobtrusive survey among college students. This initial exploration took the form of a questionnaire entitled "Remembered Persons" (a label designed to be less dramatic or less humorous in tone than *social ghosts* might seem to them). The definition of "Remembered Persons" was placed at the beginning of the first page. The questionnaire then asked respondents if there were people whom they remembered from the past, either real or fictitious, whom they had known personally or read about, who entered into their thoughts about current life activities. If so, they were asked to name each of these persons, with a maximum of three, and to identify their relationship with each of them. They were then asked to describe the ways in which each of these persons affected "your daily life at present." The attempt in the introductory paragraph of the questionnaire was to define the idea of a social ghost as clearly and as neutrally as possible and then to elicit from the respondents a few examples of social ghosts in their own lives. The survey then addressed the question of the function of social ghosts in the respondents' lives by asking for effects on daily life of these imaginal interactions. The questionnaires were administered to 76 college students of varying economic and ethnic backgrounds.

[Social ghost:] Speed Racer. I used to think Speed was a great guy when I was 6. I wanted to be a champion in the Mach 5 like him.

The surveys were content analyzed, with the aforementioned questions of whether people did have imagined interactions and, if so, with what kind of social ghosts and for what purposes. The identities of these social ghosts were assessed, as well as the relationships they had to the respondents and the functions that these imagined interactions with the social ghosts had in terms of affecting these respondents in their daily lives.

Prevalence of Imagined Interactions

The initial question to which the research was directed concerned the prevalence of the experience of imagined interactions with others. As previously mentioned, many developmental and clinical psychologists have suggested that only people with very unsatisfactory social lives and those who are mentally or emotionally disabled or immature would report experiences of interaction with absent social figures. Normal people would be unlikely to carry out an extended set of imagined relationships. However, these data support the view that imaginal interactions with social ghosts are commonplace. In fact, except for one respondent, all those surveyed indicated imagined relationships with at least one person. The majority of the respondents wrote about three relationships, which was the space provided for them on the questionnaire, although some people added more experiences. It is difficult from the results of this questionnaire to draw any conclusions about how many social ghosts people might be able to recall. Perhaps there is no finite limit to the possibilities. From my own experience, I would be inclined to agree with Mary Watkins's (1986) comment that there is a "very din of imaginal voices in adulthood" (p. 173). Clearly, young adults who are intellectually and socially competent and relatively stable emotionally can, with ease, write about their relationships with social ghosts. Support for the notion of the normalcy of these subjects comes from a similar study among adults in which, of the 20 people solicited, only one could not recall ever having had an imagined interaction. (This subject had eight children, however, and she credited the extensive nature of her actual daily relationships with her lack of imagined ones) (M. M. Gergen, 1987).

[Social ghost:] My grandmother, Eunice Mann, a model. Sometimes when I dress up I think I look like her or I carry myself like her. Often I try to act in a way that would please her. I imagine her giving me compliments.

Identity of the Social Ghosts

Who was selected to be a social ghost? The next significant question concerned the identity of these social ghosts. Psychoanalytic literature would suggest that such significant others should primarily be family members with whom one interacted in early childhood. Symbolic interactionist theory would hold that any important persons who influenced one's early formation of self-concept would be likely to serve as social ghosts. Developmental and social psychologists, especially social learning theorists, might well emphasize the importance of those figures who have high status, power, or diverse resources, such as fictional characters or famous people—entertainers, athletic stars, and other public figures who are idolized and imitated by adolescents.

As the findings demonstrated, the major proportion (37%) of the social ghosts described were friends of the respondents with whom they no longer interacted on a regular basis. Platonic friendships accounted for approximately two thirds of those mentioned as social ghosts, with former boyfriends and girlfriends generating the remainder. Family members were mentioned second most frequently, with 23% of the social ghosts being a family relative. Among the immediate family, fathers were mentioned most frequently (39%), followed by mothers (13%) and siblings (8%). However, many of these relatives were not members of the nuclear family. Grandparents, cousins, aunts, and uncles accounted for almost all the of the remaining social ghosts in this group. Former teachers were named in 11% of the cases. Among these, the predominant group, chosen in 50% of the cases, was that of high school teachers. The remaining 29% of the social ghosts were people with whom the respondent had almost never had direct interactions. These included religious figures, fictitious characters, celebrities, and others. Among the famous social ghosts unknown to the respondent, entertainers were chosen over 80% of the time.

Thus, family members were not the primary social ghosts for this sample. Friends and media-mediated personalities were more likely to be named. Interestingly, the preschool period of life was second only to high school as the time in life in which the social ghosts were most likely to be mentioned. Approximately one third of the social ghosts were recalled from early childhood, and about one half were chosen from the high school period. Very few social ghosts were named from elementary school, junior high, or college periods. This lends some support to the notion that the periods of early childhood and late adolescence are important for development, if one also assumes that one of the functions of interaction with social ghosts is to be reconnected with figures that had an important impact on one during critical periods of identity formation. Perhaps there are other reasons for these periods to be crucial for the development of imaginal relationships as well. The age of the sample precludes possibilities for later time periods. Research with an aging sample would be important in determining what periods of life might most stand out as a source of remembrance.

Interestingly, men were chosen as social ghosts to a greater extent than women by both sexes. Of the 200 social ghosts mentioned, 124 (60%) were male figures. These results may reflect the extent to which men are seen as more powerful than women in our society, especially among youth. In addition, men's positions may be more distinct and make a greater impression on young people than women's. One might also speculate that men would be more absent or emotionally distant from them. Thus, one might speculate that conversations take place in fantasy because actual dialogues are not feasible, or because they would be awkward or contentious if actually attempted or because many facets of relatedness are insufficiently developed to allow for intimacies that the subjects wish to achieve.

My mother always wanted to be a Hollywood actress. She used to always talk about Zsa Zsa Gabor as the celebrity she most identified with. I'm sure she was Mama's "social ghost." I always wondered why she couldn't have picked someone more substantial, but Zsa Zsa seemed to suit her just fine.

Functions of Social Ghosts

Given the variety of social ghosts mentioned, we might next inquire into the diversity of functions of social ghosts in daily life. Content analysis of the responses indicated numerous possibilities. In general, the ways in which social ghosts function in respondents' lives appeared largely to parallel those that psychologists have posited for ongoing relationships in "real time." Specifically, the respondents indicated that social ghosts acted as social models, facilitators in attitude formation and support, sources of esteem bolstering, providers of emotional support, and instigators of guilt and other negative feelings. A fuller description of these functions follows.

[Social ghost:] John Paul Jones. He was the bass and keyboard player for the rock group Led Zeppelin. . . . When my band practices, I feel like I'm him, and it helps me play better. It gives me more energy.

Social Ghosts as Social Models

Social ghosts set standards for behavior under wide-ranging circumstances. Respondents frequently mentioned that they either admired or wanted to behave like their social ghost. A typical response was, "When I am faced with a difficult decision, I try to face the problem as he did, despite criticism from others." Another wrote that Connie Chung "was constantly being used as a role model for me, and I found myself responding to a question about what I planned to do after graduation by saying that I wanted to go into journalism just because I had been thinking of her." Often respondents suggested that the modeling effects of social ghost interactions resulted in improvements in their social relations. As one person put it, "She showed me how to be tolerant of all people and to show respect to everyone regardless of their state in life." In general, the impact of social ghosts on social relations seemed to be one of improvement in competence or satisfaction, and no indication was found that imaginal interactions hindered social relations or served as substitutes for them. This is especially critical in light of many psychological theories that suggest that these types of interactions serve as substitutes for actual social intercourse.

I sing, and I find myself a lot of the time comparing myself to Judy Garland. Although I never knew her, I feel as if I have encouragement from her to do well.

Facilitators of Attitude Formation and Support

Social ghosts frequently were recalled by virtue of their perspectives on important matters. Almost all the respondents indicated that they were responsive to the beliefs and values of their social ghosts. The necessity of making an important decision frequently enhanced the imaginal interactions. Social ghosts seemed to have a vital role in helping people choose a course of action. Typically, respondents mentioned being positively impressed by the perspective of the social ghost. For example, of the 160 evaluations made of the attitudes of social ghosts, 120 (75%) were expressions of approval, 24 (15%) were negative, and the remaining 16 (10%) were neutral. Generally, the function of social ghosts in this regard was to bolster attitudes already held by the respondent.

Respondents also mentioned that interactions with social ghosts sometimes led to an alteration in their existing beliefs and values. Respondents made 180 mentions of ways in which they had been influenced to change their outlooks and actions as a result of imagined interactions. Most frequently, they described how their expectations for themselves had been elevated or altered either personally or professionally by these interactions. One respondent said that a social ghost of hers who was a "good Christian" was "the last link I have to Christianity at this point in my life when I am trying to determine my religious inclinations." It appears that the religious beliefs of this social ghost were recalled to help the writer form her own religious identity.

These "ghosts" have all been extremely important in my life. They have all changed me in a way, I feel, for the better.

Sources of Esteem Bolstering

Respondents often seemed to attribute to social ghosts capacities to reinforce their feelings of self-esteem. Frequently, respondents mentioned how doing what they thought their social ghosts would approve of gave them a sense of self-satisfaction and confidence that they were doing well. Many wrote of being proud to satisfy the imagined expectations or goals of the social ghost. "I think of my father and I know that he would be proud of what I have accomplished." High school teachers and coaches were particularly important in providing this type of affirmation.

Dave, my ex-boyfriend—smart, outgoing, athletic, spoke four languages frequently. An ex-druggie who overcame his sister's suicide to become a perfect, all-round, swell person. When I become depressed or sloppy, I "talk" to Dave and clean up my act.

Providers of Emotional Support

As the respondents indicated, social ghosts also served to provide emotional support in various situations. Respondents made 44 mentions of how they turned to social ghosts for comfort when in need of support. Among the results of these interactions, respondents wrote about increased feelings of well-being, hope, and security, as well as less loneliness. One person spoke of the strength she got from imagining that "my grandmother seems to be watching me and showing that she loves me even if I am not doing so well." The use of social ghosts as emotional support was echoed in the words of Meyrowitz: "The 'unreal' relationships with media friends are, ironically, often deeper and longer lasting than many real-life ties" (1994, p. 62).

Guilt and Other Negative Emotions

Although people may not wish to have sad or guilty feelings about themselves, imagined communications may function to produce them. A minority of the sample (20%) indicated that social ghosts may cause negative feelings in them. Respondents wrote of feeling inadequate, insecure, lonely, hopeless, and guilty. Among these more negative emotions, 50% of the responses were classified as nostalgia, an emotion containing both happy and sad components. "When I imagine being with him, I feel some comfort, but also some sorrow that we can never be together again." Other more clearly negative emotions, particularly regret, anger, and fear, were also mentioned. One person wrote,

> My dialogues with my dad are not as "close" or "special" because I never felt very close to him as I was growing up. My thoughts are more in trying to say perhaps that I'm sorry I didn't spend more time with him as I grew older.

Another wrote, "No matter how the 'conversation' begins, I never can keep from feeling angry at some of the things that happened between us."

In summary, respondents were generally very positive in their attitudes about their social ghosts. The majority of them mentioned the respect and regard in which they held the support and advice that their social ghosts had given them. Often they wrote of the way in which the social ghosts had stood as positive models for them. In many instances, respondents referred to the security and hope engendered by the social ghosts; in a minority of cases, instances of increased feelings of loneliness, guilt, and lack of self-confidence were described. Overall, it appears that imaginal relationships with social ghosts lead to more positive self-feelings, although a minority of the interactions seem to be painful and negative.

EXPANDING OUR INTERPRETIVE ENDEAVORS

The findings from this exploratory study are necessarily tentative and preliminary. More study is needed to construe more fully how the concept of social ghosts may be usefully applied to human conduct. In general, however, it does appear that almost all of us have experienced interactions with our social ghosts. The cast of characters is a broad one, and the functions they serve are multiple. As was initially described, theorists such as Vygotsky and Piaget have held that mature thinking is not dialogic. Rather, each of them characterized adult thinking processes as abstract and unified in perspective. In contrast, findings from this study suggest that adult thinking may be aided by dialogic processes. It appears that social ghosts may assist cognitive processes by allowing us to create multiple perspectives and divergent views and feelings within us. We can experience the advantages of talking something over with another without the disadvantages that such conversations might bring. This is an extremely important advantage. Recently, a student came to me gravely upset about an unanticipated pregnancy. In the course of talking with me, she described how conversations with her parents, her boyfriend, her boyfriend's family, and her friends at school would go if she were to tell them her secret. I think she chose me, a person she had never confided in prior to this revelation, because she thought that I would be willing to listen in a nonjudgmental way to her ruminations. I served as a mediator between her imaginal dialogues and the ones she might have had with embodied others.

Imaginal dialogues can also allow people greater ease in formulating a point of view when its source is personified as a social ghost. Instead of trying to think abstractly about the virtues of one evaluative perspective among others, of making lists and weighing and measuring the pros and cons, we can imagine being with someone who represents the views we admire or despise. Also important is the fact that most of the imagined figures are positive ones, admired or loved, and this allows one to experience a special sense of coalition with and perhaps warmth from a powerful other. Often, widows and widowers speak of the capacity of the deceased to support and advise the living partner in matters of importance (Stroebe et al., 1992). Social ghosts also are able to give immediate emotional support in a world replete with danger and ambiguity. One doesn't have to wait until the significant other is available and in the right mood. Especially in times of choice, evaluation, stress, loneliness, and loss, we may turn to agents from the past to seek guidance, affirmation, and support. The use of prayer in many religions involves conversational connections to spiritual guides and advisors. Having a personal relationship with Jesus, which is predicated on the capacity to speak and listen to him, is at the heart of most Protestant religious traditions. Words of a popular hymn sung in the Lutheran church include the phrase "And he walks with me and he talks with me, and he tells me I am his own." The Roman Catholic faith is filled with communicative potential through prayer with saints, guardian angels, and the Virgin Mary, as well as with the Blessed Trinity of Jesus, God, and the Holy Ghost. In Native American traditions, ceremonies associated with sweat lodges may include a visitation from a spirit that may bring answers to prayers, and the vision quests of the young include the expectation that spirits will communicate to them concerning their future paths. Regardless of our religious rituals, in times of success and happiness we may also turn to significant others from our pasts to share our good fortunes and receive praise from them. (And, more than is possible in ongoing interactions, we can do it without modesty.)

This is not to say that imaginal dialogues are not without risks and disadvantages. There is a danger in that we may not be able to correctly create the range of responses that others might give us in an actual conversation and thus may foreclose on opportunities that we might have had or live with uncorrected notions of what others might say to us. We may underestimate the flexibility or sensitivity of others to our concerns. Also, it is important to point out that a positive appraisal of imaginal dialogues is not made with a view to excluding actual interactions. Interactions with social ghosts can be viewed as an enhancement to social life, not as a substitute. Although there are some limitations to the positive qualities of imaginal dialogues, clearly from these interpretations one would be disinclined to accept the predominant view of much clinical and developmental psychology that they are maladaptive or immature.

The major goal of the study was merely to open a field of inquiry, not to produce a definitive end. Many other more sophisticated research endeavors might now be envisioned. This study limited the extensiveness of the information that respondents gave. With lengthy personal interviews, for example, much richer material could have been produced. Additional work could be done to address questions of particular interest to developmentalists and clinicians, as well as to other psychologists. For example, does growing older affect the quantity or change the function of imagined interaction? Can interesting new therapeutic modes be created that use various internalized voices? How might social ghosts be used to ease the pains of social adjustment to new environments, new family formations, or personal loss? A therapist recently reported to me that a widow who was being urged by her friends to "get over her grief and on with life" was greatly comforted by reading a draft of this chapter and that she speculated how she might maintain her imaginal relationship with her husband and not let go of the bonds that she so cherished. Encounters such as this suggest that people might be encouraged and trained to increase their awareness of imagined interactions and perhaps use this new dimension to enhance personal creativity and well-being.

Relating Social Ghosts to Feminism

Although this chapter appears to have strayed rather far from the feminist paths so crucial to the formation of the book, some rather interesting speculations can tie the study of social ghosts, or more precisely the lack of study of these interactions, to the more general fields of feminist psychology and women's studies. If one recalls the binary oppositions separating men and women, including the stereotypes of males and females most prevalent in the society, then the notion that the mature, emotionally stable, and rational human being is characterized by the quality of autonomy or independence from others becomes apparent. There is a presumption, fortified by object relations theory and the general notions in the developmental literature related to it, that boys and girls are raised with different orientations to separation, with boys seeking it and girls resisting it (Chodorow, 1978). If the notion of social ghosts invokes anything, it is the idea that humans are forever connected to one another, both in "real time" existence and in imaginal relations. The importance of relationships in creating healthy, normal people is at the heart of these views of social ghosts and is in stark contradiction to views of normality that stress independent, autonomous, inner-directed selves (K. J. Gergen, 1994). The discrepancy between the willingness of people to describe their social ghosts and the silence surrounding this notion in academic circles is great. That imaginal dialogues are denigrated as qualities of immature minds and emotionally unstable dispositions reminds us of the prejudice favoring masculine qualities in psychology generally (Broverman, Broverman, Clarkson, Rosenkrantz, & Vogel, 1970). That this viewpoint is undergoing challenges and changes is also an interesting development, which suggests that a certain feminizing of theory may have been subtly taking place in the last decade (Crawford, 1995). Certainly, the view that social ghosts are a sign of a healthy, thriving person is a relatively new phenomenon, but one that, if expanded, should serve both to offer new options for people to live richer lives and to affirm women's relational styles rather than men's independent ones. A greater recognition that connectedness is a desirable way to live can only benefit feminist pursuits.

Constructing Our Social Ghosts Into the Future

Finally, it is important to continue to remind ourselves that in a very important way, the study of imaginal dialogue with social ghosts is an exercise in social construction (K. J. Gergen, 1999). In this respect, the imaginal dialogue is not a new discovery of human psychological functioning but a potential element in a discourse form that might have some value for theorists, clinicians, and others interested in human behavior. It is congenial with relational theorizing of all sorts, and especially with feminist theories, including postmodern ones. By introducing clients to the notion of social ghosts, clinicians might be able to assist them in reaching new levels of accord with those who might otherwise be inaccessible or distanced. The potentials for imaginal dialogues are rich in a variety of circumstances in which clients broach the possibilities of change but are restrained by diverse limitations, including their own versions of self, as well as their understanding of their relationships with others. Through creating various imaginal dialogues, clients come to see themselves as multipotentiated. They are not as circumscribed by their pasts to be one "damaged self" as they may believe. They may regard their circumstances from various vantage points and, as a result, become detached from their particular life conditions, particularly negative ones, as they describe them. They make come to understand that they have outgrown certain imaginal relationships that once were central to their sense of self. Bakhtin (1981) described this:

> One may suppose that it is often painful to encounter a reminder—an old letter, old notes, a diary entry, . . . of how one used to orchestrate inner dialogues, because we recognize how large a role was played by voices and perspectives that we have since rejected or outgrown in ourselves and criticized in others. (p. 222)

Whether one is in a negative emotional state or is simply interested in expanding one's options for living, the encouragement to explore imaginal dialogues with one's symphony of social ghosts is likely to be beneficial. Extended explorations in the therapeutic and counseling realms should prove useful in enlarging the scope of resources available for all who engage in the enrichment of human life.

NOTES

1. "Multiculturalism," a poem by Craig Williamson, *Swarthmore College Annual Report, 1992-1993,* p. 17. Copyright © 1993. Reprinted with permission.

2. This possibility was enlivened by a conversation, in real time, with Dr. Angela Gillam, Beaver College, Feb. 1, 1999, on the LAX shuttle.

3. The use of the word *imaginal* in preference to *imagined* or *imaginary* is taken from the work of Watkins (1986). Whereas the latter two words suggest something fictional or frivolous, *imaginal* suggests other, more consequential possibilities.

4. Quotations are taken from the protocols of anonymous participants.

5. As pointed out in a recent review of work on mental simulation by Taylor, Pham, Rivkin, and Armor (1998), "Although mental simulations are imaginary, they are typically not magical" (p. 430) but rather are constrained by ordinary conventions of behavior and understandings of how the world works.

6. Among the dozens of empirical explorations in this area are those by Barclay and DeCooke (1988), Belmore and Hubbard (1987), Hastie and Kumar (1979), Taylor et al. (1998), and Wyer and Srull (1984).

7. Recent work in this area is represented by Hermans (1996), Hermans and Hermans-Jansen (1995), Hermans, Kempen, and Van Loon (1992), and Hermans, Rijks, and Kempen (1993).

6

Gaze and the Naked Maja
Si(gh)tes for Controversy

And/Or

Signification of Embodiment
When Mind Meets Matter

The Female Body and the Male Gaze
Eating Humble Pie

Power of Mystification
Stripped Tease Pays Off

Female Gaze
Blind Eye in a Vortex of Desire

Naked or Nude
The Power of the B(r)ush

Binary and Bodies
Pinning a Wench to the Wall

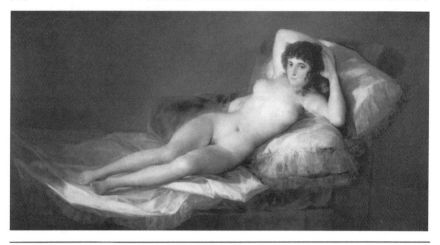

FIGURE 6.1. Goya, *The Naked Maja*
Museo del Prado, Madrid, Spain.

IN PURSUIT OF ENTITLEMENTS

The titles of the chapter suggest the direction for the reading(s) that might follow. These seven candidates encapsulate seven different narrative possibilities; each paragraph that follows contributes more and less to the satisfaction of each. One might argue that this strategy of multiple titles is very efficient. Seven stories in the space of one. Those who are easily bored might be encouraged to mix the messages within multiple story frames and thus more actively engage the text by creating innovative outcomes. Yet others who value order and precision might be unsettled or offended, with so many doors left ajar, so many jars unsealed, so much that could be jarring. The blending of so many potent queries could lead to a breakdown, with a cacophony of sensual possibilities that could not be identified. For the postmodern fan, the move is more obvious: blurring the boundaries of what is and is not the point; leaving the text in disarray; pointing to the obvious in order to disappoint it; playing serious games, with no end in sight; positioning words so that they give and take from each other, without stopping in a place to be absorbed; teasing the reader with possibilities of memories, fantasies, and dreams that belong to them, and to us as well. Making the private conundrums into public nuisances.

What are the possibilities that are teasing us with their tantalizing frames? To expand on each, just slightly, may retrieve these high-flying textual missiles before they completely escape our stratospheres. Imaginative commitments might then be facilitated, so that one could say: "This is where I wish to begin."

"Gaze and the Naked Maja: Si(gh)tes for Controversy," the premier title, is the centerpiece of the eye-metaphor as it falls upon the centerfold of the piece, Maja (Figure 6.1), a name itself to be multiply taken. How shall we unfold the tale around this studied frame? As I suggest, it is a scene of conflictual sightings and sites. The eye (I) of the beholder, the sense of sight, the distant form of knowing, the having without holding—this metaphor marks the scientist, the objectivity maker, the masculine visionary, celebrated and reviled alike (Keller, 1985). In this story, who is the seer and who is the seen is a central pole of the polemic. In the version "Signification of Embodiment: When Mind Meets Matter," the emphasis turns to the cultural binary of the (masculinized) mind versus the (feminized) body. In this context, the narrative of the chapter is transformed into questions concerning the hegemonic privilege given in the culture to male minds over female bodies. "The Female Body and the Male Gaze: Eating Humble Pie" suggests the powerful position of the viewer over the viewed. Bodies are known as part of Nature and are assigned their value through the penetrating gaze of cultural authorities. Nature in this sense belongs to culture. The subtitle, inspired by a culinary metaphor, sets the epistemology of knowing as one of consuming, and, in this case, the eater is superior in status to the eaten. The story so entitled becomes a postmodern questioning of the organization of social life around these dualities of nature/culture, consumer/consumed. Does the pie always stay on her plate? (Felski, 1995). "Power of Mystification: Stripped Tease Pays Off" corrals the contradictory and consternating currents of conversation. Perhaps the events in question display the powers of womanliness and the enchantment of feminine wiles, which are strengthened in the hint of seductive undressing and are either enlarged or stripped away in a full unveiling. Does the Maja, in her pose, exude a powerful, mysterious presence, or has she been ripped off? Has she gained in her strip tease? Or has she been taken? With this title, the story line suggests other queries: Must women become denuded of their sexuality to become free and equal? To gain social leverage, must one be missed by the roving eye, thus overlooked? Or is the power of the body too valuable to deny? (Bayer & Malone, 1996; Kaite, 1995).

"Female Gaze: Blind Eye in a Vortex of Desire" is a topic that has no text. To have no gaze of one's own is to be, in some sense, blind. How can we look upon a man, especially a man we might desire, if we are blind? The way of looking is the way in which women have been looked upon. As women, we can look upon a woman with the eyes of a man (Mulvey, 1981). Is this the only way we might wish to do so? The story of desire is not for women to tell. To be desired, to lie back and be the center in the swirl—that is the role assigned to her (Kaplan, 1983). What is it to desire? What would such a story be? "Naked or Nude: The Power of the B(r)ush" again propels the story line into the thickets of intellectual power and dispute. The focus falls on the inevitable trio of art critic, artist, and model. Art is defined as the transformation of the natural, the ordinary, the profane into the refined, the acculturated, the sublime. Through the power of the artistic imagination, a creation is produced (Curtis, 1994). The image is the feat of the artist; it belongs to him, and she, as model, is part of the raw material under construction, with no voice, no claims, no rejoinders to his aims. Art is to be assessed, not by the objects, but by the critics. Through the power of the art critic, the "masterpiece" is assigned its value. Contrary voices, those who would speak for the silenced, are profane.

"Binary and Bodies: Pinning a Wench to the Wall" turns and returns, summing the slights and slings of gendered fortunes. Every element is kept in its place, in a hegemonic frenzy of order and control. Like a butterfly in a collector's box, the Maja cannot struggle to get free of her public place. Snugly situated in the historical niche of "objet d'art," she cannot wriggle out. Nor can those who might try to release the bondage of her fame/shame. Things are stuck; to get unstuck might disrupt the universal design. Reality is fixed in representations (Kappeler, 1986). It can't be undone.

ONE VERSION OF A TALE

Once upon a time, but not so very long ago, in the fall of 1991 to be more precise, while attending a meeting of the faculty senate of my university, I heard and overheard a series of rumors, snide remarks, outraged comments, furrowed-brow conversations, and more than a few jokes about an "incident" at a branch campus of the university. The gist of the story concerned the removal of a "painting" from a classroom at the request of an instructor of English, Nancy S.[1]

[The specific object was an old and somewhat faded poster reproduction in a rather tacky wooden frame. Speaking of frames, my comments upon the story I tell are found in this framing device, which I hope readers will not find similarly tacky.] A few months later, as a result of a flurry of media reports, mostly critical of the university's actions in removing the art work from the wall, the chair of the University Faculty Senate **[also professor and chair of the Department of English]** wrote an interoffice communication addressed to the chair**[men]** of four committees of the faculty senate that seemed especially involved in such affairs. In it he enclosed a packet of materials, including newsclips from various sources, local and national, related to the event and a draft of comments that he intended to make at the next senate meeting. Among his remarks were the following: Our university "has received some national attention as a result of an incident at the S_____ Campus, where a painting, Goya's *The Nude Maja,* and four others were removed from a classroom as a result of a protest from a teacher that the painting made her and some of her students uncomfortable and was a distraction to them." He phrased the controversy as follows:

> The conflict between competing principles . . . includes those which, on the one hand, would protect students and faculty from any act that could be interpreted as sexual harassment or which contributes to a chilly climate, particularly for women . . . ; and principles on the other hand which preserve academic freedom and free speech and which protect us all from the inroads of censorship.[2]

Although in the following semester, debates, discussions, and reports to the chair were created by these various committees, no action was subsequently taken by the faculty senate as a whole on this matter.

As reported in the newspapers, the instructor had been upset because students were making lewd remarks during class about the picture, which was hung on a wall directly behind the teacher's back. She found these reactions from some of the students [presumably men] offensive not only to her but to her female students. She requested the removal of the picture from a music instructor, who had some authority over the classroom decor. When he refused, she complained to the campus branch of the University's Commission for Women. [This commission had been established by the president of the university with the mandate to protect the interests of all women in the university.] The commission members investigated the incident and noted in their report:

> Female faculty find it difficult to appear professional when forced to lecture to a class with a picture of a female nude on the wall behind them. . . . It is difficult to speak to a person whose attention is riveted to a picture of a nude female on the wall.

The campus executive officer sent a memo to the campus community announcing that the "Affirmative Action Office had decided that an art reproduction hanging in C-203 could contribute to a chilly climate in that classroom and, thus, be in violation of the law concerning sexual harassment."

Reactions to this notice were mixed. The president of the student government association at the campus, Mr. N., was reported to say, "We think it's ludicrous censorship. I find it hypocritical that the university strives for cultural diversity and then removes pieces of culture from its classrooms. . . . It's a dangerous precedent to set—what's next?"[3] On November 15, a local campus community forum was first announced and later, on November 18, canceled. The same day, the instructor in question sent the following memo to the campus community:

> Since the subject of art has been a topic of discussion on campus lately, I thought some of you might enjoy reading about some of the latest research that has been published on the topic. John Berger presents a different perspective on art in his book *Ways of Seeing,* which departs considerably from the traditional interpretations, particularly concerning paintings of nudes. . . . I learned about the book at a faculty development seminar held at University Park [the major campus of the University] last summer. . . . I would be happy to discuss the ideas in this chapter with anyone who is interested.
>
> If you are not interested in reading a new perspective on art, feel free to chuck this article into the recycling bin.

Although the controversy seemed to have subsided at the local campus, editorials sprang up elsewhere, often with a humorous jab at the actors in the event. A column in the New York City *Daily News,* with the headline "Goosestepping on Goya," proclaimed:

> Listen up Penn State: Any professor so boorish as to complain that a painting by Goya is a form of sexual harassment should be encouraged to take up another line of work, preferably in another country. Iraq could probably use a few extra thought police. . . . Any college whose officials regard the paintings of an artist like Goya as "inappropriate for the classroom" does not deserve to be called a college. It should be stripped of its accreditation and razed with bulldozers.[4]

And the *Pottsville Republican* of the same day, citing the Commission on Women's report, stated:

> "Sexually graphic images create a chilly classroom environment which makes female teachers and students embarrassed and uncomfortable and diverts student attention from the subject matter. . . ."
>   It sounds, well, just silly. Goya, Mapplethorpe from Madrid? The "Maja" is hardly Hustler.
>   What's next, Mona Lisa's lascivious smile? Or "Blue Boy"? Can't you just hear it: What kind of young man would appear in public in that kind of get-up?

The historical setting is set. Does it set right with you? It is not unbiased. Yet I have resisted pointing out many subtleties—for example, the homophobic overtones to the last line—or perhaps its transvestite dream properties?

There are many conflicting, overlapping, and multiply interpretable opinions and events circulating in this controversy. What can be said beyond the taking of a stand, either for or against the action? As a faculty senate member, a psychologist who is concerned with gender relations, and a women's studies affiliate, how do I sort through the various emotional and intellectual possibilities available? Was it wrong or right? Or is it not so simple? What are the terms of the debate? What are the sides that are in opposition? Is it necessary to have opposition? Are there only two sides? How does the language reveal and conceal power differences at play? What are the power relationships engaging in this battle? Can one see it as a playing out of power struggles that go beyond, beneath, or beside the obvious instance of conflict?

Concerns with gender, language, power, and their intersections define the postmodern feminist. From this position, what is sayable about this "incident"? What interesting underlife might be revealed if this rocky debate were overturned? In which ways might the worms turn? The potentials for conversations are vast and amorphous. This is only a small first cut.

Terms of the Conflict

As we have already noted from the chair of the senate, the debate surrounding this conflict pits two sets of principles against one another. One of these polarities concerns the principle of free speech versus censorship. Those who emphasize this set of issues tend to be the full professors, editorialists, and male students, as well as art historians and museum curators; these people all stand for "free speech." The other set of principle polarities involves sexual harassment or "chilly climates" versus a safe environment in which women can pursue academic goals. This relatively new argument is represented by the instructor in question, the Commission on Women, and the Equal Opportunities Committee, who stand for the "safe environments for women" cause. Other members of the community vacillated and split between the two positive poles of the arguments: free speech versus a "safe" climate for women. Though we may agree that these two positions are taken from different binary pairs, the antagonists may wish to define them as resting on a single base: "free speech versus censorship" or "chilly climate versus safe climate."

But is that all there is to say? Should the reader be persuaded that "chilly climate" concerns are more important than free speech? Must I make an obvious and possibly boring feminist argument championing women's concerns? Or should I side with those who insist that this is clearly a case of censorship and agree that a cultural crime has been committed?

Instead, I would like to slice the seams of the positions, pull apart the weave a bit, and look at where the knots and tangles are. I do not expect to arrive at one tidy ending place, where all the rows are finally straight. I do not want to pick up all the stitches, knit up all the sleeves of care. Rather, I want to keep the ball rolling—circulating the sequiturs, enlivening ambiguities, keeping the knotty problems, in order to engage the reader in the fibrous textures. Perhaps we can reach a fuller appreciation, but not an ultimate understanding, of why problems such as this are persistent, if unresolved.

To begin, I construe in my inner dialogue a triangle, which is equilateral: At the apex, imagine the so-called Power Elite (full professors, the president of the university and his commissions, the media, the faculty senators and directors, the chairs of departments and committees, the executive officers of campuses, the university lawyers, and the director of the ACLU). At the lower left are the Boys (the "boys will be boys" boys. Those who made the lewd remarks and gestures. Not much has been said about them!). On the lower right is the Woman—the instructor at the branch campus, Nancy S. **[Put into this form, it suddenly appears as though it's 300 against 1. No wonder it seems so overwhelming.]** As for the Girls—they are outside the analysis. They are at the margins, good girls, better seen than heard. Girls serve two roles: audience and assumed victims. They do not dare to be on the woman's side. They are observing and learning, as one local women's commissioner said, "to keep their mouths shut if they don't like something."

Once I imagine this triangulation of power/relational lines, parallels with the historical beginnings of the painting come to mind. Now my triangle takes on a third dimension—one of historical time. The power struggles I conjure up today reverberated in the Spanish court almost 200 years ago. Issues of gender, status,

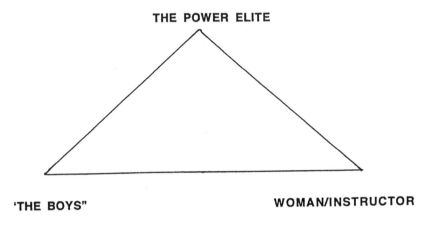

Figure 6.2. Triangulated Relationships, 1991 and 1801

and influence resound. I picture this image in Figure 6.2. In my story, I will explore these relationships in 1991 and then in 1801; the struggles and alliances produced today may indeed re-echo an old and familiar tale of human deeds.[5]

Let us consider that among and between each of the elements in the triangle there are power/relational lines carrying positive and negative connections— identities, complementarities, and oppositions, replete with dominations and submissions. Below the texts of censorship and "chilly climates" are power struggles/alliances that cannot surface without exposing and breaking the structural boundaries of authority and rules. Some things cannot be admitted; some things must be denied. Some who dare to challenge the system must be silenced; some who try to preserve the system must also be kept in line; some take a bit of comfort in the distress of others.

Each party of each triumvirate also struggles with the uneasy relations of its own separate substrates. No contestant is unified. Confusion and diffusion mask and betray the seeming solidity of each. Within the multiplicity of their voices alliances can be struck with others. Each one's enemy is also each one's friend. Each can help to defend against an Other. Yet power is not equally dispersed. The Power Elite will not tumble, at least not today. The tempest roils the waters of the shallows; damage control keeps stillness in the deep. The Power Elite may appear to have lost the battle, yet the system prevails. Let us look more closely at this array of forces. We shall start from below.

The Boys

The instigators of this dilemma, the male students in the class, are exposed to an art poster that creates ambivalent response possibilities for them. On the one hand, *The Naked Maja* is hung among four other reproductions whose subjects are not nude women; the presence in the classroom of these particular reprints suggests that they are valued cultural artifacts, quite likely masterpieces, which are to be respected, perhaps even revered. On the other hand, *The Naked Maja* looks very much like sexually arousing materials with which they are familiar, the prototype *Playboy* centerfold. The upstretched arms, the frontal nudity, the breasts and pubic hair displayed, the beguiling facial pose, lying on a bed—this is familiar stuff indeed. Yet if it is an erotic picture, don't they have a duty to respond, in keeping with their identities as sexually active young men? Isn't this what the cultural climate demands (Whatley, 1991)? The subject matter, the nudity, the bodily pose indicate that this is an object of lust.

[One might think twice about the word: Masterpiece. The master's piece? Something that the master finds erotic? Something belonging to the master? The piece who is mastered by another?]

By hanging it in a classroom, the adult authorities present this object as a challenge to this audience. "The meaning of this object is Culture," the Power Elite have declared. Do not dare to say that it is otherwise. **[Yes, the emperor is wearing beautiful clothes!]** The curriculum of the patriarchy requires this discipline. Yield to the judgments of your elders. The sexual aspect is to be silenced and denied.

[Ironically, if it is agreed that this is a masterpiece, then the possibility of enjoying the erotic aspects of the art is perpetuated. If the sexualized aspect of the painting is revealed, it must be condemned. Indeed, if the cultural value is threatened, then so too are those who established it as a "masterpiece" in the first place. It is undesirable to question authority figures.]

But the Boys do just that! Why? Perhaps it is just in order to undercut the authority figure before them. In this classroom, the male students are subjugated to a female professor. As a result, the identities of the parties are dual (at least), and they conflict with one another. Male is superordinate over female, as the painting suggests, but professor is superordinate over student. By defining the painting as an object of lust, the Boys emphasize heterosexual distinctions and the teacher's own femininity, and thus her concordance with the painting. By exposing her potential to become a naked Woman, they reduce their status deficit before her authority. She is embarrassed in a way that a male professor would not be because she cannot escape the identification with the model who is lying stretched naked in the frame behind her. By making remarks, the Boys suggest to her that she is not a real professor after all but just a Woman, who in the historical dimension of things is a permanent underclass to their designation. Though they may temporarily be adolescent students, eventually they will outgrow this youthful inconvenience. She, on the other hand, cannot outgrow her marked state.

The sexual remarks and innuendoes also threaten the stability of the male students' relationships with the professional men at the apex of the power triangle. In reacting to the sexuality of *The Naked Maja,* they tamper with the subterranean eroticism that is suppressed by the label *masterpiece.* As they threaten this definition, they potentially undermine those in authority over them. The Boys might be seen to be teasing their bosses with this play. Yet their "mischievousness" goes unpunished. No report, newspaper article, or commentary in this entire episode remarks on their questionable behavior. No male authority figure publicly chastises them or utters a condemning word about their actions. A silence settles. Their behavior passes as though it never happened. **[Why are they ignored?]** What happened **[read the newspapers]** is that a teacher lost control! Here is where the attention rests.

Eventually the rebellion is put down, in that the posters are removed from the classroom. Interestingly, the campus executive officer decides to remove all of the posters in the classroom, including a Madonna and Child, a still life, and a landscape, perhaps to suggest that he cannot tell what is so disturbing about the Goya print; he could be suggesting that something else may be offensive to this teacher next week, or to some other "difficult woman" in the future. The edict to remove the *Maja* comes via "soft" sources of power, the Commission on Women. Though the commission operates at the request of the president and thus is subject to his goodwill, it is normally not in the mainstream of power politics in the university. By allowing the Boys to lose their "centerfold" through women's offices, the perpetrators are rebuked, but not by the actual male authorities. If they had protested against male authority more directly, they would have faced more traditional male/male punishments, such as banishment (suspension), or "academic" death (expulsion).[6]

The Woman/Instructor

The Woman is clearly a fragmented person from the start. She is a hermaphrodite, a member of the male elite in drag. (In power terms, professors are stereotypically male, whereas students are female.) As a female, she is the object of the painter's delight. She shares the bodily form of the maja, despite the "dress for success" suit in which she may be disguised. But she is also a scholar, a representative of the Establishment. Playing these roles, she vacillates in her allegiances. But in neither imago can she find refuge. As Woman, she bears the brunt of the Boys' lascivious remarks. As Professor, she must control them. When she seeks assistance from her "fellows," she finds that she is rebuked. What is her problem? they want to know. Professor of English Michael B., one of her departmental colleagues at the main campus **[note the three status differences: male; professor; main campus]**, sums up the rejection of her: "I think it's ridiculous that people **[Nancy S., in this case]** can't tell the difference between culture and sexual harassment."

But the gaze of the master's is not her gaze. The female gaze is double. As a Woman who looks at *The Naked Maja,* or other such portrayals of a nude, she cannot "see straight." Her visions are twofold, as the object of the painting and as the viewer. Identifying oneself as the object can induce many feelings—shame, pride, envy, desire. As object, she knows that she has become a spectacle by proxy. "Making a spectacle out of oneself seems a specifically feminine danger. The danger . . . of an exposure . . . [of being] caught out by fate and blameworthy. . . . Any woman could make a spectacle out of herself if she was not careful" (Russo, 1986, p. 213). Gil Saunders (1989), art critic and author, has described what it means to be a spectacle: "The nude female body is commonly presented as sexual spectacle, the picture set up as an invitation to voyeurism. . . . Nakedness is regarded as a culpable incitement to male lust" (p. 23).

Being blamed for inciting men to lust is fraught with problems.

To appear naked before men is to make a spectacle of oneself. One becomes ashamed if one is seen to entice the gaze of men. One can be punished.

There is also a mocking pride that comes of knowing that you can capture the gaze of the powerful. To be capable of upsetting the order of the male establishment by lying naked would be almost humorous, a joke on them, if one were safe.

The other seeing is also complex—as viewer, as a spectator rather than a spectacle. What is the nature of her female gaze? Does she have one? I think not, or only barely. As voyeur, she has learned to look with male eyes. She cannot "see for herself." She too can see only what has been defined as the seeable (Grosz, 1994). Women are indoctrinated with the same categories of the real as men. Yet for women this becomes a paradox. When looking at a painting, a woman sees the object with her "male" gaze, but she also recognizes herself as the object that is seen. In this sense, she does a "double take": responding to the demands to see the painting as a cultural product, as a masterpiece perhaps, yet also responding as the exposed model attracting gaze. She is aware from all of her other experiences in the culture of the multiple meanings of a naked woman. Under what circumstances are naked women observed by the populace, especially of men? Except for "art," in sexual-eyed circumstances. She vacillates among these views.[7] As the viewer, she can respond to the artistic merits of the "piece." She can also resonate to the sensual desires that a naked woman can arouse. [**The easy access to lesbian desire in our culture, its naturalness, is prepared for in this gaze.**] The sensual pleasures of the naked woman are as available to women as to men when they see/feel through the same gaze, yet desiring as a woman is a missing discourse (Fine, 1992). One can also understand the taboo on naked males as artistic objects and the homophobic responses and shame when "straight" men and women look upon the picture of a naked man (Figure 6.3).[8]

To see with a male gaze a painting of a nude female model requires the denial of identification with the painting's object and the suppression of any negativity derived from possessing such a flawed vision. To admit to discomfort is to expose oneself to ridicule: Only the ignorant take a masterpiece for a personalized object of sexual consequence. Denial of the "fact" that one, as woman, is also objectified puts one on the side of the power brokers and away from the object itself. Louise K., associate professor of art history at the main campus, plays this part: "If Nude Maja is sexual harassment, every nude painting is sexual harassment. I think sexual harassment is out of hand. . . . Where's it going? Some professor could find paintings of trees offensive."[9] Another woman art critic, who must decide whether to dismiss her identification with the model or be "exposed" as an ignorant professor, takes a middle ground. She rejects the Maja as a "victim," despite her nakedness, and thus is also able to defend her own precarious double birth: "La Maja is sexual in its connotation. . . . It's more than a naked woman with upstretched arms. . . . The woman possesses dignity and confidence. She's nobody's victim."[10] Another voice, one that might raise the eyebrows of the Establishment, is heard from a woman who is the associate curator of education at the Allentown Art Museum:

> The Maja paintings "are great works. But let's face it; the standards were set by white men. . . . We cannot ignore the fact that values are involved in art and that women have been portrayed as whores, lovers, madonnas, and virgins. . . . Artistic images are responsible for perpetuating stereotypes."[11]

Despite the antagonisms of the Boys and the Woman/Instructor for each other, it is important to mention that they are also allies, at least partially and temporarily; they are both subjugated by their superiors within the Power Elite. All of them in their own way need the alliance of each other to stand against the enforcement of

Figure 6.3. Male Nude

the High Culture authority. Most often, this is a productive relationship. The teachers at the branch campuses assist their young students to gain access to the main campus and to "higher" levels of education. This is their mutual aim. This time, the alliance has broken down. The Power Elite sides with the Boys against the Woman, who also represents the Girls—or at least thinks she does. Yet the Girls never give her that satisfaction, at least not in any recorded form. The only female student quoted in the news clippings had this to say: "The guys don't make us feel like sex objects or mothers, and I didn't feel that way when I looked at the painting."[12]

The Power Elite: A View From the Top

The male establishment [**let me try not to make them sound like the forces of the Evil Empire**] effects control by defining the nature of cultural resources and their distribution. It supports the view that *The Naked Maja* is a respectable element in the dominant culture. This position is developed via intellectual argumentation and bolstered by claims to traditional authorities. This position is exemplified in a comment from a professor of art history and the director of the Institute for the Arts and Humanistic Studies that seems designed to educate as well as to rebuke the instructor, her supporters, and the "naughty" children:

> What is most distressing about this incident . . . was the panic reaction of a University committee and the administration. . . . The *Naked Maja* is, in fact, is half of a double masterpiece, the other half being a representation of the same figure fully clothed. . . . It is possible, for instance, that the pictures constituted a nineteenth-century restatement of the old theme of sacred and profane love. [**The professor then goes on to suggest that in a clever reversal on the painter's part, the naked woman may actually represent sacred, rather than profane, love.**] . . . A discussion of this kind of the eternal human dilemma (see Plato and St. Paul) [**two great feminist authors and friends to women, I note tongue in cheek**] as manifested in art would have been a far more useful . . . approach at the university level to questions raised by a venerable masterpiece on view. . . . All uneducated fantasies stimulated by a prurient television culture could have been instantly dispelled.[13]

We may note the creative lengths to which the professor goes to bury any suggestion of eroticism in the painting. Not only is it a great masterpiece, but it may represent the highest type of love, as manifested by Christ and his disciples. Only the victims of television drivel would think otherwise.

The professor is not alone in his condemnation of the prudish, repressive, and possibly ignorant authorities who supported the removal of the picture. Amitai Etzioni, well-known sociologist and editor of *The Responsive Community: Rights and Responsibilities,* added to this theme in an editorial for the *Philadelphia Inquirer*[14] in which he critically denied the suggestion that one could be humiliated by a piece of art: "Above all I find it very difficult to see how a classical painting is capable of *harassing* anyone."

Yet why is it so important for the Power Elite to stand firmly behind the legitimacy of showing this cheap and faded reproduction of a painting of a naked woman? John Berger (1972), art critic and author, had this to say: "Art . . . justifies most other forms of authority. . . . Art makes inequality seem noble, and hierarchies seem thrilling" (p. 29). Berger also argued that the power conveyed in attributing masterpiece status to a work of art is also distributed to the entire setting in which it is placed. To degrade the status of a masterpiece is to threaten the power structure of the university. Recall the concerns of the student government president. How revealing of the masculine dilemma he is when he parrots the Power Elite's stand for free speech: "It's a dangerous precedent to set—what's next?" This comment puts into words the fears of a patriarchal order. One day it's *The Naked Maja*; the next, it may be some other privilege that "they" will seek to challenge.

The paradoxical task of emphasizing the cultural value of the image while denying its rhetorical power as a sex object is important to the maintenance of structural orders. Classifying the painting as art is necessary to allow its display. Culture demands that erotic desire be controlled. It must be rationed, according to the provisions of the cultural elite. One must go to the right places and know the right people to see sexualized imagery. Only that which is denied status as sexual can be easily displayed; "pornography"—which is by definition prurient—becomes illegal. The benefits of this control of meaning—that is, defining what is art and what is pornography—adhere to the elite. It is suspected that if the masses were allowed easy and open access to sexuality, order might be undercut, thereby threatening the controlling privileges of the elite. Thus, denial of the overt nature of the sexual imagery is rampant. An example of denial in this case is evident in the remarks of the legal director of the Pennsylvania Chapter of the ACLU:"There's no case law that would apply to the display of a Goya nude. . . . My sense is that any court would probably reject [that] it's sexually explicit out of hand" (*The Morning Call*, Nov. 24, 1991, p. B8). The courts support the supposition that *The Naked Maja* is not erotic.

If we look at the dilemmas at the top from a more sympathetic view, it is very possible that we can take the Father-Professors at their word. They do not find *The Naked Maja* a turn-on. Its value as erotica has been spent over the ages since its unveiling. Its status as masterpiece is the respectful residue of the dying flame of desire. It no longer moves the groin of the experienced man. Only freshmen (is it redundant here to write *boys*?) trapped in an English class could generate this kind of sexual response. The issue then becomes one of discipline, indoctrination into the values of Western civilization and submission to the order of the university, "for their own good." The conflict between the Boys and the Instructor is only ostensibly about *The Naked Maja*. It is actually about who has power and authority. The authorities must side with the female professor, and her status must be upheld, but she is a damn nuisance if she cannot control these boys better than that. (Why can't she just convinced them via "discussion"?)

Finally, the Power Elite must contend with the shame that occurs when a father cannot keep peace in his own household. What originally was a "housekeeping" chore at a minor campus became international headline news. This media blitz was very unsettling to the image-conscious administrators. The major concern of the university Power Elite has been to look good in the eyes of the public world. If you have recently been accepted into the Big Ten (a conference of universities that is first of all about athletics) and are jockeying to be considered one of the elite public universities in the nation, it is embarrassing to have your dirty linen washed in public. Note the comments from two professors on the outcome of the hearing: "It's . . . a knee jerk reaction that makes us look very small town" ("Controversy," 1991, p. 2) and

> When Penn State's reaction to complaints about Goya's *Maja Desnuda* [note the formal title] not only made the local and national press but was also given space in the newspapers of England and Japan, the attitude toward the humanities at the University as well as the international perception of our cultural level were very poorly served. ("Director's Editorial," 1991, p. 1)

At the same time, professors who have devoted their lives to open inquiry, defending free speech and working for justice and truth, are appalled at the march to oppression they see in the removal of a piece of art from a classroom. As one instructor said, "No matter what guise or avenue is taken here, it's censorship. . . . These are crazy times . . . chilling times."

HISTORICAL REMINISCENCES: A TALE OF POWER/RELATIONAL REINSCRIPTIONS

There are parallels to this complicated story in the hazy history of the painting itself. The tensions of power that stress the parties of Penn State are replicated in the distant past. What happened then is a matter of historical speculations, but this is one possible narrative.

In the time before photography, kings, prime ministers, and nobles enjoyed the pleasures of sexually explicit images via paintings, often of their lovers and concubines (Lucie-Smith, 1972). These private pictures were commissioned and shared among the noblemen of Europe as Parisian postcards might have been traded in Les Halles 50 years ago and as pornographic pictures are displayed on the Internet today. As Gil Saunders (1989) has said,

> As a genre the female nude (there is no male equivalent) has no purpose beyond the more or less erotic depiction of nakedness for male consumption. The male artist constructs for his own or for his male patron's enjoyment the perfect partner—passive, receptive, available. (p. 23)

It is likely that *The Naked Maja* was one of these sexual paintings. (The fully clothed *Maja* too had strong erotic overtones. The model was not as modestly attired as the title may suggest; she was robed in a flimsy gown, much in the way a modern stripper might be covered in a veil.)

The Boys

In the shadow of this triangle, we can glimpse a repetitions of struggles found in the Penn State case. Goya in this parallel play takes the same position as the Boys in the previous example. Rather than reacting with sexual remarks, as the Boys did, Goya painted the Duchess of Alba for the pleasures of the Prime Minister of Spain. This commission served Goya well in all facets of his life. By pleasing his patron, the prime minister, he stabilized his position as court painter; his portraits of the royal family and others in high positions gained him money and prestige. His relationship with the prime minister ensured his son a financially secure future, even after Goya's death. Yet Goya's actions as an artist were also rebellious toward authority, and painting lewd pictures of a member of the aristocracy was shocking and offensive to many high-ranking people in the court and in the ecclesiastical orders. His relationship to his model, the Duchess of Alba, was complex. Like the male students, Goya experienced the dual conflicting relations of masculine dominance over her femininity and social inferiority to her noble heritage. Goya's associations with the duchess's family included painting formal portraits of her husband and herself. After her husband died, the duchess invited Goya to her country place, where he painted a portrait of her wearing two rings, one engraved with the name of her husband and the other with Goya's. In the sand at her feet, she points with her bejeweled finger, to the words *solo [only] Goya* lightly sketched there (Trapier, 1964). It has been speculated that Goya used the portrait to prove the lady's love and loyalty to him despite their social differences. As for the *Maja* paintings, he may have been motivated by many influences—to celebrate their liaison, to please the prime minister, or possibly to seek revenge against her.[15] That their relationship ended badly is suggested by several of his sketches. One that seems to recall their alienation, *Sueño de la Mentira y de la Inconstancia* ("A Dream of Lying and Inconstancy"), seems to depict Goya and the duchess (Trapier, 1964, p. 14). Goya often used his artistic talent to diminish his social superiors, and he satirized the noble families that he painted, including the queen, who was often the subject of his most critical caricatures.

Some art critics have suggested that the portrait of *The Naked Maja* is a fake. That is, it has been conjectured that Goya painted the duchess's face on the nude body of another model; this possibility is enhanced by the knowledge that in this same period, a similar painting purportedly of a nude "Marie Antoinette" was discovered to be fraudulent. It is clear the family of the duchess was distressed by the notion that the nude body portrayed in the painting was hers. In 1945, over 100 years after the painting was created, the family of the duchess, denying that she was Goya's nude model, had her casket exhumed to prove that the bodily measurements of the model could not have been hers; nothing conclusive was established in the examination of her corpse, however (Schickel, 1968).

Though we may be unaware of the historical importance of this nude painting, and rather inured to its effects, what must have been the reactions of those who saw it when it was newly painted? Contrary to the claims of some art historians, in 18th-century Spain paintings of nudes were extremely rare and almost always prohibited from being shown. When the authorities of the Inquisition became aware of the *Maja* paintings, Goya was called before their court. As fortunate as the Boys of Penn State, he was apparently not convicted of any crime, his status was not impaired, and no fine was levied. Historians suspect that interventions by unnamed high-ranking authorities protected him (Schickel, 1968).

The Woman

Turning to the Woman's side of the triangle, we see the sole representative here, the Duchess of Alba. The duchess was a prominent noblewoman who had an international reputation for her beauty, charm, and daring. "A French traveler described her: 'The Duchess of Alba has not a single hair on her head that does not awaken desire. Nothing on earth is as beautiful as she is.'" (Trapier, 1964, p. 14). She was prone to emotional shifts and was easily bored with her companions. She seems to have been attracted to Goya, became involved with him, and posed for him on several occasions. She also may have been involved in a romantic affair with the prime minister; at least, the paintings suggest that possibility. Her relationships with both men are full of the potential for attraction and revenge. The social position of the duchess parallels that of the Woman/Instructor in the university situation. The duchess had, on the one hand, social power over Goya and was on a par, at least theoretically, with the prime minister. The prime minister, in fact, had much more political power than she. As a woman, she occupied a subordinate role to both Goya and the prime minister. Yet in terms of personal power, she may have challenged each of them, and they may have colluded in defiling her reputation with this painting. Other possibilities also are imaginable.

Like the Woman/Instructor in the contemporary story, who also has institutional authority, the duchess is in an ambiguous position. She cannot control the response to her image, and she cannot escape it. Even 200 years later, boys are making fun at the expense of her body placed in view by the Power Elite. The right to reveal or conceal still belongs to the established authorities.[16]

The Male Power Elite

At the apex of this fantasy triangle we can place the prime minister of Spain, whose family was registered as the owner of the *Maja* paintings from the early 1800s. The sexual appetites and conquests of this man were infamous in his day, and he had a liaison with the queen, as well as with most of the women in the court whom he desired. He was a powerful man in both private and public spheres, handsome, youthful, and vigorous. The prime minister controlled the major power avenues in Spain and was influential with the forces of the Inquisition. He was supported in his position by artists such as Goya who could realize his prurient fantasies, as well as signify in paintings the importance of the nobility in Spain. He also depended on his liaisons with powerful women to seal his position and to prove his ascendancy over them. The *Maja* paintings may have served as trophies, proving his intimacy with the popular and elusive duchess; they may also have been cherished relics of an intense love affair. Or they may have served as fraudulent indicators of either. The power of his family and later arbiters of taste to endorse them as cultural icons secreted from historical view their private erotic significance to the prime minister and thus saved the family from potential embarrassment. Today, the erotic elements of the story are deeply suppressed. The family was simply fortunate enough to inherit Goya masterpieces (Schickel, 1968). In this sense, the prime minister's family, like the patriarchal "family" of the university, constructs the paintings as masterpieces in order to maintain their respect, suppress or deny their own erotic fantasies, and keep the cultural order intact.

SOME CONCLUDING COMMENTS

Regardless of the times, the tensions between youth and maturity among people of different social ranks and interests and between men and women, with all of their connections and antagonisms, cannot easily be clarified or resolved. Despite the commingling of contradictory desires, necessities, and resistances, it would appear that the investment in the status quo is strongest among the senior male elite. For them, the power to marshal and control cultural resources is never far from hand. Whether moving a painting constitutes a threat to that stability is, perhaps, a strange question. Yet, clearly, revering or challenging a painting is a political act, with many ramifications for the negotiation of power relations.

Though it may seem from these stories that the Power Elites are well in control and enjoying their privileges, it is also worth considering the extent to which they become trapped into their roles, recognize the limitations of their powers, and desire more flexibility in their activities (Armstrong, 1989; Snow, 1989). Are there fissures, overlaps, gaps, and contradictions in the discourses of aesthetic valuing that might allow male gazes to become unfixed from their authorized positions? Can the possibilities of what is seeable be expanded? Some are optimistic: "Once the dominant male gaze becomes introspective, is averted because of shame or understanding, it can no longer maintain its innocent superiority atop the hierarchical pyramid" (Nochlin, 1991, p. 14). Can a democratic vision be created in which dominance can be replaced by an egalitarian or sympathetic perspective (Curtis, 1994)? How might this unsettlement be effected?

Beyond the questioning of whose powers are being maintained by these gendered and status-bound processes of negotiating and who loses in the process is the question of how these differences of gender, generation, and status themselves become constructed (K. J. Gergen, 1996). Instead of merely adjudicating between these competing groups, might we step back to contest the categories themselves that separate each from each? What power/relations might be collapsed if we were to question the firmness of these identity frames and formulating practices? If identities are multiple, fluid, and situated in time and place, can new relational bonds be forged? Could a psychology that engaged in relational forms instigate a new beginning for gendered politics?

Once these issues are addressed, the possibility of disrupting "the foundations that cover over alternative cultural configurations" is begun (Butler, 1990, p. 147). The breaking down of established categories, traditional oppositions and binaries such as mind versus body, culture versus nature, and the viewer versus the viewed, allows the tendrils of unification and commonalities across these former divides to take root. Within each identifiable difference are elements of sameness. The nonunity of each claimed unit produces the option of reorganizing that can produce different, and temporary, identities. The potential for people to slide among positions in such a space becomes tantalizingly clear. Of particular fascination in the case of *The Naked Maja* is the "political" issue of how "desire" is created, instigated, and controlled (Davies, 1994). The struggle over meaning and the definition of reality within forms of popular culture is ultimately over the investment of desire (McWilliam & Jones, 1996). Thus, "The mobilizing and controlling of desire becomes a contradictory politics of pleasure, subject to the processes of hegemony and ideology" (Gotfrit, 1991, p. 185). What factors contain our desires, and how might we wiggle free? Can desire be constructed as an emanation of relatedness, beyond the fixity of sexual categories? Shall desire remain a unitary category or be construed differently or not at all?

This speculative closure is merely to suggest how "de-binary" processes can subvert the certitudes of reality claims. Questioning the natural divisions of binary oppositions leads to a dynamic tumult. And there is much potential for envisioning new dis-orders in the ensuing flux (M. M. Gergen, 1992b; Hekman, 1990). We might revel in the possibility of inducing a bit of chaos into the world. As Jane Flax (1987) has put it, in a now familiar phrase, "If we do our work well, 'reality' will appear even more unstable, complex, and disorderly than it does now" (p. 643). In the appeal of this dictum, we discover new beginnings. From the chaotic, new relations can be born, with new potentials for harmony.

NOTES

1. Though Ms. S.'s name was used in early newspaper reports and in interoffice correspondence, it was later dropped for reasons of confidentiality. The names of others involved in the controversy have also been shielded in similar fashion.

2. The headlines of the stories that the chair included with the memo generally centered on the censorship issue, and most decried the action: "Removal of Goya Instigates Cries of Censorship"; " 'Offensive' Art's Removal Disturbs Some Experts"; "Painting Yanked After Sexual Harassment Plea"; "Students: Removal of Classroom Art Censorship"; "If You Enjoy 'Maja' Fine; If You Don't, Look the Other Way"; "Goya Classic Yanked as 'Sexual' No-No"; and "Challenges to Artworks Raise Questions of Censor-

ship." Only one headline, an editorial from the student newspaper *Intercom,* November 21, 1991, referred to the harassment issue: "Not Censorship, University Made Right Choice in Removing Painting From Room."

3. *Collegian,* November 15, 1991, p. 10. The phrase *ludicrous censorship* was repeated in *Newsweek,* November 25, 1991, p. 6, and *USA Today,* November 15, 1991, Lifeline.

4. November 16, 1990, p. C-10.

5. Drawing upon Michel Foucault's analysis of power/knowledge relations (1979), I suggest here the desirability of defining interpersonal life as existing with power as a constitutive aspect of all relationships.

6. The loss was only temporary, however. Through legal niggling on the part of the administration, the "boys" and their supporters, in some sense, evaded the ban; the poster was rehung in a student lounge area that was hastily relabeled a "gallery."

7. Susan Hekman (1990) argued that new subjectivities can be fashioned through the spaces and contradictions in existing language forms. These gaps, openings, silences, and ambiguities, which provide resistance against dominant discourse, offer the possibility of formulating new languages that challenge the status quo. Perhaps women can see otherwise if they use their "peripheral" vision.

8. What happens if the powerful male gaze falls upon the male genitals when they are displayed in a fashion similar to female nudes? According to the *Philadelphia Inquirer* (June 23, 1992), Rupert Murdoch fired Fox Broadcasting President Stephen Chao on the spot for hiring a male model to strip at a network management conference in Aspen, Colorado. . . . A witness who spoke yesterday on condition of anonymity said the stripper walked into the meeting wearing a business suit and removed all his clothes, standing a few feet from [Secretary of Defense, Dick] Cheney. Chao was giving a speech on network censorship. Murdoch called it a tremendous misjudgment.

Again according to the *Philadelphia Inquirer* (June 27, 1992), in Buffalo, New York, the major ordered a Billie Lawless sculpture *Green Lightning* taken down just 5 days after it was installed. Major James Griffin said, "The sculpture was embarrassing." The statue was of dancing penises wearing top hats!

9. *Collegian,* November 15, 1991.

10. *Morning Call,* November 24, 1991, p. B8.

11. *Morning Call,* November 24, 1991, p. B8.

12. *Morning Call,* November 24, 1991, p. B8.

13. *Newsletter for the Institute for the Arts and Humanistic Studies,* Spring 1992.

14. June 22, 1992, p. A11.

15. It is also interesting to note that *Venus in the Looking Glass,* the only nude painting by Velázquez, the great Spanish master of the 17th century, was the property of the Alba family until 1808. Certainly Goya was familiar with this painting and may also have been inspired by it to create his own painting of a nude woman on a divan.

16. One might note a certain parallel between the lives of Princess Diana and the Duchess of Alba in terms of efforts to both reveal and conceal their private lives. Perhaps the major difference in these triangles between the court life of 1800 and 2000 is that the camera has replaced paint and canvas.

PART II

Performative Psychology

Whys and Whereabouts

The last two chapters of this volume are forms of theatrical presentations that have been developed in recent years under the rubric of performative psychology. As mentioned in the introductory chapter, performative psychology serves as a medium through which psychology as a discipline is expanding. The turn toward the performative is correlated with the breakdown in the assumption of traditional science that language is an accurate reflection of reality. It is important to acknowledge that the gap cannot be bridged between what there is in the so-called "real world" and how we present it in symbolic terms. If this is so, then there is no one right way of presentation, no privileged vocabulary, not even the primacy of the word over other forms of representation. At the same time, it is generally agreed that it is through language and other symbolic forms that our sense of the real is produced. Language is no longer thought to be inconsequential in the development of factual statements. Rather, all language becomes performative. And the performance is the creation of the real. How communities implement discursive practices is critical to how they produce and engage with each other and what they take to be "reality."

Once this perspective is taken, the boundary between performance as an art form and as a generative source of scientific activity becomes blurred. That is, there is no a priori justification for requiring one set of symbolic forms for doing research and presentation over another. The reasons for engaging in a particular manner of presentation must come from elsewhere. In the case of a performatively oriented psychology, these rationales emerge both from within the community that creates and nurtures the practice and from beyond, from other intellectual streams. In this sense, one does not do performative psychology alone. Others must be willing to coengage and affirm the practices. We generate meaning and significance together. How we go on together is something we cannot as individuals predict or control. Meanings emerge from our togetherness. The forms of meaning we create can be expanded beyond our own individual dreams. They may lead us into fearful nightmares as well.

A key feature of this orientation is its emphasis on the arbitrary nature of any enactment. Nothing is required in terms of defining our worlds, except as our community demands. Actors and audiences are sensitive to the process of interaction itself and of the context shared in such activity. This awareness fosters reflexivity among them. They ask: What is it we are doing here right now? Part of this reflexivity is to reckon with the perspective of the performers themselves, including their value investments, tactics of persuasion, and place/time limits. Thus, performative psychology can be critical or appreciative, with no pretenses of value neutrality or indifference to the subject matter or to the formal qualities of the performance. In this manner, the knowledge/power nexus is acknowledged; one can, for example, express one's feminist positions unabashedly.

A performance is always open-ended in itself and subject to the wills and won'ts of participants, observers, and authorities. The boundaries between the roles of researcher, researched, and reviewer are blurred in performative psychology. Where research begins and ends also becomes unclear once the participatory aspect of performative psychology is taken seriously. If research is about generating knowledge, and if the performance of an activity among participants is a generative process, then the performance itself can be considered part of the discovery component of research.

What are the advantages of expanding and transforming existing modes of doing research to include performance? Some of the most significant are to facilitate the creation of new and potentially more desired forms of reality through enhancing the repertoire of linguistic and symbolic resources available to various communities; to join in the dialogues attracting the attention of other communities of discourse, especially those involving postmodern ideas; and to reach out to an expanded audience of participants beyond the academy.

Performative psychology supports the notion that human communication is embodied and affective, as well as intellectual, and that all our sense modalities operate at once during communication activity. If we wish to communicate what it is like for a woman to miscarry a much longed-for child during the second trimester, as has happened to two of my friends in recent months, is a report of a depression scale score the best way to do this? Do we want to limit ourselves to statistics, "objective" case study descriptions, or other scientific modes of address? Or might dances, poems, diary entries, sonograms, or songs be as or more appropriate and compelling? Why should we have to exclude any of them, in principle? By combining affective and bodily elements with intellectual ones, performative psychology expands the range of possibilities for producing, interpreting, and displaying psychological research. Visual images, dance, poetry, role play, music, drama, and sounds, among other means, expand the rhetorical strength of a performance and allow the actors and audience to work intuitively as well as logically.

Performative psychology is also responsive to the general climate of activities and ideas in other scholarly arenas, especially within the postmodern. As mentioned in Chapter 1, researchers in anthropology, sociology, women's studies, and other neighboring disciplines have been producing works that are performative in nature. Each of them is borrowing heavily from the humanities and the arts. Recently, a special discipline called performative studies has emerged. It has been defined by Marvin Carlson (1996) in his text *Performance* as follows:

> Performance . . . is a specific event with its liminoid nature foregrounded, almost invariably clearly separated from the rest of life, presented by performers and attended by audiences both of whom regard the experience as made up of material to be interpreted, to be reflected upon, to be engaged in—emotionally, mentally, perhaps even physically. This particular sense of occasion and focus as well as the overarching social envelope combine with the physicality of theatrical performance to make it one of the most powerful and efficacious procedures that human society has developed for the endlessly fascinating process of cultural and personal self-reflection and experimentation. (pp. 198-199)

The work of Laurie Anderson, both live performances and installations of interactive performance art, is a fascinating exemplar of how performance can be effective in promoting ideas that connect diverse disciplinary interests, including those of psychology.

In terms of reaching out to diverse audiences, one of the appealing aspects of a performative style in which artistic and entertainment devices are used is that it is often more familiar to a broad audience than ordinary scientific writings. Generally, investigations of readership have indicated that most articles in highly esteemed scientific journals are read thoroughly by very few. Surely one reason for this is that they are so difficult and unappealing linguistically that only those heavily invested in a particular topic plunge ahead through the thickets of arcane language and statistics. Performative pieces trade in the currency of everyday encounters, the performing arts, and the media, which allows them to be more accessible to people outside academic enclaves as well as within. Researchers who wish to make a difference in the society are likely to be attracted to this possibility. One dramatic illustration of this approach is the work of psychologists Glenda Russell and Janis Bohan (1999), who organized an oratorio from data collected in interviews regarding the psychological consequences of anti-gay politics. The piece was performed by a professional chorus for a broad public audience.[1] Through the production of new forms of presentations, the sense of what can be said to exist is altered, and thus new options for action are created.

Despite these intriguing advantages, one of the apparent disadvantages of performance psychology is its ephemeral quality. Although performative psychology is often a live performance in "real time," as is now said, this need not be an attribute of the endeavor. It is still possible to codify, videotape, and store performances so that they can be archived for future use. Not only do the scripts I have written as Chapters 7 and 8 stabilize my performances, but the written text allows time for reflection, which is missing in a visual staging of the piece. In this sense, the visual and the textual forms can complement each other.

The performative pieces in the chapters to follow have been presented in a variety of settings in the United States, Europe, and Australia. I have included many of the theatrical aspects through stage directions and descriptions of how the performance is to occur. As is the case when we read a play designed to be acted on a stage, much is missing from this particular form. My experience has been that the audience often cannot "make sense" with me to the degree that I have desired because there is too much that is unfamiliar and complex. For this reason, the written text holds some advantages over the staged one. Given the nature of the chapters as dramatic readings, some readers might like to reproduce them in some fashion. You have my permission to make of them what you will. You may play with the plays.

Chapter 7, "Woman as Spectacle," is designed to foster interest in the manner in which psychology deals with the topic of "women over 40." It functions as a literature review, emphasizing the lack of attention in psychology to this period of life and the negativity of the few psychological theories that are related to them. My script challenges conventional notions that the proper woman should disappear after she has begun to age. Drawing on literary, philosophical, and psychological sources, I enact ways that women might fight against the societal pressures that try to force them out of the dance of life and into the wallpaper.

The counterposition I take involves wearing startlingly bright and sexualized clothes, a big curly blond wig, and gobs of jewelry and makeup. The script is accompanied by a "limited" striptease. All of the physical gestures and clothes are designed to provoke audience responses related to the central issues of the performance.

"Against Mod Mascu-linity and Post-Mod Macho: A Feminist End-Game," the concluding chapter, is introduced from within. The first performative piece I wrote, it was presented in 1989 at a conference on postmodernity in Aarhus, Denmark. With its complex interplay of word games and double entendres, it is easier read aloud than heard. Because the chapter promotes a strong positive stance toward value-invested work, it is especially harmonious with feminist views. There are many rewards and plentiful dangers in engaging in this kind of enterprise, but from the general response it has received among curious graduate students and new doctorates, as well as active midcareer professionals in diverse fields, I believe that performance modes are among the innovative methods that will continue to grow in size, diversity, and respectability into this century; in addition it is exciting, challenging, and fun to do. I hope to entice readers and future performers into further explorations of this genre with this exposure.[2]

NOTES

1. A summary of this research activity is found in a special issue of *Psychology of Women Quarterly* on innovative methods, edited by Mary Crawford and Ellen Kimmel (1999), along with a review piece by Gergen, Joan Chrisler, and Alice LoCicero (1999) that includes references relevant to performative psychology as well as other forms of innovative methods.

2. Perhaps it is fitting to list some of the other writers who are developing this area with, and for, as well as within psychology: Barry (1996), Billig (1994), Blumenfeld-Jones (1995), Carlson (1996), Case (1997), Case, Brett, and Foster (1995), Cochran (1986), Denzin (1997), Donmoyer and Yennie-Donmoyer (1995), Dudek (1996), Ellis and Bochner (1996), Finley and Knowles (1995), Game (1988), Lather and Smithies (1997), Letherby (1995), McCall (2000), Mienczakowski (1996), Mienczakowski, Smith, and Sinclair (1996), Morris (1995), Newman and Holzman (1996), Smyth (1991), Tierney (1995), and Ussher (1994).

7

Woman as Spectacle[1]

or,

Facing Off
Cavorting With Carn-ival Knowledge

Woman as Spectacle. This is me, as I am here, as I am pictured (Figure 7.1). It is important that I am gaspingly noticeable. I attract attention. The attention is not altogether admiring. In fact, it is shocking to many in the audience that a woman past 50 would wear such colors, in such combinations, with sexual overtones in her demeanor and garments, engaging in mildly impolite activities, such as chewing gum, swigging brandy from a flask, carrying a cigar, telling jokes. I call myself POMO, a play on postmodern, and Mama, and other things.

The second title, "Facing Off: Cavorting With Carn-ival Knowledge," which I have used on occasion, suggests the process of losing face—that is, of discarding the mask of propriety, which I am doing in my performance. At the same time, *facing off* is a hockey term, in which two players of opposite teams face each other and vie for the puck through their stick handling. Facing off suggests an aggressive posture and metaphorically can be stretched to include standing up for one's right to reveal a self beyond the constraints of social propriety. Cavorting—having fun, moving about in a playful manner—is always an important part of any performative occasion. *Carn-ival* is a play on *carne,* meat, my meat in particular—the body as flesh, and also the last part of the word, "ival" or evil—the body contrasted with the spirit. *Carnival* can also be read as a totality, the festival in which good and evil are transposed. Carnival, as Michael Bakhtin (1981) described it, treasures the ambiguity and the transgressive potentials of the charade, yet as Bakhtin has warned, in a final ironic twist, upheavals, such as carnival, are sanctioned by the ruling bodies; by accepting carnival, the rulers

Figure 7.1. The Author as Spectacle
Elizabeth Hechtman, photographer.

reinstate their own power.[2] Thus, there is an irony in this performance as well. One cannot so easily escape the place society has "meted" out for one.

As the house lights dim, and the spotlight falls upon me, I begin.

ACT I: STRIPPING DOWN TO BASICS

POMO   *[Chewing gum, blowing bubbles, takes the gum out and places it somewhere convenient, but impolite]* How I love an audience. What a place for a starstruck kid.

Kid, I said. Do I hear some snickering? "Who is she kidding? She's more like an old goat than a starstruck kid."

[Takes off hat and gloves. Sets down gold lamé purse full of things to eat and drink and smoke, perhaps]

In March 1998, Beatrice Wood, the Mama of Dada, died in her studio in California, just days after she gave a party in honor of the director of the movie *Titanic*. The obituary said she was 105, but she quarreled with the calculation. She always said that if scientists have showed that time is relative, then she was 32. The secret to a long life depended on two things, she said: chocolate and young men. (Not much to disagree with there, although what means young? And maybe men aren't the only choice, but otherwise Beatrice was right on.) Let's dedicate this performance to the Mama of Dada, may her spirit live forever.

Age is a social construction. So like Beatrice, I'm somewhere between 6 and 60 today, depending on how we get along together. We'll see.

Still, at whatever age, this is a pretty formidable place to be standing, given that some of you have other expectations about how a proper woman (and professor) should behave. It's a tough balancing act—to do what I do in such sacred territory. But I'll give it a whirl. *[Swirling about with arms out]*

[She takes a slug of brandy from a silver flask. It is real brandy]

Ah, just a drop of "Koolaid" to get the juices flowing.

I'm warming up. *[Takes off cape]*

But before I get too far along, let me just thank you for coming and joining in our conversation. You make a girl's day. That is what all this relational stuff is all about. I couldn't be standing up here without you. And, of course, if you are wondering how come you are listening to me, and watching me, and puzzling out what I'm up to, then you just better reflect back and consider what you did to deserve me. 'Cause I certainly didn't make this up all by myself.

But you might ask: "What is this 'Woman as Spectacle' thing all about? What is she going to do? And why?" Here I am . . . a nice girl from Lake Wobegon, looking like a raspberry tart, and we ain't celebrating Mardi Gras here. What's the psychology of being outlandish . . . outside the customs, peculiar . . . provocative . . . verging on the weird, the grotesque, the carnivalesque. A woman on the edge of feminine respectability—or way over the line.

One thing is for sure. I'm here to amuse you . . . and bemuse you . . . even confuse you. All those ooze words . . . is that sexy or what?

[*I point to a corner of the stage*] Over there in an imaginary circle of my textual friends. My social ghosts, I call them. One of them, Mary Russo,[3] has charted the dangers of what I attempt: "Making a spectacle out of oneself seem[s] a specifically feminine danger. The danger . . . of an exposure. . . . Women who make spectacles of themselves have done something wrong, have stepped, as it were, into the limelight out of turn—too young or too old, too early or too late—and yet anyone, any woman, can make a spectacle out of herself if she is not careful."

[*Addressing the audience*]

WHAT IS THE WORST SPECTACLE YOU MADE OF YOURSELF? Arguing with somebody more important than you in public? Belching, or, God forbid, farting in company, or even alone? Getting caught eating like you were hungry? Being rude to somebody, even if he was molesting you?

DO YOUR CHEEKS BURN TO THINK OF IT? EVERYONE WHISPERING BEHIND YOUR BACK . . . HOW EMBARRASSING . . . IF ONLY YOU COULD DISAPPEAR INTO THIN AIR. (IF ONLY I HAD NOT BROUGHT IT UP!)

[*Pauses, points to the corner*]

Peggy Penn, over there in my magic circle, has spelled out one of those moments in a poem called *Omen for Women*.[4] Here is one:

At twelve my russet blood rolled out,
Everyone on the bus to Latrobe, PA,
whispered, "See, her eggs are multiplying!
Her insides sloughing off! See! it's dripping on her knees!

It ain't been called the Curse for nothing. Is there no recourse but to relive our endless anguishes? Peggy's no Pollyanna, but she saves herself from humiliation in the final lines of this poem anyway:

Leaving a trail
for you to find me in eleven years.

(There's a positive spin if I've ever seen one. Hansel and Gretel for the pubescent set. Follow my droplets and you'll find your way home.)

COULD *YOUR* SPECTACLE EVER BE REVALUED? MIGHT THERE BE SOMETHING TO SALVAGE IN YOUR STORY? EVEN POLITICAL POTENTIAL? (Or is this feminist jive?)

Mary Russo also said: "In contemplating these dangers, I grew to admire . . . the lewd, exuberant . . . Mae West. . . . Her bold affirmations of feminine performance, imposture, and masquerade . . . suggest cultural politics for women."[5]

Wasn't her line: "Is that a banana in your pocket or are you just glad to see me?"

bell hooks[6] —I admire her outlandish starlight—concurs in her rap about African American women: "When we give expression . . . to those aspects of our identity forged in marginality, we may be seen as 'spectacle.' Yet, . . . this is a risk we must run, . . . It is a means by which culture is transformed and not simply reproduced with different players in the same game."

Transformation, re-creation, even recreation, the politics of fun. Let us move from living with "fear, the most elegant weapon," as artist Jenny Holzer's neon sign proclaims, to a raucous appreciation of our right to be. And to be in violations of the codes by which we are told to live.

If we want to strip away the bars holding us in place, the corset stays of respectability, and tease the audience with our unbounded flesh, how shall we begin? [*POMO taking off some clothes—in some performances stockings, in others a boa, a jacket; or putting a leg up on a chair to check stocking seams*] We walk a thin line in this little striptease . . . slathering the seams of sentences so they all run soothingly into one; smoothing out the ragged edges that might catch us up. Snag our hemlines. . . . stub our toes, or sliver our heels on the runways of our stage of life. Beryl Curt warns that "such words [should] . . . always arouse suspicion. Their very ease . . . beguiles the [listener] . . . into believing they are merely mirroring the world 'as it really is', and obscures their ability to glamour that reality into being."[7]

I am guilty. I do wish to glamour a reality into being, preening these words into worlds. You have been forewarned. [*POMO waves her magic wand*]

The spectacle under construction: needs more introduction. Over there [*POMO points to another part of the stage*] are people who would want to strip me of my style. At my age (chronological, that is), I am meant to disappear. I should have been gone long ago. In the dance of the life cycle, I am being propelled against the wall. [*Moving backwards as though being pushed from the front, arms extended, curled in the middle*] Centrifugal forces spin me to the chairs, from which I rose so long ago . . . arms that circled me, and kept me on the floor. Oh, how I could dance. [*POMO does a bit of a cha cha, then takes up a sheer purple scarf that is tucked into the purse*] Now they've let me go. My dance card is empty. [*Pomo places the large scarf over her head, covering her face*] Now I'm melding with the walls . . . pressing into paper . . . melting with the glue . . . Stuck, not pinned and wriggling like Eliot's Prufrock, but misting into mottled lavender, without a muscle's twitch. [*Standing with arms out, covered by the veil of purple*] This is the fate of a woman of a mature age. [*Removes scarf, keeps it in hand*] She is somewhere over 40 and, according to some, about as useful as a fruit fly (at least they have the courtesy to die swiftly when their breeding days are done). If she cannot procreate, she is lifeless, you see, but not dead. She never should attract attention. She learns to be the antispectacle. Yet she is the object of our gaze.

Such hatred we sometimes feel for her [*Wringing scarf like a neck*]. That shameful blot on the image of our youth. Couldn't we just wring her neck? Be done with her. No one needs her . . . hoarder of Medicare . . . Social Security sad sack . . . our tax dollars feeding a body no one wants to see.

But lest we discard her so quickly, she is also me, and perhaps you. She is our destiny, those of the female persuasion. Ugghhh, should we call for our pills, ply ourselves with hormones? Slather on our creams? Invite the knife to cut into our own throats, and pay for that pleasure? [*Making slitting gestures*]

Or shall we tipple into our drugs of sweet forgetting? [*Takes another brandy sip*]

Is there anyone to call? Will 911 give us any help?

Today she is the creature under construction. And I, in my spectacular role, a Postmodern Mama, with nothing to lose but my invisibility, I challenge those who would erase these fine lines. [*Motions over body*]

ACT II: FACING OFF

On the face of it, it's a challenging task. How do we claim a space on the floor when we are told that the music has stopped? How can we face up to this rejection? It is a challenging task.

Let's play on words of faces . . . on the face of it . . . face values, those of sameness, of identities, of what identities are worth. Facing off . . . challenging the status quo, . . . taking off identities, . . . losing one's face, . . . losing face, the name of shame . . . but this time . . . how can we do it without dread?

We spin over possibilities . . . questioning identities, selfhoods, the singles of selves. Poised for the face off, we lose who we are.

The face becomes the mask . . . masking the face . . . facing our masks.

Who else can we become?

Is this only a Midsummer Night's Dream? We struggle for meaning and mistaken identity. In this struggle for meaning, can we ring up a hat trick? Pull the rabbit out of the hat? Change her luck?

Or in the moments of spectacle will we be defaced?

Or are we off sides here? Betraying one's own . . . a feminist involved in the postmod game . . . losing one's self in the flux of the game. Playing with the dialogic. Giving up or losing one's place. . . . Shimmering and shaking, we shuck our old selves.

In this masquerade, where parody is paramount, we must fake it as we go. Well, at least we have some talent and experience there. In the politics of spectacle, we will reclaim a space.

[*Pauses*]

[*Points to an aisle seat*]

The man on the aisle is trying to understand what all the fuss is about. Why are we men accused? Why blame us if we are swayed by the beauty of youth? We are mere animals, after all. Yearning to spread our seeds abroad. Who can quarrel with the dictates of fate? Sooner or later we are all victims of the game. Nature's call is wild. It's not political, it's biological.

In the dominant world of science, support for the gentleman endures. Doctor Freud had this to say: "A man of about thirty seems youthful. . . . A woman of about the same age frequently staggers us by her psychological rigidity. . . .

There are no paths open to her for further development."[8] Sociobiologists are crawling out from under every rock, claiming that our fates are in our genes, and they ain't talking Levis.

As evolutionary psychologist David Buss has said, "All around the world men are more interested in the youth and beauty of their sexual partners and less discriminating in their choice of partners than women are."[9]

So be it?

We hear feminist researchers lament the discourse of science on our wall-flower women:

"Images of disease and deficiency . . . become the basis of discourse about women's lives in general."[10]

Every woman over 50 years of age becomes a patient.

The disease, of course, is menopause. [*Takes out a fan*] I always say the best treatment, next to chocolate and young men, is a fan.

"The characterization of women as different and pathological . . . tends to provide a . . . justification for misogyny in the wider culture. . . . It is basically a political phenomenon disguised as medical science."[11]

Egglets and Wigglets—the whole world reduced to microscopic protoplasmic difference. And "the Whigs" have it.

I will not wait for Science to come to its senses. We haven't got all day. We must de-face its smug veneer. Graffiti its granting agencies. Pull the plug on its polemics.

Yet how is it possible?

It is dangerous business to mess with the master's discourse. Audre Lorde warned, "The master's tools will never dismantle the master's house."[12] But is language the master's tool, or does language encompass the master as well? Can we not twist his tools into tinsel? Tools into toys? Tools into tinderboxes?

(I've always hated the metaphor of tools. . . . Ludwig may roll over in his grave at this. Tools are forcers. They are required when even brute strength will not get the job done. Tools are instruments of torture—wrenching, pounding, screwing, drilling, chiseling. We do not necessarily want tools.)

Other voices, singing on the sidelines, support us, suggesting scripts for us to follow.

They create the possibility of the woman of means . . . and ways. They can help us to blast out of our prisons—created from low-burning tempers, lolling libidos, lackluster liberalism, loser labels, and ladylikeness.

They give us ruses, diversions, lighthearted banter. We must elude the mainsayers, with no confrontations, no arguments, no logical lies.

It is time for carnival—for glamour, disguise, mystery, and Puckish surprise.

ACT III: ACTING OUT

Can making a spectacle create cultural change?

"Through discourses we construct our selves, our desires, our erotic orientations and our possibilities."[13] How can we create and be created through discourses that bring potential for change?

As Michelle Fine and Susan Gordon suggest, we "need to disrupt prevailing notions of what is inevitable, what is natural, and what is impossible . . . to invent and publish images of what is not now, and what could be."[14]

(We need to draw dirty pictures . . . do unruly things . . . un-ruly . . . against the rulers, against the rules.)

Making it up as we go along.

Woman under construction. Or on Top of?

Topsy turvy, turning the world upside down . . . or perhaps more potently, sidling up . . . saddling up. [*POMO straddles a chair or a stool*]

Women on Top . . . Controlling the pace . . . taking in as much as she wants. Finding a hip bone for her lipbone.

A missionary in her position, evading the law.

A butterfly wing stroking in sweet rebellion. Stirring up the airwaves in spunky surrender.

The image of the disorderly woman stirring the cauldron . . . widens options for women—a temporary release, there's no grand solution anymore.

But Lady Godiva rides, and politics are rampant. [*Throughout this speech, it is possible to rock on the chair or stool*]

So what might we do about the opposite sexes? Can we only count to two? Or can there be boy-girls and girl-boys, and everything else in between? Sugary snakes and spicy snails, and leave the nice puppy dog tails for the puppies?

Let's make some "gender trouble," as Judith Butler says.

"Myths of gender, however alluring, are the bane of women's lives."[15]

Weapon One in our wayward wars of transgression: Fool with Mother Nature: Rub on the line that divides the sexes. (MMMMmm that always feels good to rub on that line.)

Cross over the line, erase the line, blur the line? Is there a politics of lines? Watch out for the dangerous curves.

[Possible to insert a slightly off-colored joke here. "Have you heard the one about . . . ?"]

But if gender is performance, there are certain things we've got to learn. We become the dramatic effect of our performances. We act out the gestures of gender and age. We are fantasies whose bodies are inscribed through our performances. We, whoever we are, can affirm ourselves, while destabilizing the ideal of female beauty and realigning desire.

Although we are trapped in social orderings, tattooed within our proper place . . . in outlandish moments we are freed to create the possibility of cultural change. . . . Let us go on from here:

To revel in our specialness. To blush only when it suits us. To hold our heads up and be proud, no matter where and how we are.

To celebrate the lifted yoke of fertility and rejoice in our wholeness again. [*Fans again*] Like girls, to prance in moonlight and in sun.

To remember that the calendar is only one—bureaucratic—measurement of time. It cannot tell the age of spirit, heart, and mind.

Our spectacles are opportunities to glamour into being other forms of life. As we soar over the edge of respectability . . . (with a bow to Thelma and Louise) . . . let us make a joyful noise and be glad of our excesses. Let us find a way to celebrate. Let us dare to strut our stuff and when we die, die laughing.

NOTES

1. There is no one text of this performance. Each time I prepare for a presentation, I go over this script, edit it for the occasion, add new lines, and remove parts I do not feel resonate with the context or with my own mood. Even on stage I improvise. This chapter does not exist except here. I have never enacted this particular piece.

2. Bakhtin (1981).

3. Russo (1986, p. 213).

4. Personal communication, January 1996.

5. Russo (1986, p. 213).

6. Quoted in Bordo (1992, p. 164).

7. Curt (1994, p. 14). This book has the collective author Beryl C. Curt (no relation to Cyril Burt, of course).

8. See Freud (1933, p. 134).

9. Buss (1995, p. 155).

10. Rostosky and Travis (1996, p. 288).

11. Rostosky and Travis (1996, p. 301).

12. Lorde (1984a, p. 112).

13. Condor (1993, p. 256).

14. Fine and Gordon (1991, p. 24).

15. Sayers (1993, p. 257). "The false idea that gender is fixed and immutable is all too often used to keep women in their place, to justify all manner of discrimination against them" (Sayers, 1993, p. 257).

8

Against Mod Mascu-linity and Post-Mod Macho
A Feminist End-Game

Let's begin with a scare tactic: What we've all been on the edge of our seats to bring up and to deny. Face to face, can we stare it down? Will it get us down? Or are we starry-eyed from too much gazing? Then what will become of us?

Has the end of history come? Nothing left but to demystify and deconstruct the illusory claims to knowledge made by the long track of wisemen stretching from now to once upon a time. The task is to unmask. To rid the world of the pretense behind the propositions—demonstrating knowledge makers as fools after all. Nothing will be left, a charred shell, a burnt-out book, a leveled plain. Then the ending comes: He "beholds the world blankly, with a knowingness that dissolves feeling and commitment into irony" (or so said Todd Gitlin, in 1988 [p. 35]). And do we take it lie-ing down? Do we disappear?

Although there is much to be said for critical unmasking, the present text advocates a feminist a-version to this as the end game. Does it all come down to this? I don't think so. Yet, in a postmodern-feminist moment, I am on this side and am often simultaneously repelled. Feminists cannot hold the deconstructive posture (it makes us tense, and often past tense at that). We long for movement. And in our dance, as postmodern mimes, we might just renovate, restore, and refurnish the social sciences. Faithfully faithless, we can play with the context but not lose our way in the motion. As Marilyn Strathern (1987) noted, we can employ ironic gestures, in a "deliberate juxtaposition of contexts, pastiche perhaps but no jumble" (p. 268).

It is within such a postmodernist moment that this piece is set.[1] The script that follows was originally designed as a dramatic reading.[2] It is intentionally not

181

"straight talk" and is often difficult to follow. The reasons for this shift in linguistic styling are several and significant. First, as feminist postmodernists have come to realize, most of the forms of intelligible discourse in Western culture are suffused with androcentric biases (Butler, 1990; Crawford, 1995; K. J. Gergen, 1991; Heilbrun, 1988; Lather, 1995). Grammar, logic, and narrative structures, for example, lend themselves to certain problematic ends (such as hierarchy and separation). For feminists such as Luce Irigaray (1985b), Julia Kristeva (1980), and Patti Lather (1995), the conclusion argues for a breaking with the prevailing traditions of discourse. With Mary Daly (1978) on our side, we can slip into bewitchery.

Second, to adopt the customary forms of " straight talk" is, for the postmodern, to invite the reader again into the cul-de-sac of traditionalism—that is, into the belief that language maps the terrain. To avoid such objectification, one is invited to play with the traditions, unsettle the words, so that consciousness is never lost that the postmodern's language is itself subject to deconstruction (St. Pierre, 1997). Finally, from the postmodern standpoint, "straight talk" restricts the signifiers (or the meaning of words) in arbitrary ways that may pass unnoticed. For the "postmodern," social science writing should, in principle, be shaken loose from its authorized source. The language should be liberated and allowed to rove more evocatively.[3]

The immediate inspiration for this refrain (he might say, the target) was a plenary address at the Conference on Critical Anthropology at the University of Amsterdam in December 1989, given by Stephen Tyler, professor of anthropology at Rice University, a leading hot-rodder in the postmodern turn. Freed from the boundaries of convention, alert to linguistic snares, Tyler pursues a course that roams helter-skelter over those left, discipline bound, behind. My text is a reaction to the solitary stance (t)he(y) take(s). A lament couched in ironic teasing, as well as an angry chastisement of his text, it re-sounds as a yelp of the Big Bear against her errant sons, and all those who assume ontological freedom, transitivity, and solipsistic solitude; it is addressed to those who proclaim the immediacy of one/two/selfness—of separation and dissolution—and who revel in a phallic superfluidity that denies connections, relationships, and the possibility of love.[4]

THE STAGE DIRECTIONS

Setting for the Original Performance

A typical academic auditorium in darkness, with bright lights illuminating the stage. A podium is set upon a desk, which may be used or not by the reader as a chair, table, or stand. An overhead projector screen is illuminated behind the area stage left of the desk where the words are projected as they are spoken.

The Characters

First woman, as feminist postmodern critic
Second woman, her companion
PM [or postmodern] man

The Reader's Costume

Black turtleneck, pants, and heels (optional). one-and-a-half meters of red feather boa flung about the shoulders and neck. A hand mirror, with a broken glass, face out, is strung on a ribbon or string about the neck as a necklace.

Script Notes

The performance is in two parts; (metaphorically) it is a pie, a seafood crepe, an empanada, a piñata, or perhaps a pregnant woman. Part I is the crust; Part II is the filling.

The designation of [ ] indicates stage directions. The reader may use "finger snaps" to indicate quotation marks for the audience.

The prologue of the performance is composed of the introductory lines from Tyler's (1987) written text "A Post-Modern for Instance." It describes Tyler's two mental selves, his mind as the book and his mind as the word processor/computer.

THE PERFORMANCE

Prologue

Tyler: I'm of two minds about this . . . the unmoved one and the moving continuum, Apollo and Dionysus . . . the mind as a book . . .
a passionate attention that . . . joins life and experience in an act
of production/reproduction/creativity, a conceit that we call the
concept . . . and thus note the role of Eros in the sexual act of
conceiving the concept, the perfection of form, the fixed entity
of the idea, the achieved whole of the inner psyche that makes
the integrity of the private mind and repeats itself in the solitude
of the book, in the trance-like stasis of reading and writing.
. . . My other mind . . . the mind of the word processor/com-
puter . . . replaces the steadiness of contemplative formulation
with an excess of dynamic possibilities, turning my private solitude into the public network, destroying my authorship by making a totalized textuality in which the text is only ancillary.[5]

Part I: The Crust

First Woman:	Mille Feuille for the Fruits de Mer. How to make sense of the senses to follow. How many sheets can we layer, to make "womb" for the filling to fit? A winding sheet around the carcass of words.
Second Woman:	[*Aside*] It would be much easier (and more to the point) to talk about hot dogs and hot dog buns.
First Woman:	But much less elegant, and much less French. The problem . . . my problem: How to compos(t)e a postmodernist pose, one that does not crush my feminist folds.
Second Woman:	Irigaray speaks of the folds of femininity in perpetual embrace. As women, in a constant caress, caressing ourselves, and maybe each other.
First Woman:	No wonder we do not come to the point the way men claim to do! My question: Can there be a Re-Union with Difference? Is it possible to conceive of A FEMINIST POSTMODERN/POSTMODERN FEMINIST/FEMINIST-FEMME/POSTMODERN MODIFIED?
Second Woman:	Let's say yes, but it's a High-Anxiety situation. There is much to criticize, and I've done my share. Donna Haraway said it with in-tension: "The further I get in describing . . . postmodernism . . . the more nervous I get. The imagery of . . . high-tech military fields, . . . where blips of light called players disintegrate (what a metaphor!) each other in order to stay in the knowledge and power game."[6]
First Woman:	Where does the Ray-a-thon become a Rhoda-thon? Is this another squeeze play? And we're still the marginal mayo and mustard?
Second Woman:	Craig Owens noticed it too: "Few women have engaged in the modernism/postmodernism debate. . . . Postmodernism may be another masculine invention engineered to exclude women."[7]
First Woman:	If he says it, can my intuition be totally untracked?
Second Woman:	My dream would be a wedlock, not a deadlock. To have the best of both worlds and leave the modern one behind. To throw a curve ball that knots the haves and the have-nots into a spinning wheel of dense desire.
First Woman:	Whose desire? That's another course to pursue. Theresa de Lauretis speaks of a story as a question of desire: "But

whose desire is it that speaks, and whom does that desire address?"[8] Is it unreal to imagine: [*Read across the rows here*]

Letting go of	taking	and	combining:
Modernist	*Postmod*		*Feminist*
Stability	Partiality		Connection
Linearity	Playfulness		Construction
Control/manipulation	Pastiche		Commitment
Polar opposites	Parody		Dialogue
"Real world"	Difference		Politics
Value neutrality	Deconstruction		Caring
?	?		?

Second Woman: As Edward Said said, "Transform binary opposition into an economy in which terms circulate."[9] *Or,* as a chaoticist might insist, let the boiling pot of words break the liminarity and the clarity of orderly flow. Uncongeal categories, Both and And. "Have your cake and eat it"—two. (There's a Mari-ann'ette, French again, a puppet game for you and me. Let us probe for the Un-said.)

First Woman: Postmodernism . . . Is it just another sport to add to the Academic Olympics? Who can deconstruct the fastest and the mostest? Bring on the muscle men, and let them strain. Steroid doses and noselogic poses. GOLD/SILVER/BRONZE [she sings a phrase of "La Marseillaise": *"Allons enfants de la patrie"* . . . [*Pauses*].

Second Woman: Did anybody say anything about anyone who wasn't playing their game?

First Woman: There was some mention of women, at least of their bodies. They're the supplement, the ex-centrics. Without phALL-USes they can't go very far, especially in this game.

Second Woman: No body seemed to notice that all the players are "IN" the establishment. From the Sorbonne to Santa Cruz, the same old tricks, ruses, disguises, they use them to kick the OLD GUARD OUT of power. Re-Volving door policy—so that they could be INNER. More IN, less OUT. They won't hold a door open for anyone.

Just the same old "sexual politics" (The old IN and OUT).

First Woman: Well, that's what got me going! It's a love/hate relationship—postmodernism/feminism—How perfectly PM/PMS. Their endless discourses colliding in one conundrumatic phrase. But two isms don't make an are, or do they?

Second Woman: Collapsing the opposition of love and hate. Collapsing the opposition: Femme and them, me and he.

First Woman: Collapsing the opposition (by taking the wind out of their sails?). Co-LAP-SING the (T)OP-POSition. (All missionaries are being recalled for faulty transmissions.) Or is it "Co-Lapsinging"—a name for conjoining. Let our laps sing together. . . . Much better.

Second Woman: No one needs to be "on top." We don't have to listen to what those dick-shunaries told us.

First Woman: Then let's start a deconstruction. It can happen anywhere. How about here? Perhaps the Zen master is right. It all/ nothing makes sense.

Second Woman: A word about Stephen Tyler, to whom this piece is daddy-kated. He's a cover-boy[10] (do you think I'm covering something up?), an under-cover (anthro)-agent; looking to discover; running for cover. But there are no more hiding places. It's all on the surface, now. Nothing can hide under pre-texts any more.

First Woman: Tyler is a PM magician . . . talks and even writes PM-ese. Read *The Unspeakable*[11] if you don't believe me. I admire him.

   Yet he is the target. I am after the pack. He is the random one whose number came up. My ode is to and with and through him.

   In the intertextuality of things, he is a woof and I am a "Whorf." Now I shall spin us together in a centrifuge of text. Come follow me along, over and under we go, shuttles on the shades of weaving words.

[First Woman reads]: Part II: "The Filling"

PM Man: All I ever wanted to do was to stay in my room and "play with IT."[12]

First Woman: Behold. S.T., one in a new chain of linguistic magistics . . . U.V.W.X.Y.Z. The end of the line . . . where we all have to get off now. How to "get off" ah, there's the rub. 'Tis nobler in the minds of men perhaps, but is that enough? That is also the question.

	The PM Man, torn apart . . . full of contra-DICK-shun. Of two minds. . . . Platonist, left hemispheric, the "ur-form of the scribal hand" . . . "taking in hand" . . . E-Man-cipate . . . "UNMOVED," AND the other mind, Dionysian, "the boundless" one (do you anticipate MOVED? Yes, why not? We were brought up on opposition). "Moved . . . E-Moved . . . E-MOTION" . . .
Second Woman:	Emotion. . . . Now we get to the heart of the matter.
First Woman:	Sorry to disappoint you, but it's a wrong spelling; don't forget the hyphen. It's E (hyphen) Motion. His motion is not from the heart; it's from the hardware.
PM Man:	Give me SPACE! Keep it all separate. That's where it's com-FORT-able. (One Man, One FORT!) E-MOTION . . . the "moving continuum." E-Motion on the screen. "The mind of the word processor/computer . . . poke at . . . monkey." (Get the French connection? It's all in the tongue.) Losing the self-consciousness of the left brain, peeling down the cortex to the electronic core . . . fingering "mon" key, the magic wand that opens doors, boxes, hidden files . . . mesmerized by the flickering shadow-images, dancing naked on the screen. . . .
First Woman:	He's CELL-Eee-Brate-ing alone, total-(itarian)-ly in "calculative power, total manipulative control, abundant resource, speed, complete management . . . hypnotized by the phosphorescent glow of moving symbols. . . . Listen to him hum.
PM Man:	[*Shouting*] Power is mine! . . . I have the instantaneous and total knowledge of god and am ONE with the movement of thought. . . . I AM THE MOVING MATRIX! . . .
First Woman:	CLIMAX, cut, end of paragraph . . . CURTAIN.
Second Woman:	[*Softly*] Should we pull the shades? Cigarette?
PM Man:	[*Tired*] It is dawn by now. No one can see in. Everyone is asleep. Besides, we are not ashamed. We are scholars. It's the thing now. Left or Right: The Thing Was Always It.
First Woman:	PM, Poor Man, just trying to get his head together. Or heads together? Is a Man of two heads or three? It's a trinity . . . three in one . . . indivisible . . . a miracle, the priest said. We should all respect it, even if we can't understand.

Second Woman:	And be forgiven if we envy. (Who will forgive us? Our Sigmund who art in heaven?)

First Woman:	But it's no fun when they won't let you play. Or when all you can be is the nurse, or the patient, or the ground they measure and inspect.

    Always peeking, then they say, "Is that all there is?"

    When will they learn? [*Forcefully*] Don't mess with Mother Nature!

Second Woman:	E-movement. . . . B-movement . . . Re-movement. "When the boys came out to play, Georgie Porgie ran away."

First Woman:	Who are they trying to scare off? Full of Power and Manipulative Control, Abundant Resources, Speed, Complete Management. The New Army, complete with portable Zenises.[13] Pulling the rug out from under the OLD GUARD. (Didn't we all want to run out of the stands and CHEER!!!?) Down with the OLD ORDER. . . . Foundations of Modernity, split into Gravity's Rainbow/Rules shredded ribbons adorning the May POLE, wavering in the Breeze of breathtaking words/ ABSOLUTE-ly nothinged by the shock-ing PM tropes/ smashing icons with iron(ic)s/Wreaking CON-SENSE with NON-SENSE/

      PARODYING

       PARADING

        PANDERING

         PARADOXING

         PLAYING

          POUNDING

         PRIMPING

         PUMPING

    What fun! [*Singing*] . . . London Bridges Falling Down. [*Then shouting*] (DE-CONSTRUCT-ED) [*Resume singing*] MY FAIR LADY.

    Where can WE jump in? Shall we twirl your batons? Can we all form a circle? Dance around the fire? the Pole? The falling bridges? Give us a hand. Give us a hand? Give us a hand. . .

PM Man:	All they ever want are handouts. . . Give 'em an inch they'll take a mile. How many inches do they think we've got? [*A brief pause, then, addressing Women*] Besides, can't you see we've got play to do? It's not easy just going off to play each day. It takes practice . . . dedication . . . grace. It's not something you can just join in like that. We've got our formation. Can't you see you'll just muck it up? We're in the wrecking business. What business is that of yours? "You make, we break": We can write it on the truck. Next thing you'll want us to settle down and play house. We've got to be movin' on. It's part of the code. Girls can't be in combat. Besides, John Wayne doesn't talk to them, so adios. Don't call us, we'll call you.

First Woman: That call has a familiar ring to it. The call of the WILD.

PM Man: We aren't animals; and don't call us an army! Better a merry dis-band-ment of (dis) Con-victors;
    (dis) Con-artists; (dis)co-dandies;
      (dis)iden-ticals;
    (dis)-sent-uals; (dis)-coursers;
      (dis)i-paters; (dis)contents; (dis)-ap-pere-ers. . .
        (Dig that French)
  cr
  ac
    king
    up (by any meaning you like)
      c
    rac
    king
  up (whatever other meaning(s) you like). . . .
THE JOINT

First Woman: How many joints you got in mind?

PM Man: Hey, it's not personal. No hard feelings?

First Woman: How do you mean that?

Second Woman: Makes you wonder if she has a "double entendre" in mind. Those Frenchies are at it again.

PM Man: If you wanna make an omelette, you gotta break some eggs.

First Woman: But we've got the eggs.

PM Man: Which comes first, the chicks or the eggs? Sorry, I couldn't help it. Old gag line, part of the new PM ritual: Say whatever comes into your head, especially if it's a dumb "yoke." [*Laughs at his own joke*]

First Woman: Which head?

Second Woman: Another double entendre?!

PM Man: One for all and all for one. At least for the moment. That's another thing. We don't make promises. Just another word for COMMITMENT (the really big C-word, the one that

	gets you behind bars, and I don't mean mixing martinis). A rolling stone gathers no moss and no mille-deux.
First Woman:	Mick Jagger has children.
PM Man:	Babies are phallic. If you need one, get one.
First Woman:	But your phallus doesn't need bread.
PM Man:	"Let them eat cake," as good ol' Marie put it. She had a feel for our rap.
First Woman:	That doesn't solve the problem.
PM Man:	It's not my problem. Postmodern life is, as Deleuze sez, nomadic.[14] And S.T. added, "We are all homeless wanderers on the featureless, post-industrial steppe, tentless nomads, home packed up."[15] And as a NATO tank commander once said, "You can't have an army when you gotta bring along the outhouse for the dames."
First Woman:	Looks like its going to be a short revolution—about one generation.
PM Man:	Au contraire, Baby, we've just begun. I mean the trashing is in dis-progress. Disciplines to dismantle/methods to maul/ Truth to trample/origins to emasculate.
First Woman:	Who's on the cleanup committee?
PM Man:	You sound like somebody's mother. Whose side are you on anyway? Few minutes ago you wanted to dance in the streets. Down with the old, up with the new. (Never satisfied; always want something ya can't get. . . . Bitch, bitch, bitch).
First Woman:	You sound de-fence-i've. Have I got your goat?
PM Man:	Now you're getting down to something. Thanks, but no thanks. I get off graphically. Who needs flesh. And I can log off any time any time any time. . . . Let's leave it at that. Stephen Tyler has said: "Postmodernism accepts the para-doxical CONsequences of . . . irreconcilable ambiguity without attempting to end the CONflict by imposing CLOSURE."[16]. . .
	We're a-dispersing . . . "dis-pursing" . . . we are getting further and further away. Space is beautiful.
First Woman:	It's gonna be mighty COLD out there. . . .

PM Man: Earthling, do you read me? . . . Do you read me? . . . Do you
. . . reeeeead. . .?

First Woman: You're fading, Major Tom.

The signal is getting weaker and weaker. It is running out in space. It is running out of space. Soon there is nothing but

SILENCE

NOTES

1. Other feminist critiques in more traditional forms tangentially or solidly share these concerns (see Flax, 1987, 1990; Fraser & Nicholson, 1988; Hekman, 1990; Hollway, 1989; Lather, 1986, 1995; Lorber & Farrell, 1991; Mascia-Lees, Sharpe, & Cohen, 1989; Moi, 1988; Nielsen, 1990; Roberts, 1981; Weedon, 1987).

2. Performed at the Postmodernity and Psychology Conference held at the Center for Qualitative Methodology, the University of Aarhus, Denmark, in June 1989.

3. Besides, it is more fun to talk associatively. If you read it aloud, you can join the authorial stream and create new meanings and new lines. I give my permission now.

4. For Tyler, according to Mascia-Lees et al. (1989),

Ethnographic discourse is not part of a project whose aim is to create universal knowledge, but rather the "consumed fragment" of an understanding that is only experienced in the text, the text which is evocative and participatory, bringing the joint work of the ethnographer and his native partners together with the hermeneutic process of the reader. (p. 31)

5. Tyler (1989, p. 1).

6. Haraway (1988, p. 577).

7. Owens (1983, p. 61).

8. de Lauretis (1984, p. 113).

9. Said (1983, p. 155).

10. The front-cover photograph of Clifford and Marcus's (1986) book shows a young anthropologist (Stephen Tyler) writing his field notes as an older man of the village looks on.

11. Tyler (1987).

12. The Lacanian sign transposed as the Word, the Object, PC, the Thing of Things, or "whatever turns you and it on."

13. Donna Haraway (1988) has written with similar feelings:

The further I get in describing . . . postmodernism . . . , the more nervous I get. The imagery of force fields, of moves in a fully textualized and coded world . . . is, just for starters, an imagery of high-tech military fields, of automated academic battlefields, where blips of light called players disintegrate (what a metaphor!) each other in order to stay in the knowledge and power game. Technoscience and science fiction collapse into the sun of their radiant (ir)reality-war. (p. 577)

14. Deleuze (1978).
15. Tyler (1991, p. 84).
16. Tyler (1991, p. 89).

PART III

A Closing

Invitations to Commence

As we come to an ending place, and the dialogues contained and commenced within continue, there are more words that I would like to add. Endless streams of possibilities appear before me at this watershed moment. Perhaps my reluctance to close is about never having to say goodbye. The chapters here have heralded both gains and losses that are in store for all of us who want to travel along the untrod paths leading into the predictable, unpredictable postmodern future. The postmodern moment has proclaimed the loss of the grand narratives and, with this, the end of the search for the final answers, truths, theories, or ways of discovering them. Everything is not going to be packed up, with loose pieces fitted perfectly into some preprogrammed puzzle. The metaphor of the jack-in-the-box may be more apt than the puzzle to describe what we may anticipate ahead, with chaotic disruptions undermining any potential ordering effects. What is lost is also what is gained. Instead of one great and coherent story, there is the potential for multiple stories, with many characters and plots and themes and endings. And instead of the telescope that allows us to bring distant objects into sharp focus, we have kaleidoscopes that can shift the perspectives, alter the arrangements, and provide endless speculations about what is, was, and could be. The theorist becomes the twister and not the televangelist. The adoption of this postmodern stance has been liberating for me as a feminist, and I believe for many others. I, for one, no longer wish that women could conquer the world! Nor do I wish us to be either Goddesses or Cyborgs—except, perhaps, in just the right moments. From an intellectual standpoint, I now seek a vision of a feminist psychology based on the notion of a relational science: that is, one that would emphasize the collaborative nature of knowledge making and be more inclusive rather than less. But this is not all that is suggested by a relational science. The opportunity exists for creating a study of human life that would focus as much or more on the study of relationships as on discrete individuals. Let me describe this bold step in the words of Kum-Kum Bhavnani and Donna Haraway (1994):

> The whole question of what counts as the unit of analysis is in play. . . . So the subject of psychology, . . . produced by the discourse, . . . has to be an object . . . whose boundaries are configured in the kinds of relationships being examined. And now we can see that what counts as an individual is far from self evident. (p. 34)

This would indeed be a daring step into an interesting future. Instead of theorizing and doing research on how *individuals* think, feel, and act, one might study how relationships evolve to create human activity (K. J. Gergen, 1994). Beyond that, we might fruitfully examine how our individual subjectivities, our sense of individuality, our identities as whoever we think we are, become fixed or altered. The work of Judith Butler (1990, 1993) is of great interest here. Butler suggests that we both produce and are produced out of our social interactions; this dynamic image has inspired me to consider a new psychology along these lines. As she suggests, we create and are simultaneously created within our constructed worlds. For me, pursuing this vision of what relational beings might be is a very fruitful idea for feminists. For others, it may provide inspiration for other modes of creative action. Having a commitment to feminist values, as I explore various avenues of relational theory, is reassuring. Exactly how this commitment plays out in any particular moment is, however, an open question. Each of the chapters in this book has been a way of exploring, inventing, appropriating, and disrupting the existing milieu of activities within feminist psychology. Much more can be accomplished, and I hope something of this book will encourage those endeavors. But I hope more than anything else that these words will encourage relationships that will enhance life for all creatures, great and small, on this planet and that they will provide a greater impetus to continue in the quest for a more loving and just world.

> Did these words seem to be mine? They belong to others. We share in this construction. Some words get blurred and others obliterated. No one is understood fully. Many voices have not be heard within this telling. They may be calling. Other books will be written; other voices heard. This is for my time, being.

References

Adams, Ansel (with Mary Street Alinder). (1985). *Ansel Adams: An autobiography.* Boston: Little, Brown.

Alcoff, Linda. (1988). Cultural feminism versus post-structuralism: The identity crisis in feminist theory. *Signs: Journal of Women in Culture and Society, 13,* 405-436.

Alcoff, Linda. (1994). The problem of speaking for others. In S. O. Weisser & J. Fleischner (Eds.), *Feminist nightmares—Women at odds: Feminism and the problem of sisterhood* (pp. 285-309). New York: New York University Press.

American Psychiatric Association. (1994). *Diagnostic and statistical manual of mental disorders* (4th ed.). Washington, DC: Author.

Anderson, Harlene. (1997). *Conversation, language, and possibilities: A postmodern approach to therapy.* New York: HarperCollins.

Apfelbaum, Erika. (1993). Norwegian and French women in high leadership positions: The importance of cultural contexts upon gendered relations. *Psychology of Women Quarterly, 17,* 409-430.

Armstrong, Carol D. (1989). The reflexive and the possessive view: Thought on Kertesz, Brandt, and the photographic nude. *representations, 25,* 57-71.

Baez, Joan. (1987). *And a voice to sing with: A memoir.* New York: New American Library.

Bakhtin, Michael M. (1981). *The dialogical imagination.* (M. Holquist, Ed.; C. Emerson, Trans.). Minneapolis: University of Minnesota Press.

Bakhtin, Michael M. (1986). *Speech genres and other late essays* (M. Holquist, Ed.; C. Emerson & M. Holquist, Trans.). Austin: University of Texas Press.

Barclay, Craig R., & DeCooke, Peggy A. (1988). Ordinary everyday memories: Some of the things of which selves are made. In U. Neisser & E. Winograd (Eds.), *Remembering reconsidered: Ecological and traditional approaches to the study of memory* (pp. 91-125). New York: Cambridge University Press.

Barrows, Sydney Biddle. (1987). *Mayflower madam.* Sydney, Australia: Futura Press.

Barry, David. (1996). Artful inquiry: A symbolic constructivist approach to social science research. *Qualitative Inquiry, 2,* 411-438.

Bart, Pauline. (1971). Depression in middle-aged women. In V. Gornick & B. K. Moran (Eds.), *Women in sexist society*. New York: Basic Books.

Bayer, Betty M., & Malone, Kareen Ror. (1996). Feminism, psychology and matters of the body. *Theory & Psychology, 6,* 667-692.

Becker, E. (1964). *The revolution in psychiatry*. Glencoe, IL: Free Press.

Belenky, Mary Field, Clinchy, Blythe McVicker, Goldberger, Nancy Rule, & Tarule, Jill Mattuck. (1986). *Women's ways of knowing: The development of self, voice, and mind*. New York: Basic Books.

Belmore, S. M., & Hubbard, M. L. (1987). The role of advance expectancies in person memory. *Journal of Personality and Social Psychology, 53,* 61-70.

Bem, Sandra. (1974). The measurement of psychological androgyny. *Journal of Consulting and Clinical Psychology, 42,* 155-162.

Bem, Sandra. (1993). *The lenses of gender, Transforming the debate on sexual inequality*. New Haven, CT: Yale University Press.

Benhabib, Seyla, & Cornell, Drucilla (Eds.). (1987). *Feminism as critique*. Minneapolis: University of Minnesota Press.

Benstock, Shari. (1988). Authorizing the autobiography. In S. Benstock (Ed.), *The private self: Theory and practice in women's autobiographical writings* (pp. 1-13). London: Routledge.

Berger, John. (1972). *Ways of seeing*. Harmondsworth, UK: Penguin.

Berger, Peter, & Luckmann, Thomas. (1967). *The social construction of reality*. New York: Doubleday.

Bernard, Jessica. (1973). My four revolutions: An autobiographical history of the American Sociological Association. *American Journal of Sociology, 78,* 773-791.

Bhavnani, Kum-Kum, & Haraway, Donna. (1994). Shifting the subject: A conversation between Kum-Kum Bhavnani and Donna Haraway on 12 April, 1993, Santa Cruz, California (Transcribed by Justine Meyers). *Feminism & Psychology, 4,* 19-39.

Billig, Michael. (1994). Repopulating the depopulated pages of social psychology. *Theory & Psychology, 4,* 307-335.

Billig, Michael, Condor, S., Edward, D., Gane, A., Middleton, D. & Radley, A. (1988). *Ideological dilemmas: A social psychology of everyday thinking*. Newbury Park, CA: Sage.

Black, Naomi. (1989). *Social feminism*. Ithaca, NY: Cornell University Press.

Bleier, Ruth. (1984). *Science and gender: A critique of biology and its theories of women*. New York: Pergamon.

Bleier, Ruth (Ed.). (1986). *Feminist approaches to science*. New York: Pergamon.

Bleuler, E. (1951). Autistic thinking. In D. Rapaport (Ed.), *The organization and pathology of thought*. New York: Columbia University Press. (Original work published 1912)

Blumenfeld-Jones, Donald S. (1995). Dance as a mode of research representation. *Qualitative Inquiry, 1,* 391-401.

Bohan, Janet (Ed.). (1992). *Seldom seen, rarely heard: Women's place in psychology*. Boulder, Co: Westview.

Bohan, Janet. (1993). Regarding gender: Essentialism, constructionism, and feminist psychology. *Psychology of Women Quarterly, 17,* 5-21.

Bohan, Janet. (1996). *Psychology and sexual orientation: Coming to terms*. New York: Routledge.

Bordo, Susan. (1992). Postmodern subjects, postmodern bodies. *Feminist Studies, 18,* 159-175.

Braidotti, Rosi. (1991). *Patterns of dissonance.* New York: Routledge.

Braidotti, Rosi. (1994). *Nomadic subjects: Embodiment and sexual difference in contemporary feminist theory.* New York: Columbia University Press.

Brodribb, Somer. (1992). *Nothing mat(t)ers: A feminist critique of postmodernism.* Melbourne, Australia: Spinifex.

Broverman, J. K., Broverman, D. M., Clarkson, F. E., Rosenkrantz, P. S., & Vogel, S. R. (1970). Sex role stereotypes and clinical judgments of mental health. *Journal of Consulting and Clinical Psychology, 34,* 1-7.

Brown, Laura S., & Root, Maria (Eds.). (1990). *Complexity and diversity in feminist theory and therapy.* New York: Haworth.

Brown, Lyn Mikel. (1994). VII. Standing in the crossfire: A response to Tavris, Gremmen, Lykes, Davis and Contratto. *Feminism and Psychology, 4,* 382-398.

Brown, Lyn Mikel, Argyris, D., Attanucci, J., Bardige, B., Gilligan, C., Johnston, D. K., Miller, B., Osborne, R., Tappan, M., Ward, J., Wiggins, G., & Wilcox, D. (1988). *A guide to reading narratives of conflict and choice for self and relational voice* (Monograph No. 1). Cambridge, MA: Harvard Graduate School of Education, Project on the Psychology of Women and the Development of Girls.

Brown, Lyn Mikel, & Gilligan, Carol. (1992). *Meeting at the crossroads: Women's psychology and girls' development.* Cambridge, MA: Harvard University Press.

Bruss, Elizabeth. (1980). Eye for I: Making and unmaking autobiography in film. In J. Olney (Ed.), *Autobiography: Essays, theoretical and critical.* Princeton, NJ: Princeton University Press.

Burke, Carolyn G. (1978). Report from Paris: Women's writing the women's movement. *Signs: Journal of Women in Culture and Society, 3.* 844-853.

Burman, Erica, Aitken, Gill, Alldred, Pam, Billington, Tom, Goldberg, Brenda, Gordo Lopez, Angel, Heenan, Colleen, Marks, Deb, & Warner, Sam. (1996). *Psychology discourse practice: From regulation to resistance.* Bristol, PA: Taylor & Francis.

Buss, Alan (Ed.). (1979). *Psychology in social context.* New York: Irvington.

Buss, Alan. (1995). Psychological sex differences: Origins through sexual selection. *American Psychologist, 50,* 164-167.

Butler, Judith. (1990). *Gender trouble: Feminism and the subversion of identity.* London: Routledge.

Butler, Judith. (1993). *Bodies that matter: On the discursive limits of "sex."* London: Routledge.

Campbell, Joseph. (1956). *The hero with a thousand faces.* New York: Bollingen.

Carlson, Marvin. (1996). *Performance: A critical introduction.* London, NY: Routledge.

Case, S.-E., Brett, P., & Foster, S. L. (Eds.). (1995). *Cruising the performative: Interventions into the representation of ethnicity, nationality, and sexuality.* Bloomington: University of Indiana Press.

Caughey, John. (1984). *Imaginary social worlds.* Lincoln: University of Nebraska Press.

Cheng, Nien. (1986). *Life and death in Shanghai.* New York: Penguin.

Chodorow, Nancy J. (1978). *The reproduction of mothering and the sociology of gender.* Berkeley: University of California Press.

Chodorow, Nancy J. (1989). *Feminism and psychoanalytic theory.* Berkeley: University of California Press.

Christian, Barbara. (1989). The race for theory. In L. Kauffman (Ed.). *Gender and theory: Dialogues on feminist criticism* (pp. 225-237). Oxford, UK: Basil Blackwell.

Circourel, Aaron V. (1968). *The social organization of juvenile justice.* New York: John Wiley.

Clifford, James. (1983). On ethnographic authority. *representations, 2,* 132-143.

Clifford, James. (1986). Introduction: Partial truths. In J. Clifford & G. Marcus (Eds.), *Writing cultures: The poetics and politics of ethnography.* Berkeley: University of California Press.

Clifford, James, & Marcus, George (Eds.). (1986). *Writing cultures: The poetics and politics of ethnography.* Berkeley: University of California Press.

Cochran, Larry. (1986). *Portrait and story: Dramaturgical approaches to the study of persons.* Westport, CT: Greenwood.

Collins, Patricia. Hill. (1986). Learning from the outsider within: The sociological significance of black feminist thought. *Social Problems, 33,* S14-S32.

Collins, Patricia Hill. (1991). *Black feminist thought: Knowledge, consciousness, and the politics of empowerment.* New York: Routledge.

Condor, S. (1993). Book review, Jessica, Benjamin, *The Bonds of Love: Psychoanalysis, Feminism and the Problem of Domination. Feminism & Psychology, 3,* 256.

Controversy over censorship continues. (1991, November 23). *Intercom [Pennsylvania State University student newspaper],* p. 2.

Cooley, Charles Horton. (1902). *Human nature and the social order.* New York: Scribners.

Cooper, H. M. (1979). Statistically combining independent studies: A meta-analysis of sex differences in conformity research. *Journal of Personality and Social Psychology, 37,* 131-146.

Cooperrider, David L. (1998, August). *A positive revolution in change: Capturing what matters most in the practice of appreciative inquiry.* Paper presented at the 1998 Academy of Management Symposium, Appreciative Inquiry: Capturing What Matters Most—A Review and Assessment, Chicago.

Cooperrider, David L., & Dutton, Jane (Eds.). (1998). *No limits to cooperation: The organization dimensions of global change.* Thousand Oaks, CA: Sage.

Cooperrider, David L., & Srivastva, Suresh. (1998). An invitation to organizational wisdom and executive courage. In S. Srivastva & D. L. Cooperrider (Eds.), *Organizational wisdom and executive courage* (pp. 1-22). San Francisco, CA: New Lexington Press.

Cowan, G., Warren, L. W., & Young, J. L. (1985). Medical perceptions of menopausal symptoms. *Psychology of Women Quarterly, 9,* 3-14.

Crapanzano, V. (1980). *Tuhami: Portrait of a Moroccan.* Chicago: University of Chicago Press.

Crawford, June, Kippax, Susan, Onyx, Jenny, Vault, Una, & Benton, Pam. (1992). *Emotion and gender: Constructing meaning from memory.* London: Sage.

Crawford, Mary. (1995). *Talking difference: On gender and language.* Thousand Oaks, CA: Sage.

Crawford, Mary, & Kimmel, Ellen (Eds.). (1999). Innovative methods [Special issue]. *Psychology of Women Quarterly, 22*(1), *23*(2).

Culley, Margo. (1991). "We are here to stay": Curriculum transformation in the 90s. *Transformations, 2,* 4-13.

Curt, Beryl C. (1994). *Textuality and tectonics: Troubling social and psychological science.* Milton Keynes, UK: Open University Press.

Curtis, Bruce. (1994). Men and masculinities in American art and illustration. *Masculinities, 2,* 10-37.

Daly, Mary. (1978). *Gyn/ecology: The metaethics of radical feminism.* Boston: Beacon.

Datan, Nancy. (1997). Corpses, lepers, and menstruating women: Tradition, transition, and the sociology of knowledge. In M. M. Gergen & S. N. Davis (Eds.), *Toward a new psychology of gender* (pp. 285-294). New York, London: Routledge.

Davies, Nicola. (1994). Portrait of woman as artist and art object. *Feminism & Psychology, 3,* 430-438.

de Beauvoir, Simone. (1953). *The second sex* (H. M. Parshley, Trans.). New York: Knopf.

de Lauretis, Theresa. (1984). *Alice doesn't: Feminism, semiotics, cinema.* Bloomington: Indiana University Press.

de Man, Paul. (1979). Autobiography as de-facement. *Modern Language Notes, 94,* 920.

Deaux, Kay. (1985). Sex and gender. *Annual Review of Psychology, 36,* 49-81.

Deaux, Kay, & Major, Brenda. (1987). Putting gender into context: An interactive model of gender-related behavior. *Psychological Review, 94,* 369-397.

Deleuze, Gilles. (1978). Nomad thought (J. Wallace, Trans.). *Semiotext(e), 3,* 12-20.

Derrida, Jacques. (1978). *Writing and difference.* (A. Bass, Trans.). Chicago: University of Chicago Press.

Derrida, Jacques. (1981). *Positions* (A. Bass, Trans.). Chicago: University of Chicago Press. (Original work published 1972)

Diamond, Irene, & Quinby, Lee (Eds.). (1988). *Feminism and Foucault: Reflections on resistance.* Boston: Northeastern University Press.

Dinnerstein, Dorothy. (1976). *The mermaid and the minotaur.* New York: Harper & Row.

Director's editorial. (1991, December). *Newsletter of the Institute for the Humanities [Pennsylvania State University],* p. 1.

Donmoyer, R., & Yennie-Donmoyer, J. (1995). Data as drama: Reflections on the use of reader's theater as a mode qualitative data display. *Qualitative Inquiry, 1,* 402-428.

Douglas, Mary. (1980). *Purity and danger: An analysis of the concepts of pollution and taboo.* London: Routledge.

Dudek, S. (Ed.). (1996, Fall/Winter). *Performative psychology, psychology and the arts* [Special section]. Washington, DC: American Psychological Association, Division 10.

DuPlessis, Rachel Blau. (1985). *Writing beyond the ending.* Bloomington: Indiana University Press.

Eagly, Alice H. (1987). *Sex differences in behavior: A social-role interpretation.* Hillsdale, NJ: Lawrence Erlbaum.

Eagly, Alice H. (1995). The science and policies of comparing women and men. *American Psychologist, 50,* 145-158.

Eagly, Alice H., & Carli, L. L. (1981). Sex of researchers and sex-typed communications as determinants of sex differences in influenceability: A meta-analysis of social influence studies. *Psychological Bulletin, 90,* 1-20.

Eagly, Alice H., & Crowley, M. (1986). Gender and helping behavior: A meta-analytic review of the social psychological literature. *Psychological Bulletin, 100,* 283-308.

Eagly, Alice H., & Johnson, Blair T. (1990). Gender and leadership style: A meta-analysis. *Psychological Bulletin, 108,* 233-256.

Eagly, Alice H., & Steffen, V. J. 1984). Gender and aggressive behavior: A meta-analytic review of the social psychological literature. *Psychological Bulletin, 100,* 309-330.

Eliot, T. S. (1963). The love song of J. Alfred Prufrock. In *Collected poems: 1909-1962.* London: Faber & Faber.

Ellerbee, Linda. (1986). *And so it goes: Adventures in television.* New York: Berkley.

Ellis, Carolyn, & Bochner, Arthur P. (Eds.). (1996). *Composing ethnography: Alternative forms of qualitative writing.* Walnut Creek, CA: Alta Mira.

Elms, Alan. (1975). The crisis of confidence in social psychology. *American Psychologist, 30,* 967-976.

Emerson, Caryl. (1983). The outer word and inner speech: Bakhtin, Vygotsky, and the internalization of language. *Critical Inquiry, 10,* 245-264.

Fals-Borda, O., & Rahman, M. A. (1991). *Action and knowledge: Breaking the monopoly with participatory action-research.* New York: Apex.

Farganis, Sandra. (1994). *Situating feminism: From thought to action* (Vol. 2). London: Sage.

Fausto-Sterling, A. (1981). Women and science. *Women's Studies International Quarterly, 4,* 41-50.

Favret-Saadia, J. (1980). *Deadly words: Witchcraft in the Bocage.* Cambridge, UK: Cambridge University Press.

Felski, Rita. (1995). *The gender of modernity.* Cambridge, MA: Harvard University Press.

Feynman, Richard P. (1986). *"Surely you're joking, Mr. Feynman!* New York: Bantam Books. (Originally published in 1985)

Fine, Michelle. (1980). Reflections on a feminist psychology of women: Paradoxes and prospects. *Psychology of Women Quarterly, 9,* 167-183.

Fine, Michelle. (1992). *Disruptive voices.* Ann Arbor: University of Michigan Press.

Fine, Michelle. (1997). Sexuality, schooling, and adolescent females: The missing discourse of desire. In M. M. Gergen & S. N. Davis (Eds.), *Toward a new psychology of gender* (pp. 375-402). New York: Routledge.

Fine, Michelle, & Gordon, Susan Merle. (1991). Effacing the center and the margins: Life at the intersection of psychology and feminism. *Feminism & Psychology, 1,* 19-28.

Fine, Michele, Weis, Lois, Powell, L. C., & Wong, L. M. (Eds.). (1997). *Off white: Readings on race, power, and society.* New York: Routledge.

Flax, Jane. (1983). Political philosophy and the patriarchal unconscious: A psychoanalytic perspective on epistemology and metaphysics. In S. Harding & M. Hintikka (Eds.), *Discovering reality* (pp. 245-282). Dordrecht, the Netherlands: D. Reidel.

Flax, Jane. (1987). Postmodernism and gender relations in feminist theory. *Signs: Journal of Women in Culture and Society, 12,* 621-643.

Flax, Jane. (1990). *Thinking fragments: Psychoanalysis, feminism, & postmodernism in the contemporary west.* Berkeley: University of California Press.

Flax, Jane. (1993a). *Disputed subjects: Essays on psychoanalysis, politics and philosophy.* New York: Routledge.

Flax, Jane. (1993b). Multiples: On the contemporary politics of subjectivity. *Human Studies, 16,* 33-49.

Foster, Hal (Ed.). (1983). *The anti-aesthetic: Essays on postmodern culture.* Port Townsend, WA: Bay Press.

Foucault, Michel. (1979). *Discipline and punish: The birth of the prison* (A. Sheridan, Trans.). New York: Vintage.

Fox, Karen V. (1996). Silent voices: A subversive reading of child sexual abuse. In C. Ellis & A. Bochner (Eds.), *Composing ethnography: Alternative forms of qualitative writing* (pp. 330-356). Thousand Oaks, CA: Sage.

Fraser, Nancy. (1989). *Unruly practices: Power, discourse, and gender in contemporary social theory.* Minneapolis: University of Minnesota Press.

Fraser, Nancy, & Nicholson, Linda. (1988). Social criticism without philosophy: An encounter between feminism and postmodernism. In A. Ross (Ed.), *Universal abandon: The politics of postmodernism* (pp. 83-104). Minneapolis: University of Minnesota Press.

Freud, Sigmund. (1933). Femininity (Lecture 33). In *New introductory lectures on psychoanalysis* (J. Strachey, Trans. & Ed.; Standard ed., Vol. 22, pp. 112-135). London: Hogarth.

Fuss, D. (1989). *Essentially speaking: Feminism, nature and difference.* New York: Routledge.

Gadamer, Hans Georg. (1976). *Philosophical hermeneutics* (D. E. Linge, Trans.). Berkeley: University of California Press.

Gagnon, John H., & Simon, William. (1973). *Sexual conduct: The social sources of human sexuality.* Chicago: Aldine.

Gallop, Jane. (1988). *Thinking through the body.* New York: Columbia University Press.

Game, A. (1988). Research and writing: Secretaries and bosses. *Journal of Pragmatics, 13,* 92-104.

Gannon, Linda R. (1985). *Menstrual disorders and menopause: Biological, psychological, cultural research.* New York: Praeger.

Gannon, Linda R. (1990). Endocrinology of menopause. In R. Formanek (Ed.), *The meanings of menopause: Historical, medical and clinical perspectives.* Hillsdale, HJ: Analytic Press.

Gannon, Linda, & Ekstrom, Bonnie. (1993). Attitudes toward menopause: The influence of sociocultural paradigms. *Psychology of Women Quarterly, 17,* 275-288.

Garfinkel, Harold. (1967). *Studies in ethnomethodology.* Englewood Cliffs, NJ: Prentice Hall.

Garratt, Dean, & Hodkinson, Phil. (1998). Criteria for selecting research criteria? A hermeneutical analysis of an inescapable dilemma. *Qualitative Inquiry, 4,* 515-539.

Gavey, Nicola. (1989). Feminist poststructuralism and discourse analysis. *Psychology of Women Quarterly, 13,* 459-475.

Gee, James. (1991). A linguistic approach to narrative. *Journal of Narrative and Life History, 1,* 15-39.

Gergen, Kenneth J. (1973). Social psychology as history. *Journal of Personality and Social Psychology, 26,* 309-320.

Gergen, Kenneth J. (1978). Toward generative psychology. *Journal of Personality and Social Psychology, 36,* 1344-1360.

Gergen, Kenneth J. (1985). The social constructionist movement in modern psychology. *American Psychologist, 40,* 266-275.

Gergen, Kenneth J. (1988). Feminist critique of science and the challenge of social epistemology. In M. M. Gergen (Ed.), *Feminist thought and the structure of knowledge* (pp. 27-48). New York: New York University Press.

Gergen, Kenneth J. (1991). *The saturated self: Dilemmas of identity in contemporary life.* New York: Basic Books.

Gergen, Kenneth J. (1994). *Realities and relationships.* Cambridge, MA: Harvard University Press.

Gergen, Kenneth J. (Chair). (1996, August). *Performative psychology.* Symposium conducted at the annual meeting of the American Psychological Association, Toronto.

Gergen, Kenneth J. (1999). *Invitation to social construction.* Thousand Oaks, CA: Sage.

Gergen, Kenneth J., & Gergen, Mary M. (1983). *Narrative of the self.* In T. Sarbin & K. Schiebe (Eds.), *Studies in social identity* (pp. 254-273). New York: Praeger.

Gergen, Kenneth J., & Gergen, Mary M. (1988). Narrative and the self as relationship. In L. Berkowitz (Ed.), *Advances in Experimental Social Psychology, 21,* 17-56.

Gergen, Mary M. (1987). *Social ghosts of the middle-aged: A pilot study.* Unpublished manuscript, Pennsylvania State University.

Gergen, Mary M. (Ed.). (1988a). *Feminist thought and the structure of knowledge.* New York: New York University Press.

Gergen, Mary M. (1988b). Toward a feminist methodology. In M. M. Gergen (Ed.), *Feminist thought and the structure of knowledge* (pp. 87-104). New York: New York University Press.

Gergen, Mary M. (1992a). Life stories: Pieces of a dream. In G. Rosenwald & R. Ochbert (Eds.), *Storied lives* (pp. 127-144). New Haven, CT: Yale University Press.

Gergen, Mary M. (1992b). Metaphors for chaos, stories of continuity: Building a new organizational theory (pp. 40-71). In S. Srivastva, & P. Frey (Eds.), *Executive and organizational continuity; Managing the paradoxes of stability and change.* San Francisco: Jossey-Bass.

Gergen, Mary M. (1994). Free Will and psychotherapy: Complaints of the draughtsmen's daughters. *Journal of Theoretical and Philosophical Psychology, 14,* 13-24.

Gergen, Mary M., Chrisler, Joan C., & LoCicero, Alice. (1999). Innovative methods: Resources for research, teaching, and publishing. *Psychology of Women Quarterly, 23,* 431-456.

Gergen, Mary M., & Davis, Sara N. (Eds.). (1997). *Toward a new psychology of gender.* New York: Routledge.

Gergen, Mary M., & Gergen, Kenneth J. (1984). Narrative structure and their social construction. In K. J. Gergen & M. M. Gergen (Eds.), *Historical social psychology.* Hillsdale, NJ: Lawrence Erlbaum.

Gergen, Mary M., & Gergen, Kenneth J. (2000). Qualitative inquiry: Tensions and transformations. In N. Denzin & Y. Lincoln (Eds.), *Handbook of qualitative research* (2nd ed., pp. 1025-1046). Thousand Oaks, CA: Sage.

Getty, J. Paul (1986). *As I see it: An autobiography of J. Paul Getty.* New York: Berkley.

Gilbert, G. N., & Mulkay, M. (1984). *Opening Pandora's box: A sociological analysis of scientists' discourse.* Cambridge, UK: Cambridge University Press.

Gilligan, Carol. (1979). Woman's place in man's life cycle. *Harvard Educational Review, 49,* 431-446.

Gilligan, Carol. (1982). *In a different voice: Psychological theory and women's development.* Cambridge, MA: Harvard University Press.

Gilligan, Carol, Lyons, Nona, & Hanmer, Trudy (Eds.). (1990). *Making connections: The relational worlds of adolescent girls at Emma Willard School.* Cambridge, MA: Harvard University Press.

Gilligan, Carol, Rogers, Annie, & Tolman, Deborah, (Eds.). (1991). *Women, girls and psychotherapy: Reframing resistance.* New York: Haworth.

Gitlin, Todd. (1988, November 6). Hip-deep in post-modernism. *New York Times Book Review,* pp. 1, 35-36.

Goffman, Erving. (1959). *The presentation of self in everyday life.* Garden City, NY: Doubleday.

Goldner, Virginia, Penn, Peggy, Sheinberg, Marcia, & Walker, Gillian. (1990). Love and violence: Gender paradoxes in volatile attachments. *Family Process, 29,* 343-364.

Goolishian, Harry, & Anderson, Harlene. (1987). Language systems and therapy: An evolving idea. *Psychotherapy: Theory, Research and Practice, 24,* 529-538.

Gordon, Chad, & Gergen, Kenneth J. (1968). *The self in social interaction.* New York: John Wiley.

Gotfrit, Leslie. (1991). Women dancing back: Disruption and the politics of pleasure. In H. A. Giroux (Ed.), *Postmodernism, feminism, and cultural politics* (pp. 174-195). Albany: State University of New York Press.

Grady, Kathleen E. (1981). Sex bias in research design. *Psychology of Women Quarterly, 5,* 628-636.

Griffin, Susan. (1993). *A chorus of stones: The private life of war.* New York: Doubleday.

Griffith, James L., & Griffith, Melissa Elliott. (1994). *The body speaks: Therapeutic dialogues for mind-body problems.* New York: Basic Books.

Griscom, Joan. (1992). Women and power. Definition, dualism, and difference. *Psychology of Women Quarterly, 16,* 389-414.

Grosz, Elizabeth. (1994). *Volatile bodies: Towards a corporeal feminism.* Sydney: Allen & Unwin.

Hammond, Sue. (1996). *The thin book of appreciative inquiry.* Plano, TX: Thin Book.

Hammond, Sue, & Royal, Cathy (Eds.). (1998). *Lessons from the field: Applying appreciative inquiry.* Plano, TX: Practical Press.

Haraway, Donna J. (1988). Situated knowledges: The science question in feminism and the privilege of partial perspective. *Feminist Studies, 14,* 575-599.

Haraway, Donna J. (1997). *Modest witness @second millennium: FemaleMan meets OncoMouse.* New York: Routledge.

Harding, Sandra. (1986a). The instability of the analytical categories of feminist theory. *Signs: Journal of Women in Culture and Society, 11,* 645-664.

Harding, Sandra. (1986b). *The science question in feminism.* Ithaca, NY: Cornell University Press.

Harding, Sandra. (1987a). Conclusion: Epistemological questions. In S. Harding (Ed.), *Feminism and methodology (pp. 3-14). Bloomington: University of Indiana Press.*

Harding, Sandra. (1987b). Introduction: Is there a feminist method? In S. Harding (Ed.), *Feminism and methodology (pp. 3-14). Bloomington: University of Indiana Press.*

Harding, Sandra. (1991). *Whose science, whose knowledge?* Milton Keynes, UK: Open University Press.

Harding, Sandra, & Hintikka, M. B. (Eds.). (1983). *Discovering reality: Feminist perspectives on epistemology, metaphysics, methodology and philosophy of science.* Dordrecht, the Netherlands: D. Reidel.

Hare-Mustin, Rachel. (1991, May). *Discourse in the mirrored room.* Paper presented at the International Conference on Narrative and Psychotherapy: New Directions in Theory and Practice for the 21st Century, Houston, TX.

Hare-Mustin, Rachel. (1994). Discourse in a mirrored room: A postmodern analysis of therapy. *Family Process, 33,* 199-236.

Hare-Mustin, Rachel, & Marecek, Jeanne. (1986). Autonomy and gender: Some questions for therapists. *Psychotherapy, 23,* 205-212.

Hare-Mustin, Rachel, & Marecek, Jeanne (Eds.). (1990). *Making a difference: Psychology and the construction of gender.* New Haven, CT: Yale University Press.

Harré, Rom. (1986). *The social construction of emotion.* Oxford, UK: Basil Blackwell.

Harré, Rom, & Secord, Paul. (1972). *The explanation of social behaviour.* Oxford, UK: Basil Blackwell.

Hartsock, Nancy. (1983). *Money, sex and power.* New York: Longman.

Hastie, Reid, & Kumar, P. A. (Eds.). (1979). Person memory: Personality traits as organizing principles in memory for behavior. *Journal of Personality and Social Psychology, 37,* 25-38.

Hawksworth, Mary. (1989). Knower, knowing, and known: Feminist theory and claims of truth. *Signs: Journal of Women in Culture and Society, 14,* 550.

Heilbrun, Carolyn. (1988). *Writing a woman's life.* San Francisco: Woman's Press.

Hekman, Susan. (1990). *Gender and knowledge: Elements of a postmodern feminism.* Boston: Northeastern University Press.

Henriques, J., Hollway, Wendy, Urwin, Cathy, Venn, C., & Walkerdine, Valerie. (1984). *Changing the subject: Psychology, social regulation, and subjectivity.* London: Methuen.

Hermans, Hubert J. M. (1996). Opposites in a dialogical self: Constructs as characters. *Journal of Constructivist Psychology, 9,* 1-26.

Hermans, Hubert J. M., & Hermans-Jansen, E. (1995). *Self-narratives: The construction of meaning in psychotherapy.* New York: Guilford.

Hermans, Hubert J. M., Kempen, Harry, & Van Loon, R. J. P. (1992). The dialogical self: Beyond individualism and rationalism. *American Psychologist, 47,* 23-33.

Hermans, Hubert J. M., Rijks, T. I., & Kempen, Harry J. G. (1993). Imaginal dialogues in the self: Theory and method. *Journal of Personality, 61,* 207-236.

Higgins, E. Tory, & Kruglanski, Arie (Eds.). (1996). *Social psychology: Handbook of basic principles.* New York: Guilford.

Hollway, Wendy. (1989). *Subjectivity and method in psychology: Gender meaning and science.* London: Sage.

hooks, bell. (1990). *Yearning: Peace, gender and cultural politics.* Toronto: Between the Lines.

Howard, Ann, Pion, G. M., Gottfredson, G. D., Flattau, P. E., Oskamp, S., Pfafflin, S. M., Bray, D. W., & Burstein, A. G. (1986). The changing face of American psychology: A report from the Committee on Employment and Human Resources. *American Psychologist, 41,* 1311-1327.

Hubbard, Ruth. (1982). Have only men evolved? In R. Hubbard, M. S. Henifin, & B. Fried (Eds.), *Biological woman: The convenient myth* (pp. 17-46). Cambridge, MA: Schenkman.

Hubbard, Ruth. (1988). Some thoughts about the masculinity of the natural sciences. In M. M. Gergen (Ed.), *Feminist thought and the structure of knowledge* (pp. 1-15). New York: New York University Press.

Hurd, Tracey L. (1998, August). *"I'm a second mom": The intricacies of mothering other people's children.* Presented at the annual meeting of the American Psychological Association, San Francisco.

Hyde, Janet, & Linn, Marcia (Eds.). (1986). *The psychology of gender: Advances through meta-analysis.* Baltimore, MD: Johns Hopkins University Press.

Iacocca, Lee (with William Novak). (1984). *Iacocca: An autobiography.* New York: Bantam.

Irigaray, Luce. (1985a). *Speculum of the other woman.* (G. C. Gill, Trans.). Ithaca, NY: Cornell University Press.

Irigaray, Luce. (1985b). *This sex which is not one.* (C. Porter, Trans.). Ithaca, NY: Cornell University Press.

Israel, Jochim, & Tajfel, Henri (Eds.). (1972). *The context of social psychology: A critical assessment.* New York: Academic Press.

Jack, Dana Crowley. (1991). *Silencing the self: Women and depression.* Cambridge, MA: Harvard University Press.

Jack, Dana Crowley, & Dill, D. (1992). The Silencing of Self Scale: Schemas of intimacy associated with depression in women. *Psychology of Women Quarterly, 16,* 97-106.

Jaggar, Allison M. (1983). *Feminist politics and human nature.* Totowa, NJ: Rowman & Allanheld.

Jameson, Fredric. (1984, Fall). The politics of theory: Ideological positions in the postmodernism debate. *New German Critique, 33,* 34-41.

Janet, Pierre. (1928). *L'evolution de la memoire et la notion du temps.* Paris: L. Alcan.

Jelinek, Estelle C. (1980). *Women's autobiography: Essays in criticism.* Bloomington: Indiana University Press.

Josselson, Ruthellen, & Lieblich, Amia (Eds.). (1993). *The narrative study of lives* (Vol. 1). Newbury Park, CA: Sage.

Josselson, Ruthellen, & Lieblich, Amia (Eds.). (1995). *Interpreting experience: The narrative study of lives.* Thousand Oaks, CA: Sage.

Kahn, Arnold S., & Yoder, Janice D. (1989). The psychology of women and conservatism: Rediscovering social change. *Psychology of Women Quarterly, 13,* 427-432.

Kaite, Berkeley. (1995). *Pornography and difference.* Bloomington: University of Indiana Press.

Kaplan, E. Ann. (1983). *Women and film: Both sides of the camera.* New York: Methuen.

Kappeler, Susanne. (1986). *The pornography of representation.* Minneapolis: University of Minnesota Press.

Kauffman, Linda S. (1986). *Discourses of desire: Gender, genre and epistolary fictions.* Ithaca, NY: Cornell University Press.

Keller, Evelyn Fox. (1983). Gender and science. In S. Harding & M. B. Hintikka (Eds.), *Discovering reality: Feminist perspectives on epistemology, metaphysics, methodology and philosophy of science* (pp. 187-205). Dordrecht, the Netherlands: D. Reidel.

Keller, Evelyn Fox. (1985). *Reflections on gender and science.* New Haven, CT: Yale University Press.

Keller, Evelyn Fox. (1992). The paradox of scientific subjectivity. *Rethinking Objectivity: Annals of Scholarship, 9*(2), 135-154.

Keller, Evelyn Fox, & Longino, Helen (Eds.). (1996). *Feminism and science.* New York: Oxford University Press.

Kelly, George. (1955). *The psychology of personal constructs.* New York: Norton

Kessler, Wendy, & McKenna, Suzanne. (1978). *Gender: An ethnomethodological approach.* New York: John Wiley.

Kiesler, Sara B., & Baral, Roberta L. (1970). The search for a romantic partner: The effects of self-esteem and physical attractiveness on romantic behavior. In K. J. Gergen & D. Marlowe (Eds.), *Personality and social behavior* (pp. 155-166). Reading, MA: Addison-Wesley.

Kimble, Gregory A. (1984). Psychology's two cultures. *American Psychologist, 39,* 833-839.

Kimble, Gregory A. (1995). *Psychology: The hope of a science.* Cambridge: MIT Press.

Kimmel, Michael S. (1994). Masculinity as homophobia. In H. Broad & M. Kaufman (Eds.), *Theorizing masculinities* (pp. 200-219). London: Sage.

Kirkland, Gelsey (with Greg Lawrence). (1986). *Dancing on my grave.* New York: Doubleday.

Kitzinger, Celia. (1987). *The social construction of lesbianism.* London: Sage.

Kitzinger, Celia. (1991a). Feminism, psychology and the paradox of power. *Feminism & Psychology, 1,* 111-130.

Kitzinger, Celia. (1991b). Politicizing psychology. *Feminism & Psychology, 1,* 49-54.

Kitzinger, Celia, & Wilkinson, Sue. (1994). Virgins and queers: Rehabilitating heterosexuality. *Gender & Society, 8,* 444-463.

Knorr-Cetina, Karin. (1981). *The manufacture of knowledge.* New York: Pergamon.

Koch, Edward I. (with William Rauch). (1984). *Mayor.* New York: Warner.

Kolody, Annette. (1980). The lady's not for spurning: Kate Millett and the critics. In E. Jelinek (Ed.), *Women's autobiography: Essays in criticism,* Bloomington: Indiana University Press.

Komesaroff, Paul, Rothfield, Philipa, & Daly, Jeanne (Eds.). (1997). *Reinterpreting menopause: Cultural and philosophical issues.* New York: Routledge.

Kristeva, Julia. (1980). *Desire in language. A semiotic approach to literature and art.* (T. Gora Trans.; A. Jardine & L. Roudiez, Eds.). New York: Columbia University Press.

Kroker, Arthur, & Kroker, Marilouise (Eds.). (1993). *The last sex: Feminism and outlaw bodies.* London: Macmillan.

Kuhn, Thomas S. (1970). *The structure of scientific revolutions* (2nd rev. ed.). Chicago: University of Chicago Press.

Kuhn, Thomas S. (1977). *The essential tension: Selected studies in scientific tradition and change.* Chicago: University of Chicago Press.

Kvale, Steiner (Ed.). (1992). *Psychology and postmodernism.* Newbury Park, CA: Sage.

LaFromboise, Teresa D., & Plake, B. (1984). A model for the concept of culture in American Indian educational research. *White Cloud Journal, 3,* 44-52.

Landrine, Hope (Ed.). (1995). *Bringing cultural diversity to feminist psychology: Theory, research, and practice.* Washington, DC: American Psychological Association.

Lather, Patti. (1986). Research as praxis. *Harvard Educational Review, 56,* 257-277.

Lather, Patti. (1991). *Getting smart: Feminist research and pedagogy within the postmodern.* New York: Routledge.

Lather, Patti. (1995). The validity of angels: Interpretive and textual strategies in researching the lives of women with HIV/AIDS. *Qualitative Inquiry, 1,* 41-68.

Lather, Patti, & Smithies, Chris. (1997). *Troubling with angels: Women living with HIV/AIDS.* Boulder, CO: Westview.

Latour, Bruno, & Woolgar, Stephen. (1979). *Laboratory life: The social construction of scientific facts.* Thousand Oaks: Sage.

Leng, Kwok Wei. (1997). Menopause and the great divide: Biomedicine, feminism, and cyborg politics. In P. Komesaroff, P. Rothfield, & J. Daly (Eds.), *Reinterpreting menopause: Cultural and philosophical issues* (pp. 255-272). New York: Routledge.

Letherby, G. (1995). "Dear researcher": The use of correspondence as a method within feminist qualitative research. *Gender & Society, 9,* 576-593.

Levinson, Daniel. (1978). *Seasons of a man's life.* New York: Knopf.

Lieblich, Amia, & Josselson, Ruthellen (Eds.). (1994). *Exploring identity and gender: The narrative study of lives* (Vol. 2). Thousand Oaks, CA: Sage.

Lieblich, Amia, Tuval-Mashiach, Rivka, & Zilber, Tamar. (1998). *Narrative research: Reading, analysis, and interpretation.* Thousand Oaks, CA: Sage.

Lincoln, Yvonne. (1995). Emerging criteria for quality in qualitative and interpretive research. *Qualitative Inquiry, 1,* 275-289.

Lockheed, M. E. (1985). Sex and social influence: A meta-analysis guided by theory. In J. Bergen & M. Zelditch, Jr. (Eds.), *Status, rewards, and influence: How expectancies organize behavior* (pp. 406-429). San Francisco: Jossey-Bass.

Longino, Helen. (1981). Scientific objectivity and feminist theorizing. *Liberal Education, 67,* 73-87.

Lopes, Lola L. (1991). The rhetoric of irrationality. *Theory & Psychology, 1,* 65-82.

Lorber, Judith, & Farrell, Susan A. (1991). *The social construction of gender.* Newbury Park, CA: Sage.

Lorde, Audre. (1984a). Comments at the Personal and Political Panel of the Second Sex Conference, New York, NY, September 29, 1979. In *Sister outsider: Essays and speeches by Audre Lorde.* New York: Crossing Press.

Lorde, Audre. (1984b). Eye to eye: Black women, hatred and anger. In *Sister outsider: Essays and speeches by Audre Lorde.* New York: Crossing Press.

Lott, Bernice. (1985). The potential enrichment of social/personality psychology through feminist research and vice versa. *American Psychologist, 40,* 155-164.

Lucie-Smith, Edward. (1972). *Eroticism in Western art.* New York: Oxford University Press.

Lykes, M. Brinton. (1985). Gender and individualistic vs. collectivist based notions about the self. *Journal of Personality, 53,* 356-383.

Lykes, M. Brinton. (1989). Dialogue with Guatemalan Indian women: Critical perspectives on constructing collaborative research. In R. Unger (Ed.), *Representations: Social construction of gender* (pp. 167-185). Amityville, NY: Baywood.

Lykes, M. Brinton. (1996). Meaning making in a context of genocide and silencing. In M. B. Lykes, A. Banuazizi, R. Liem, & M. Morris (Eds.), *Myths about the powerless: Contesting social inequalities* (pp. 159-178). Philadelphia: Temple University Press.

Lynch, Mervin D., Norem-Hebeisen, Aridity A., & Gergen, Kenneth J. (1981). *Self-concept: Advances in theory and research.* Boston: Ballinger.

Lyotard, Jean-Francis. (1984). *The postmodern condition: A report on knowledge.* Minneapolis: University of Minnesota Press.

Maccoby, Eleanor E., & Jacklin, Carol N. (1974). *The psychology of sex differences.* Stanford, CA: Stanford University Press.

Macmillan, Katie. (1990). Giving voice: The participant takes issue. *Feminism & Psychology, 5,* 547-552.

Maguire, P. (1987). *Doing participatory research: A feminist approach.* Amherst, MA: University of Massachusetts, Center for International Education.

Mahoney, Maureen A., & Yngvesson, Barbara. (1992). The construction of subjectivity and the paradox of resistance: Reintegrating feminist anthropology and psychology. *Signs: Journal of Women in Culture and Society, 18,* 44-73.

Maoz, B., Dowty, N., Antonovsky, A., & Wijsenbeck, H. (1970). Female attitudes to menopause. *Social Psychiatry, 5,* 35-40.

Marecek, Jeanne. (1993). Disappearances, silences, and anxious rhetoric: Gender in abnormal psychology textbooks. *Journal of Theoretical and Philosophical Psychology, 13,* 114-124.

Martin, Emily. (1987). *Woman in the body: A cultural analysis of reproduction.* Boston: Beacon.

Mascia-Lees, Frances E., Sharpe, Patricia, & Cohen, Colleen Ballerino. (1989). The postmodernist turn in anthropology: Cautions from a feminist perspective. *Signs: Journal of Women in Culture and Society, 15,* 7-33.

Mason, Mary G. (1980). Autobiographies of women writers. In J. Olney (Ed.), *Autobiography, essays theoretical and critical.* Princeton, NJ: Princeton University Press.

McCall, M. M. (2000). Performance ethnography: A brief history and some advice. In N. K. Denzin & Y. S. Lincoln (Eds.), *The handbook of qualitative research* (2nd ed., pp. 421-434). Thousand Oaks, CA: Sage.

McGovern, T. V., Furumoto, Laura, Halpern, Diane F., Kimble, Gregory, A., & McKeachie, Wilbert J. (1991). Liberal education, study in depth, and the arts and sciences major: Psychology. *American Psychologist, 46,* 598-606.

McIntyre, Alice, & Lykes, M. Brinton. (1998). Who's the boss? Confronting whiteness and power differences within a feminist mentoring relationship in participatory action research. *Feminism & Psychology, 8,* 427-444.

McRae, Jill F. Kealey. (1994). A woman's story: *E pluribus unum.* In A. Lieblich & R. Josselson (Eds.), *Exploring identity and gender: The narrative study of lives* (Vol. 2, pp. 195-229).Thousand Oaks, CA: Sage.

McWilliam, Erica, & Jones, Alison. (1996). Eros and pedagogical bodies: The sate of (non)affairs. In E. McWilliam & P. G. Taylor (Eds.), *Pedagogy, technology, and the body* (pp. 127-136). New York: Peter Lang.

Mead, George H. (1934). *Mind, self and society* (C. W. Morris, Ed.). Chicago: University of Chicago Press.

Mednick, Martha S., & Tangri, Sandra S. (1972). New social psychological perspectives on women. *Journal of Social Issues, 28,* 1-16.

Meyrowitz, Joshua. (1994). The life and death of media friends: New genres of intimacy and mourning. In R. Cathcart & S. Drucker (Eds.), *American heroes in a media age.* New York: Hampton.

Mienczakowski, Jim. (1996). An ethnographic act. The construction of consensual theater. In C. Ellis & A. P. Bochner (Eds.), *Composing ethnography: Alternative forms of qualitative writing* (pp. 244-266). Thousand Oaks, CA: Alta Mira.

Mienczakowski, Jim, Smith, Richard, & Sinclair, Mark. (1996). On the road to catharsis: A theoretical framework for change. *Qualitative Inquiry, 2,* 439-462.

Mies, Maria. (1987). *Patriarchy and accumulation on a world scale: Women in the international division of labour.* London: Zed.

Miller, Jean Baker. (1976). *Toward a new psychology of women.* Boston: Beacon.

Miller, Jean Baker, & Stiver, Irene Pierce. (1997). *The healing connection: How women form relationships in therapy and in life.* Boston: Beacon.

Mitroff, Ivan. (1974). *The subjective side of science.* Amsterdam: Elsevier.

Mohanty, Chandra Talpade. (1995). Feminist encounters: Locating the politics of experience. In L. Nicholson & S. Seidman (Eds.), *Social postmodernism: Beyond identity politics* (pp. 68-86). New York: Cambridge University Press.

Moi, Toril. (1985). *Sexual/textual politics*. London: Metheun.

Moi, Toril (Ed.). (1987). *French feminist thought: A reader.* Oxford, UK: Basil Blackwell.

Moi, Toril. (1988). Feminism, postmodernism, and style: Recent feminist criticism in the United States. *Cultural Critique, 9,* 3-22.

Moraga, Cherrie, & Anzaldua, Gloria (Eds.). (1981). *This bridge called my back: Writing by radical women of color.* Watertown, MA: Persephone.

Morawski, Jill G. (1987). Troubled quest for masculinity, femininity and androgyny. In P. Shaver & C. Hendrick (Eds.), *Review of personality and social psychology: Vol. 7. Sex and gender* (pp. 44-69). Newbury Park, CA: Sage.

Morawski, Jill G. (1988a). Impasse in feminist thought? In M. M. Gergen (Ed.), *Feminist thought and the structure of knowledge* (pp. 182-194). New York: New York University Press.

Morawski, Jill G. (Ed.). (1988b). *The rise of experimentation in American psychology.* New Haven, CT: Yale University Press.

Morawski, Jill G. (1994). *Practicing feminisms, reconstructing psychology: Notes on a liminal science.* Ann Arbor: University of Michigan Press.

Morawski, Jill G., & Bayer, Betty. (1995). Stirring trouble and making theory. In H. Landrine (Ed.), *Bringing cultural diversity to feminist psychology: Theory, research, and practice* (pp. 113-137). Washington, DC: American Psychological Association.

Morris, Rosalind C. (1995). All made up: Performance theory and the new anthropology of sex and gender. *Annual Review of Anthropology, 24,* 567-592.

Mouffe, Chantal. (1995). Feminism, citizenship, and radical democratic politics. In L. Nicholson & S. Seidman (Eds.), *Social postmodernism: Beyond identity politics* (pp. 315-331). New York: Cambridge University Press.

Mulvey, Laura. (1981, Summer). Afterthoughts on "Visual pleasure and narrative cinema" inspired by *Duel in the Sun. Framework, 15/16/17.*

Navratilova, Martina (with George Vecsey). (1985). *Martina.* New York: Fawcett.

Neugarten, Bernice L. (1979). Time, age, and the life cycle. *American Journal of Psychiatry, 136,* 887-894.

New, Caroline. (1998). Realism, deconstruction and the feminist standpoint. *Journal for the Theory of Social Behaviour, 28,* 349-372.

Newman, Fred, & Holzman, Lois. (1996). *Unscientific psychology: A cultural-performatory approach to understanding human life.* New York: Praeger.

Nicholson, Linda (Ed.). (1990). *Feminism/postmodernism.* New York: Routledge.

Nicholson, Linda. (1995). Interpreting gender. In L. Nicholson & S. Seidman (Eds.), *Social postmodernism: Beyond identity politics* (pp. 39-67).New York: Cambridge University Press.

Nicholson, Linda, & Seidman, Steven (Eds.). (1995). *Social postmodernism: Beyond identity politics.* New York: Cambridge University Press.

Nielsen, Joyce M. (Ed.). (1990). *Feminist research methods.* Boulder, CO: Westview.

Nochlin, Linda. (1991). Women, art, and power. In N. Bryson, M. A. Holly, & K. Moxey (Eds.), *Visual theory: Painting and interpretation* (pp. 13-46). New York: HarperCollins.

Nussbaum, Felicity. (1988). Eighteenth century women's autobiographical common-places. In S. Benstock (Ed.), *The private self* (pp. 34-51). London: Routledge.

O'Bryant, Shirley L., & Nocera, Doris. (1985). The psychological significance of "home" to older widows. *Psychology of Women Quarterly, 9,* 403-412.

Ochberg, Richard L. (1988). Life stories and the psychosocial construction of careers. *Journal of Personality, 56,* 171-202.

O'Leary, Virginia E., Unger, Rhoda K., & Wallston, Barbara S. (Eds.). (1985). *Women, gender, and social psychology.* Hillsdale, NJ: Lawrence Erlbaum.

Olney, James. (1980). *Autobiography: Essays theoretical and critical.* Princeton, NJ: Princeton University Press.

Owens, Craig. (1983). The discourse of others, feminists and postmodernism. In H. Foster (Ed.), *The anti-aesthetic: essays on postmodern culture* (pp. 57-82). Port Townsend, WA: Bay Press.

Parlee, Mary Brown. (1991). Happy birthday to *Feminism & Psychology. Feminism & Psychology, 1,* 39-48.

Penn, Peggy, & Frankfurt, Marilyn. (1994). Creating a participant text: Writing, multiple voices, narrative multiplicity. *Family Process, 33,* 3-21.

Pennebaker, James W. (1988). Confiding traumatic experiences and health. In S. Fisher & J. Reason (Eds.), *Handbook of life stress, cognition and health.* New York: John Wiley.

Pennebaker, James W. (1990). *Opening up: The healing power of confiding with others.* New York: William Morrow.

Peplau, Letitia A., & Conrad, Eva. (1989). Beyond nonsexist research: The perils of feminist methods in psychology. *Psychology of Women Quarterly, 13,* 379-400.

Perelman, C., & Olbrechts-Tyteca, L. (1969). *The new rhetoric: A treatise on argumentation* (J. Wilkinson & P. Weaver, Trans.). Notre Dame, IN: University of Notre Dame Press.

Piaget, Jean. (1955). *The language and thought of the child.* New York: New American Library.

Piaget, Jean. (1960). *The child's conception of the world.* Totowa, NJ: Littlefield Adams.

Pickens, T. Boone, Jr. (1987). *Boone.* Boston: Houghton Mifflin.

Poland, Blake, & Pederson, Ann. (1998). Reading between the lines: Interpreting silences in qualitative research. *Qualitative Inquiry, 4,* 293-312.

Poovey, Mary. (1988). Feminism and deconstruction. *Feminist Studies, 14,* 51-65.

Potter, Jonathan. (1996). *Representing reality, discourse, rhetoric and social construction.* Thousand Oaks, CA: Sage.

Potter, Jonathan, & Wetherell, Margaret. (1987). *Discourse and social psychology: Beyond attitudes and behavior.* London: Sage.

Rabuzzi, Kathryn Allen. (1988). *Motherself: A mythic analysis of motherhood.* Bloomington: Indiana University Press.

Rappoport, Leon. (1984). Dialectical analysis and psychosocial epistemology. In K. J. Gergen & M. M. Gergen (Eds.), *Historical social psychology* (pp. 103-124). Hillsdale, NJ: Lawrence Erlbaum.

Rashad, Ahmad (with Peter Bodo). (1988). *Rashad.* New York: Penguin.

Red Horse, J. G. (1980). Family structure and value orientation in American Indians. *Social Casework, 61,* 462-467.

Reid, Pamela T. (1993). Poor women in psychological research: Shut up and shut out. *Psychology of Women Quarterly, 17,* 133-150.

Reid, Pamela T., & Comas-Diaz, Lillian. (1990). Gender and ethnicity. *Sex Roles, 22,* 397-408.

Reinharz, Shulamit. (1985). Feminist distrust. Problems of context and content in sociological work. In D. Berg & K. Smith (Eds.), *Exploring clinical methods for social research* (pp. 153-172). Beverly Hills, CA: Sage.

Reinharz, Shulamit. (1992). *Feminist methods in social research.* New York: Oxford University Press.

Rich, Adrienne. (1977). *Of woman born.* New York: Norton.

Rivers, Joan (with Richard Meryman). (1986). *Enter talking.* New York: Delacorte.

Roberts, Helen (Ed.). (1981). *Doing feminist research.* London: Routledge.

Rommetveit, Ragnar. (1980). On "meanings" of acts and what is meant and made known by what is said in a pluralistic social world. In M. Brenner (Ed.), *The structure of action* (pp. 108-149). Oxford, UK: Basil Blackwell.

Rosaldo, Michelle, & Lamphere, Louise (Eds.). (1974). *Women, culture, and society.* Stanford, CA: Stanford University Press.

Rosenblatt, Paul C. (1990). *Metaphors of family systems theory: Toward new constructions.* New York: Guilford.

Rosenblatt, Paul C., & Meyer, Cynthia. (1986). Imagined interactions and the family. *Family Relations, 35,* 319-324.

Rosenwald, George C. (1988). A theory of multiple-case research. *Journal of Personality, 56,* 239-264.

Rostosky, Sharon Scales, & Travis, Cheryl Brown. (1996). Menopause research and the dominance of the biomedical model, 1984-1994. *Psychology of Women Quarterly, 20,* 285-312.

Roth, Sallyann, & Chasin, Richard. (1994). Entering one another's worlds of meaning and imagination: Dramatic enactment and narrative couple therapy. In M. F. Hoyt (Ed.), *Constructive therapies* (pp. 189-216). New York: Guilford.

Russ, Joanna. (1972). What can a heroine do? Or why women can't write. In S. Koppelman Cornillon (Ed.), *Images of women in fiction* (pp. 42-55). Bowling Green, OH: University Popular Press.

Russell, Glenda M., & Bohan, Janis S. (1999). Hearing voices: The use of research and the politics of change. *Psychology of Women Quarterly, 23,* 3.

Russo, Mary. (1986). Female grotesques: Carnival and theory. In T. de Lauretis (Ed.), *Feminist studies, critical studies* (pp. 213-229). Milwaukee: University of Wisconsin Press.

Russo, Nancy Felipe. (1995). Editorial *PWQ:* A scientific voice in feminist psychology. *Psychology of Women Quarterly, 19,* 1-3.

Russo, Nancy Felipe, & Dumont, B. Angela. (1997). Division 35: Origins, activities, future. In D. Dewsbury (Ed.), *A history of the divisions of the American Psychological Association* (pp. 211-238). Washington, DC: American Psychological Association.

Said, Edward W. (1983). Opponents, audiences, constituencies and community. In H. Foster (Ed.), *The anti-aesthetic: Essays on postmodern culture (pp. 135-159). Port Townsend, WA: Bay Press.*

Sampson, Edward E. (1977). Psychology and the American ideal. *Journal of Personality and Social Psychology, 36,* 1332-1343.

Sampson, Edward E. (1981). Cognitive psychology as ideology. *American Psychologist, 36,* 730-743.

Sampson, Edward E. (1991). The democratization of psychology. *Theory and Psychology, 1,* 275-298.

Sampson, Edward E. (1993). *Celebrating the other: A dialogic accounting of human nature.* Boulder, CO: Westview.

Saunders, Gill. (1989). *The nude: A new perspective.* London: Herbert.

Sayers, Janet. (1993). Book reviews of Patricia Elliot, *From mastery to analysis: Theories of gender in psychoanalytic feminism,* and Richard Feldstein and Judith Roof (Eds.), *Femininity and psychoanalysis. Feminism & Psychology, 3,* 257.

Sayre, Robert F. (1980). Autobiography and the making of America. In J. Olney (Ed.), *Autobiography: Essays theoretical and critical* (pp. 43-67). Princeton, NJ: Princeton University Press.

Schafer, Roy. (1992). *Retelling a life: Narrative and dialogue in psychoanalysis.* New York: Basic Books.

Schickel, Richard. (1968). *The world of Goya, 1746-1828.* New York: Time Life.

Scott, Joan W. (1988). Deconstructing equality-versus-difference: Or, the use of poststructuralist theory for feminism. *Feminist Studies, 14,* 33-50.

Sherif, Carolyn W. (1979). Bias in psychology. In J. A. Sherman & E. T. Beck (Eds.), *The prism of sex: Essays in the sociology of knowledge* (pp. 93-133). Madison: University of Wisconsin Press.

Shields, Stephanie A. (1975). Functionalism, Darwinism, and the psychology of women: A study in social myth. *American Psychologist, 30,* 739-754.

Shotter, John. (1984). *Social accountability and selfhood.* Oxford, UK: Basil Blackwell.

Shotter, John. (1993). *Cultural politics of everyday life: Social constructionism, rhetoric and knowing of the third kind.* Toronto: University of Toronto Press.

Shotter, John. (1995). In conversation: Joint shared intentionality and ethics. *Theory and Psychology, 5,* 49-73.

Sills, Beverly, & Linderman, Lawrence. (1987). *Beverly.* New York: Bantam.

Simon, William. (1996). *Postmodern sexualities.* New York: Routledge.

Simon, William, & Gagnon, John H. (1986). Sexual scripts: Permanence and change. *Archives of Sexual Behavior, 15,* 97-120.

Smith, Dorothy E. (1991). Writing women's experience into social science. *Feminism & Psychology, 1,* 155-170.

Smith, Sidonie A. (1974). *Where I'm bound: Patterns of slavery and freedom in Black American autobiography.* Westport, CT: Greenwood.

Smith, Sidonie A. (1987). *A poetics of women's autobiography: Marginality and the functions of self-representation.* Bloomington: Indiana University Press.

Smythe, A. (1991). The floozie in the Jacuzzi: The problematics of culture and identity for an Irish woman. *Feminist Studies, 17,* 7-28.

Snow, Edward. (1989). Theorizing the male gaze: Some problems. *Representations, 25,* 30-42.

Spelman, E. (1988). *Inessential woman: Problems of exclusion in feminist thought.* Boston: Beacon.

Spence, Janet T., & Helmreich, Robert L. (1978). *Masculinity and femininity.* Austin: University of Texas Press.

Spender, Dale. (1980). *Man made language.* London: Routledge.

Sprinkler, Michael. (1980). Fictions of the self: The end of autobiography. In J. Olney (Ed.), *Autobiography: Essays theoretical and critical.* Princeton, NJ: Princeton University Press.

Squire, Corinne. (1989). *Significant differences: Feminism in psychology.* London: Routledge.

St. Pierre, Elizabeth. (1997). Circling the text: Nomadic writing practices. *Qualitative Inquiry, 3,* 403-417.

Stam, Henderikus J. (Ed.). (1996). The body and psychology [Special issue]. *Theory & Psychology, 6.*

Stanley, Liz, & Wise, Sue. (1983). *Breaking out: Feminist consciousness and feminist research.* London: Routledge.

Stanton, Domna. (1984). *The female autograph.* Chicago: University of Chicago Press.

Strathern, Marilyn. (1987). Out of context: The persuasive fictions of anthropology. *Current Anthropology, 28,* 251-270.

Strickland, Lloyd (Ed.). (1984). *Directions in Soviet social psychology.* New York: Springer-Verlag.

Strickland, Lloyd, Aboud, Francis, & Gergen, Kenneth J. (1976). *Social psychology in transition.* New York: Plenum.

Stroebe, Margaret, Gergen, Mary M., Gergen, Kenneth J., & Stroebe, Wolfgang. (1992). Broken hearts or broken bonds: Love and death in historical perspective. *American Psychologist, 47,* 1205-1212.

Stroebe, Wolfgang, & Stroebe, Margaret. (1988). *Bereavement and health: The psychological and physical consequences of partner loss.* New York: Cambridge University Press.

Suleiman, Susan Rubin. (1990). *Subversive intent: Gender, politics, and the avant-garde.* Cambridge, MA: Harvard University Press.

Suls, Jerry (Ed.). (1982). *Psychological perspectives on the self.* Hillsdale, NJ: Lawrence Erlbaum.

Sutton-Smith, B. (1971). Piaget on play: A critique. In R. E. Herron & B. Sutton-Smith (Eds.), *Child's play* (pp. 217-231). New York: John Wiley.

Tappan, Mark. (1991). Narrative, language and moral experience. *Journal of Moral Education, 21,* 243-256.

Tavris, Carol. (1992). *The mismeasure of woman: Why women are not the better sex, the inferior sex, or the opposite sex.* New York: Simon & Schuster.

Taylor, Shelley E., Pham, Lien B., Rivkin, Inna D., & Armor, David A. (1998). Harnessing the imagination: Mental simulation, self-regulation, and coping. *American Psychologist, 53,* 429-439.

Tetlock, Philip E. (1994). Political psychology or politicized psychology: Is the road to scientific hell paved with good moral intentions? *International Society of Political Psychology, 10,* 509-529.

Thorne, Barrie. (1990). Children and gender: Constructions of difference. In D. Rhode (Ed.), *Theoretical perspectives in sexual difference* (pp. 100-113). New Haven, CT: Yale University Press.

Tiefer, Leonore. (1988). A feminist perspective on sexology and sexuality. In M. M. Gergen (Ed.), *Feminist thought and the structure of knowledge* (pp. 16-26). New York: New York University Press.

Tiefer, Leonore. (1995). *Sex is not a natural act, and other essays.* Boulder, CO: Westview.

Tiefer, Leonore. (1997). Sexual biology and the symbolism of the natural. In M. M. Gergen & S. N. Davis (Eds.), *Toward a new psychology of gender* (pp. 363-376). New York: Routledge.

Tierney, William G. (1995). (Re)Presentation and voice. *Qualitative Inquiry, 1,* 379-390.

Tong, Rosemary. (1989). *Feminist thought: A comprehensive introduction.* Boulder, CO: Westview.

Trapier, Elizabeth du Gue. (1964). *Goya and his sitters. A study of his style as a portraitist.* New York: Hispanic Society of America.

Trebilcot, Joyce. (1994). *Dyke ideas: Process, politics, daily life.* Albany: State University of New York Press.

Trump, Donald (with Tony Schwartz). (1987). *Trump: The art of the deal.* New York: Warner.

Tyler, Stephen. (1986). Post-modern ethnography: From document of the occult to occult documents. In J. Clifford & G. Marcus (Eds.), *Writing culture.* Berkeley: University of California Press.

Tyler, Stephen. (1987). *The unspeakable: Discourse, dialogue, and rhetoric in the postmodern world.* Madison: University of Wisconsin Press.

Tyler, Stephen. (1989, April). *A postmodern (for) instance.* Paper presented at the Conference on Critical Anthropology, Amsterdam.

Tyler, Stephen. (1991). A post-modern in-stance. In L. Nencel & P. Pels (Eds.), *Constructing knowledge: Authority and critique in social science* (pp. 78-94). Newbury Park, CA: Sage.

Unger, Rhoda. (1983). Through the looking glass: No Wonderland yet! (The reciprocal relationship between methodology and models of reality). *Psychology of Women Quarterly, 8,* 9-32.

Unger, Rhoda. (1988). Psychological, feminist, and personal epistemology: Transcending contradiction. In M. M. Gergen (Ed.), *Feminist thought and the structure of knowledge* (pp. 124-141). New York: New York University Press.

Unger, Rhoda (Ed.). (1989). *Representations: Social construction of gender.* Amityville, NY: Baywood.

Vance, Carole S. (Ed.). (1984). *Pleasure and danger: Exploring female sexuality.* London: Routledge.

Vaughter, R. (1976). Psychology: Review essay. *Signs: Journal of Women in Culture and Society, 2,* 120-146.

Vygotsky, L. S. (1962). *Thought and language.* Cambridge: MIT Press.

Wagner, R. (1975). *The invention of culture.* Englewood Cliffs, NJ: Prentice Hall.

Walkerdine, Valerie. (1986). Post-structuralist theory and everyday social practices: The family and the school. In S. Wilkinson (Ed.), *Feminist social psychology: Developing theory and practice* (pp. 57-76). Milton Keynes, UK: Open University Press.

Walkerdine, Valerie. (1990). *Schoolgirl fictions.* London: Verso.

Walsh-Bowers, Richard. (1999). Fundamentalism in psychological science: The APA *Publication Manual* as bible. *Psychology of Women Quarterly, 23*(2), 375-398.

Walster, Elaine. (1965). The effect of self-esteem on romantic liking. *Journal of Experimental Social Psychology, 1,* 184-197.

Walster, Elaine, Aronson, V., Abrahams, D., & Rottman, L. (1966). Importance of physical attractiveness in dating behavior. *Journal of Personality and Social Psychology, 4,* 508-516.

Watkins, Mary. (1986). *Invisible guests, the development of imaginal dialogues.* Hillsdale, NJ: Analytic Press.

Watson, Thomas J., Jr., & Petre, Peter. (1990). *Father Son & Co.: My life at IBM and beyond.* New York: Bantam.

Weedon, Chris. (1987). *Feminist practice and post-structuralist theory.* Oxford, UK: Basil Blackwell.

Weisstein, Naomi. (1971). Psychology constructs the female. In V. Gornick & B. K. Moran (Eds.), *Woman in sexist society* (pp. 133-146). New York: Signet.

Weisstein, Naomi. (1993). Power, resistance, and science: A call for a revitalized feminist psychology. *Feminism & Psychology, 3,* 239-245.

Weitz, Rose. (1998). *The politics of women's bodies: Sexuality, appearance, and behavior.* New York: Oxford University Press.

Wetherell, Margaret (Ed.). (1996). *Identities, groups and social issues.* Milton Keynes, UK: Open University Press.

Whatley, Marianne H. (1991). Raging hormones and powerful cars: The construction of men's sexuality in school sex education and popular adolescent films. In H. Giroux (Ed.), *Postmodernism, feminism, and cultural politics* (pp. 119-143). Albany: State University of New York Press.

White, Jacquelyn W., Bondurant, Barrie, & Travis, Cheryl Brown. (2000). Social constructions of sexuality: Unpacking hidden meanings. In C. B. Travis & J. W. White (Eds.), *Sexuality, society, and feminism* (pp. 11-33). Washington, DC: American Psychological Association.

White, Michael, & Epston, David. (1990). *Narrative means to therapeutic ends.* New York: Norton.

Wilkinson, Sue (Ed.). (1986). *Feminist social psychology.* Milton Keynes, UK: Open University Press.

Williams, Linda. (1989). *Hard core: Power, pleasure, and the frenzy of the visible.* Berkeley: University of California Press.

Wood, W. (1987). Meta-analytic review of sex differences in group performance. *Psychological Bulletin, 102,* 53-71.

Woolf, Virginia. (1957). *A room of one's own.* New York: Harcourt, Brace, Jovanovich. (Original work published 1929)

Woolf, Virginia. (1958). *Granite and rainbow.* New York: Harcourt, Brace, Jovanovich.

Woolgar, Steven (Ed.). (1987). *Knowledge and reflexivity.* London: Sage.

Woolgar, Steven. (1988). *Science, the very idea.* New York: Tavistock.

Wyatt, Gayle. (1992). The sociocultural context of African American and white women's rape. *Journal of Social Issues, 48,* 77-91.

Wyer, R. S., & Srull, T. K. (Eds.). (1984). *Handbook of social cognition.* Hillsdale, NJ: Lawrence Erlbaum.

Yeager, Chuck, & Janos, Leo. (1985). *Yeager, an autobiography.* New York: Bantam.

Yoder, Janice D., & Kahn, Arnold S. (1993). Working toward an inclusive psychology of women. *American Psychologist, 48,* 846-850.

Young, Iris Marion. (1990). *Justice and the politics of difference.* Princeton, NJ: Princeton University Press.

Young, Katharine (Ed.). (1993). *Bodylore.* Knoxville: University of Tennessee Press.

ADDITIONAL SUGGESTED READINGS

Barratt, Barnaby, & Straus, Barrie Ruth. (1994). Toward postmodern masculinities. *American Imago, 51,* 37-67.

Bhavnani, Kum-Kum. (1990). What's power got to do with it? Empowerment and social research. In I. Parker & J. Shotter (Eds.), *Deconstructing social psychology* (pp. 141-152). London: Routledge.

Boone, Joseph A., & Cadden, Michael (Eds.). (1990). *Engendering men, The question of male feminist criticism.* New York: Routledge.

Bordo, Susan. (1993). Anorexia nervosa. Psychopathology as the crystallization of culture. *Unbearable weight: Feminism, Western culture and the body.* Berkeley: University of California Press.

Brittan, Arthur. (1989). *Masculinity and power.* Oxford, UK: Basil Blackwell.

Brown, Laura S. (1989). New voices, new visions: Toward a lesbian/gay paradigm for psychology. *Psychology of Women Quarterly, 13,* 445-458.

Bruner, Jerome. (1990). *Acts of meaning.* Cambridge, MA: Harvard University Press.

Burman, Erica. (1990). The spec(tac)ular economy of difference. *Feminism & Psychology, 5,* 543-546.

Burman, Erica. (1991). Power, gender, and developmental psychology. *Feminism & Psychology, 1,* 131-153.

Chasin, Richard, & Roth, Sallyann. (1994, March). *Reinventing the past: An action/narrative approach to couples therapy.* Paper presented at the Annual *Family Therapy Networker* Symposium, Washington, DC.

Code, Lorraine. (1992). Who cares? The poverty of objectivism for moral epistemology. *Rethinking Objectivity II, Annals of Scholarship, 9,* 1-18.

Cooperrider, David L. (1995). Introduction to appreciative inquiry. In W. French & C. Bell (Eds.), *Organization development* (5th ed.). New York: Prentice Hall.

Cooperrider, David L. (1998). Getting started. In S. Hammond & C. Royal (Eds.), *Lessons from the field: Applying appreciative inquiry.* Plano, TX: Practical Press.

Crawford, Mary, & Maracek, Jeanne. (1989). Psychology reconstructs the female, 1968-1988. *Psychology of Women Quarterly, 13,* 147-165.

Danziger, Kurt. (1985). The methodological imperative in psychology. *Philosophy of Social Sciences, 15,* 1-13.

Danziger, Kurt. (1997). *Naming the mind: How psychology found its language.* London, Thousand Oaks, CA: Sage.

Davis, Kathy. (1997). *Embodied practices: Feminist perspectives on the body.* Thousand Oaks, CA: Sage.

Derrida, Jacques. (1979). *Spurs: Nietzsche's styles* (B. Harlow, Trans.). Chicago: University of Chicago Press.

Elam, Diane. (1994). *Feminism and deconstruction: Ms. en abyme.* New York: Routledge.

Epstein, Cynthia F. (1990). *Deceptive distinctions: Sex, gender and the social order.* New Haven, CT: Yale University Press.

Faith, Kareen. (1994). Resistance: Lessons from Foucault and feminism. In H. Lorraine Radtke & Henderikus J. Stam (Eds.), *Power/gender, social relations in theory and practice* (pp. 36-66). London: Sage.

Fonow, Mary Margaret, & Cook, Judith A. (1991). *Beyond methodology: Feminist scholarship as lived research.* Bloomington: Indiana University Press.

Foucault, Michel. (1978). *The history of sexuality: Vol. 1. An introduction* (R. Hurley, Trans.). New York: Vintage.

Foucault, Michel. (1980). *Power/knowledge* (C. Gordon, Ed. & Trans.). New York: Pantheon.

Furomoto, Laurel, & Scarsborough, Elizabeth. (1986). Placing women in the history of psychology: The first American women psychologists. *American Psychologist, 41,* 35-42.

Gergen, Kenneth J., & Gergen, Mary M. (1986). The discourse of control and the maintenance of well-being. In M. Baltes & P. Baltes (Eds.), *Aging and control* (pp. 119-137). Hillsdale, NJ: Lawrence Erlbaum.

Gergen, Kenneth J., & Gergen, Mary M. (1993). Narratives of the gendered body in the popular autobiography. In R. Josselson & A. Lieblich (Eds.), *The narrative study of lives* (pp. 191-218). Newbury Park, CA: Sage.

Gergen, Mary M. (1989). Loss of control among the aging: A feminist alternative. In P. S. Fry (Ed.), *Psychological perspectives of helplessness and control in the elderly* (pp. 261-289). New York: Elsevier.

Gergen, Mary M. (1990). Finished at 40: Women's development within the patriarchy. *Psychology of Women Quarterly, 14,* 471-493.

Gergen, Mary M. (1990). From mod masculinity to post-mod macho: A feminist re-play. *Humanistic Psychologist, 18,* 95-104.

Gergen, Mary M. (Chair). (1998, August). *Performative psychology.* Symposium conducted at the annual meeting of the American Psychological Association, San Francisco.

Gilfoyle, Jackie, Wilson, Jonathan, & Brown, A. (1992). Sex, organs and audiotape: A discourse analytic approach to talking about heterosexual sex and relationships. *Feminism & Psychology, 2,* 209-230.

Gilligan, Carol. (1994). Listening to a different voice: Celia Kitzinger interviews Carol Gilligan. *Feminism and Psychology, 4,* 408-419.

Gleason, Tracy. (1998). *Imaginary companions: A window on early childhood.* Unpublished doctoral dissertation, University of Minnesota.

Goffman, Erving. (1981). *Forms of talk.* Philadelphia: University of Pennsylvania Press.

Gorman, Jane. (1993). Postmodernism and the conduct of inquiry in social work. *Affilia, 8,* 247-264.

Harding, Sandra. (1998). *Is science multicultural? Postcolonialisms, feminisms, and epistemologies.* Bloomington: Indiana University Press.

Hare-Mustin, Rachel. (1988). Changing women, changing therapy: Clinical implications of the changing role of women. *Journal of Feminist Family Therapy, 4,* 7-18.

Haug, Friga, et al. (1987). *Female sexualization: A collective work of memory.* London: Verso.

Hekman, Susan. (1993). Moral voices, moral selves: About getting it right in moral theory. *Human Studies, 16,* 143-162.

hooks, bell. (1984). *Feminist theory: From margin to center.* Boston: South End.

hooks, bell. (1989). *Talking back: Thinking feminist, thinking black.* Boston: South End.

Hyde, Janet S. (1985). *Half the human experience: The psychology of women.* Lexington, MA: D. C. Heath.

Ibanez, Tomas, & Iniguez, Lupicinio (Eds.). (1997). *Critical social psychology.* London: Sage.

Israeli, Dafna. (1993). They have eyes and see not. Gender politics in the Diaspora Museum. *Psychology of Women Quarterly, 17,* 515-523.

Jaggar, Alison M. (1989). Love and knowledge: Emotion in feminist epistemology. In A. Jaggar & S. Bordo (Eds.), *Gender/body/knowledge: Feminist reconstructions of being and knowing.* New Brunswick, NJ: Rutgers University Press.

Jardine, Alice. (1985). *Gynesis: Configurations of woman and modernity.* Ithaca, NY: Cornell University Press.

Jones, Alison. (1993). Becoming a "girl": Post-structionalist suggestions for educational research. *Gender and Education, 5,* 157-166.

Joy, Morny. (1993). Feminism and the self. *Theory and Psychology, 3,* 275-302.

Kippax, Susan, Crawford, June, Benton, Pam, Gault, Una, & Noesjirwan, Jenny. (1988). Constructing emotions: Weaving meaning from memories. *British Journal of Social Psychology, 27,* 19-33.

Kitzinger, Celia. (1994). *Problematizing pleasure: Radical feminist deconstruction of sexuality and power.* Unpublished manuscript.

Knorr-Cetina, Karin, & Mulkay, Michael (Eds.). (1983). *Science observed: Perspectives on the social study of science.* London: Sage.

Kristeva, Julia. (1987). *The Kristeva reader* (T. Moi, Ed.). New York: Columbia University Press.

Kroker, Arthur, & Cook, David. (1988). *The postmodern scene.* New York: St. Martin's.

Lather, Patti. (1990). Postmodernism and the human sciences. *Humanistic Psychologist, 18,* 64-84.

Latour, Bruno. (1987). *Science in action: How to follow engineers through society.* Milton Keynes, UK: Open University Press.

Latour, Bruno, & Woolgar, Steve. (1986). *Laboratory life: The construction of scientific facts* (2nd ed.). Princeton, NJ: Princeton University Press.

Lloyd, Moya. (1993). The (f)utility of a feminist turn to Foucault. *Economy and Society, 22,* 437-460.

Mahoney, Michael. (1991). *Human change processes.* New York: Basic Books.

McHugh, Mary C., Koeske, Randy D., & Frieze, Irene H. (1986). Issues to consider in conducting nonsexist psychological research. *American Psychologist, 41,* 879-890.

Miles, Lesley. (1993). Women, AIDS, and power in heterosexual sex: A discourse analysis. *Women's International Forum, 16,* 497-511.

Minton, H. L. (1986). Emancipatory social psychology as a paradigm for the study of minority groups. In K. S. Larsen (Ed.), *Dialectics and ideology in psychology.* Norwood, NJ: ABLEX.

Mishler, E. (1986). *Research interviewing: Context and narrative.* Cambridge, MA: Harvard University Press.

Morawski, Jill G. (1985). The measurement of masculinity and femininity: Engendering categorical realities. *Journal of Personality, 53,* 196-223.

Moscovici, Serge. (1984). The phenomenon of social representations. In R. Farr & S. Moscovici (Eds.), *Social representations* (pp. 1-39). London: Cambridge University Press.

Mulkay, Michael J. (1979). *Science and the sociology of knowledge.* London: Allen & Unwin.

Mulkay, Michael J. (1985). *The word and the world: Explorations in the form of sociological analysis.* London: Allen & Unwin.

Neugarten, B. L. (Eds.). (1964). *Personality in middle and late life.* New York: Atherton.

Nietzsche, Friedrich. (1964). *Complete works* (Vol. 2) (O. Levy, Ed.). New York: Russell & Russell.

Nochlin, Linda (Ed.). (1973). *Woman as sex object: Studies in erotic art, 1730-1970.* London: Allen Lane.

Oakley, Ann. (1981). Interviewing women: A contradiction in terms. In H. Roberts (Ed.), *Doing feminist research* (pp. 30-61). New York: Routledge

Odeh, Lama Abu. (1993). Post-colonial feminism and the veil: Thinking the difference. *Feminist Review, 43,* 26-37.

Offerman, Lynn R., & Beil, Cheryl. (1992). Achievement styles of women leaders and their peers. *Psychology of Women Quarterly, 16,* 37-56.

Opie, Anne. (1992). Qualitative research, appropriation of the "other" and empowerment. *Feminist Review, 42,* 23-31.

Oyama, Susan. (1991). Essentialism, women and war: Protesting too much, protesting too little. In A. E. Hunter (Ed.), *Genes and gender: Vol. 6. On peace, war, and gender* (pp. 64-76). New York: Feminist Press.

Parlee, Mary Brown. (1973). The premenstrual syndrome. *Psychological Bulletin, 83,* 454-465.

Parlee, Mary Brown. (1979). Psychology and women. *Signs: Journal of Women in Culture and Society, 5,* 121-133.

Pennebaker, James W., Paez, Dario, & Rime, Bernard (Eds.). (1997). *Collective memory of political events.* Hillsdale, NJ: Lawrence Erlbaum.

Peterson, Sharyl Bender, & Kroner, Traci. (1992). Gender biases in textbooks for introductory psychology and human development. *Psychology of Women Quarterly, 16,* 17-36.

Pleck, Joseph. (1981). *The myth of masculinity.* Cambridge: MIT Press.

Popper, Karl. (1959). *The logic of scientific discovery.* New York: Basic Books.

Rabine, Leslie W. (1988). A feminist politics of non-identity. *Feminist Studies, 14,* 11-31.

Rhedding-Jones, Jeanette. (1995). What do you do after you've met poststructuralism? Research possibilities regarding feminism, ethnography and literacy. *Journal of Curriculum Studies, 27,* 479-500.

Riger, Stephanie. (1992). Epistemological debates, feminist voices: Science, social values, and the study of women. *American Psychologist, 47,* 730-740.

Rorty, Richard. (1979). *Philosophy and the mirror of nature.* Princeton, NJ: Princeton University Press.

Rosenau, Pauline Marie. (1992). *Post-modernism and the social sciences: Insights, inroads, and intrusions.* Princeton, NJ: Princeton University Press.

Scheman, Naomi. (1983). Individualism and the objects of psychology. In S. Harding & M. B. Hintikka (Eds.), *Discovering reality: Feminist perspectives on epistemology, metaphysics, methodology and philosophy of science* (pp. 225-244). Dordrecht, the Netherlands: D. Reidel.

Shalin, Dmitri. (1993). Modernity, postmodernity and pragmatist inquiry: An introduction. *Symbolic Interaction 16,* 303-332.

Shotter, John. (1993). *Conversational realities. Constructing life through language.* London: Sage.

Smith, Jonathan A. (1994). Reconstructing selves: An analysis of discrepancies between women's contemporaneous and retrospective accounts of the transition to motherhood. *British Journal of Psychology, 85,* 371-392.

Tavris, Carol. (1994). II. Reply to Brown and Gilligan. *Feminism & Psychology, 4,* 350-352.

Tiefer, Leonore. (1987). Social constructionism and the study of human sexuality. In P. Shaver & C. Hendrick (Eds.), *Review of personality and social psychology: Vol. 7. Sex and gender* (pp. 70-94). Newbury Park, CA: Sage.

Unger, Rhoda. (1989). Sex in psychological paradigms: From behavior to cognition. In R. Unger (Ed.), *Representations: Social construction of gender* (pp. 15-20). Amityville, NY: Baywood.

Venturi, Robert, Brown, Denise Scott, & Izenour, Steven. (1984). *Learning from Las Vegas.* New York: Rizzoli.

Weir, Lorraine. (1994). Post-modernizing gender: From Adrienne Rich to Judith Butler. In H. Lorraine Radtke & Henderikus J. Stam (Eds.), *Power/gender: Social relations in theory and practice* (pp. 210-218). London: Sage.

Wilkinson, Sue (with Susan Condor, Christine Griffin, Margaret Wetherell, & Jennie Williams). (1991). Feminism & psychology: From critique to reconstruction. *Feminism & Psychology, 1,* 5-18.

Wortham, Stanton. (1986). *Dialogue: Two conceptions.* New York: Teachers College Press.

Worthley, Joanna. (1992). Is science persistence a matter of values? *Psychology of Women Quarterly, 16,* 57-68.

Young, Iris Marion. (1994). Gender as seriality: Thinking about women as a social collective. *Signs: Journal of Women in Culture and Society, 19,* 713-738.

Index

About the Author

MARY GERGEN is Professor of Psychology and Women's Studies at Pennsylvania State University, Delaware County. She is primarily identified with the postmodern movement in feminist psychology, and has been involved in innovative methods in gender studies for many years. Her special fields of interest include the social construction of adulthood and aging, embodiment, and narrative psychology.